CALENDARS
OF AMERICAN LITERARY
MANUSCRIPTS

THE LITERARY MANUSCRIPTS OF

HENRY DAVID THOREAU

The Literary Manuscripts of Henry David Thoreau is the third volume in a series of CALENDARS OF AMERICAN LITERARY MANUSCRIPTS. The series is sponsored by an agency bearing the same name, and is under the control of its Editorial Board.

THE LITERARY MANUSCRIPTS OF

HENRY DAVID THOREAU

BY WILLIAM L. HOWARTH

OHIO STATE UNIVERSITY PRESS

For Jenny and Jeff

CONTENTS

ILLUSTRATIONS

(Following page 186)

All photographs courtesy of Pierpont Morgan Library, New York City.

FOREWORD

One no longer has to justify the idea of systematically presenting knowledge gained from an intensive search for American literary manuscripts. The development of a criticism based on close and sophisticated reading of texts has increased the importance of allied scholarly arts for which that knowledge is essential; and the successes of the *National Union Catalog of Manuscript Collections* (Washington, D.C., 1959–) and *American Literary Manuscripts* (Austin, Texas, 1960) have indicated the value of establishing the breadth of the available manuscript resources for the study of our national literature. There is some point, however, in introducing Calendars of American Literary Manuscripts because this project aims to contribute primary knowledge about American manuscripts in a depth greater than that attempted by those mentioned above.

The scholar's situation most often demands that he be able to locate a particular manuscript or family of manuscripts of a given literary work. Even a comprehensive list of bulk collections will indicate to him only the likely starting points for his quest. Since the manuscripts of most American authors are widely dispersed, that quest will most often involve wide correspondence and intensive research over an ever-increasing area. And, of course, one can rarely be satisfied that any discovery has terminated the hunt. To this point, almost every student who has had need of manuscript materials for an investigation in a field new to him has had to perform the quest afresh—even if, as is frequently true, the same quest had engaged others before him. It is an expensive, time-consuming, and often frustrating task; when it is performed redundantly, it is also shamefully wasteful of the resources of those in professions that can least afford waste.

Simply, Calendars of American Literary Manuscripts hopes to minimize this kind of waste by publishing the results of specialized searches for all of the available pre- and post-publication inscriptions of individual authors. With this kind of foundation, further explorations into the broad area we designate as manuscript materials should enlarge, rather than duplicate, information about the available. That is our major wish. We hope for subsidiary benefits as well: for an increase in the use of manuscript materials in scholarly and critical studies of American writers, for added impetus to research and criticism in American literature generally, and for the emergence of the incalculably large body of submerged American literary manuscripts.

Given the richness of our national literature in its quantity as well as in its quality, we are well aware that our efforts can at best be only a contribution to the necessary end. There is much to do, little time in which to do it, and almost no financial support for this kind of work. But one must begin. By definition, therefore, no volume in the series ought to be considered definitive. We both expect and desire supplementary information about material within the scope of volumes in CALM. Such addenda will be published in *Proof: The Yearbook of American Bibliographical and Textual Studies* (Columbia: University of South Carolina Press, 1971–). Contributions of that kind may be addressed directly to *Proof*. They are important, and they will be welcomed.

Joseph Katz

ACKNOWLEDGMENTS

Many individuals and institutions have contributed substantially to this volume, and to several of them I owe both gratitude and special recognition.

For their patience, sympathy, and sound advice, I thank Herbert Cahoon and Joseph Katz, of the Editorial Board of CALM; and Weldon A. Kefauver, director of the Ohio State University Press.

For their hospitality and expert assistance, I thank the following staff members of public repositories: Edwin Carpenter, Robert Dougan, Mary Isabel Fry, Herbert C. Schultz, James Thorpe (Henry E. Huntington Library and Art Gallery); Donald Gallup (Yale University); John C. Broderick (Library of Congress); Albert Perdue (University of Iowa); Kenneth W. Duckett, Thomas J. Jackson (Southern Illinois University); J. Richard Phillips (Amherst College); Kimball C. Elkins, Harley P. Holden, Carolyn E. Jakeman, Mary M. Meehan (Harvard University); William H. Harrison (Fruitlands Museum); Marcia Moss (Concord Free Public Library); Lydia Doane Newcomb (Wellfleet Historical Society); Marjory H. Drake (University of Michigan); Elsie Frievogel (Washington University); Jane D. Van Arsdale (Buffalo and Erie County Public Library); Robert B. Stone (University of New Hampshire); Kenneth A. Lohf (Columbia University); Edward Mickle (City College of New York), Marian Kahn, Jean R. McNeice, Lola S. Szladits (New York Public Library); Herbert Cahoon, Douglas Ewing, Charles Ryskamp (J. Pierpont Morgan Library); Judith Dessner (Carl H. Pforzheimer Library); Christine D. Hathaway (Brown University); Sally Leach, June Moll (University of Texas); R. W. Franklin, John D. McKenna, Edward Rosenfeld (Middlebury College); and Edmund D. Berkeley, Jr., Anne Freudenberg, Elizabeth R. Schubert (University of Virginia).

For their extraordinary interest in this project, I thank the following owners of private collections: Alexander B. Adams, Raymond Adams, Raymond R. Borst, T. Y. Davis, Grace S. Davenport, John M. Dorsey, Malcolm Ferguson, Carl B. Hansen, Walter Harding, Nancy Jackson, Edward M. Kennedy, Leonard F. Kleinfeld, Russell W. Knight, Elizabeth McDevitt, Harold S. Newton, Robert Rulon Miller, Mrs. George W. Pierce, John Seelye, Daniel Siegel, William E. Stockhausen, Wade Van Dore, William Strutz, W. Stephen Thomas, Beatrice K. Weigel, and J. Howard Woolmer.

For generously opening the manuscript census files of the Thoreau Edition, I thank Professor Walter Harding and his secretary, Marsha Britt. With their assistance I was able to contact many of the private owners listed above.

For helping to date and identify many of the various fragments in sections D and E, I thank Thomas Blanding and Linck Johnson, who readily imparted to me their notes and thoughts on this difficult series of manuscripts. I also thank Professors Joseph J. Moldenhauer and Paul O. Williams for obtaining copies of manuscripts at their university libraries.

For several grants supporting travel and research, I thank the Henry E. Huntington Library, the John E. Annan Fund, and the Princeton University Research Board. For an academic leave of absence in 1970, I thank the Trustees of Princeton University. For typing and other secretarial assistance, I especially thank Sandra Day, Janet Miller, Grace Taliaferro, and Marilyn Walden of the Princeton University Department of English. I also thank Elizabeth Friskey, my research assistant, for her help in compiling the indexes.

Finally, for unstinting aid, encouragement, and companionship during the past four years of travel and research, I thank Bonnie, to whom I always owe the greatest debt.

After all the mileage, correspondence, and study, I surrender this book with regrets, frankly admitting that perfection remains its unattained goal. Manuscripts are still coming to light, dealers and collectors will not always respond, occasionally curators cannot locate items listed in their catalogues. Nor is the author infallible; error and inconsistency seem to have threatened me every step of the way. At the least, I may have spared some readers the delays and frustrations that manuscript research often entails. If they can build on the information here provided, raising new questions about the development of Thoreau's mind and art, then the time will have been well spent, indeed.

William L. Howarth

Princeton University
Princeton, New Jersey

INTRODUCTION

The Manuscripts

When Henry Thoreau died in May 1862, he left his family almost no legacy except for a huge collection of literary manuscripts. Housed in three trunks—two wooden, one leather —of his own making, these papers covered Thoreau's entire literary career, from student compositions written at Harvard to essays dictated from his deathbed. In less than thirty years Thoreau had gathered an impressive array of materials. About sixty bound volumes, mostly *Journal* and extract books, formed the core of his archives, supplemented by several thousand single leaves of notes and rough drafts, which he had sorted into groups and fastened with ribbon or straight pins. Had it survived, the careful arrangement of these papers would have preserved something of their author's meticulous personal character. The story of their subsequent dispersal, however, still accurately reflects the growth of his literary reputation.

Thoreau appointed Sophia, his younger sister, as his literary executor, since she had worked most closely with him at the end, transcribing drafts and helping to set his manuscript collection in order. During the next four years Sophia's major task was to supervise final publication of various essays and books that Henry had partially edited: *Excursions* (1863), *The Maine Woods* (1864), *Cape Cod* (1865), and *A Yankee in Canada with Anti-Slavery and Reform Papers* (1866). She chose Ellery Channing, an eccentric but trusted friend, to assist with these volumes, but in 1864 they quarreled and parted company over Channing's demand to publish some *Journal* passages.[1]

Her own editing tasks completed, in 1866 Sophia began to consider how other manuscripts, especially the *Journal*, might be edited yet kept intact. Other than a few items given to

---

1. F. B. Sanborn, *The Life of Henry Thoreau* (Boston: Houghton Mifflin Co., 1917), p. 491; H. S. Canby, *Thoreau* (Boston: Houghton Mifflin Co., 1939), p. 441.

friends or auctioned for charitable purposes, Sophia had scrupulously preserved the papers and their final order. But perfection eluded her; often precious leaves disappeared at the printing house, where she had sent them as copy with explicit instructions for their safe return. F. B. Sanborn later charged that Sophia was too careless and impatient to submit final fair copies, as Thoreau always had.[2] Yet to a disinterested observer—which Sanborn certainly was not—Sophia's attitude toward the manuscripts seems, if anything, overprotective. To Thomas W. Higginson, who had offered to edit the *Journal* for Ticknor and Fields, she wrote in September 1866: "These papers are very sacred to me & I feel inclined to defer giving them to the public for the present." But she also asserted, *contra* Higginson, that an edition of the *Journal* would sell profitably.[3] Her fierce desire to idealize Henry's memory accounts for this ambivalence, and for her later disposition of the papers.

During the next few years only a few of Sophia's closest friends received permission to examine her brother's manuscripts. She kept Channing and Sanborn at a distance, evading their persistent offers to edit the manuscripts. But she frequently permitted Emerson and Alcott to borrow manuscripts for study, especially the various *Journal* volumes. Emerson's reactions to these papers appear in his own journal between 1867 and 1870, and by 1872 Alcott was openly calling for their publication, perhaps in an abbreviated "calendar" form.[4]

---

2. Letter to W. K. Bixby, Olin Library, Washington University. After several mishaps Emerson took to supervising the return of manuscripts to Sophia. As he reported to James Cabot, she valued the papers "religiously." See *The Letters of Ralph Waldo Emerson,* ed. R. L. Rusk (New York: Columbia University Press, 1939), 5: 307, 344.

3. Pierpont Morgan Library (MA 1443). James Fields tried to second Higginson's offer, but Sophia was in no haste to find an editor: "She did not see the man . . . but she thought he would come." Because of this initial rebuff, Higginson later accused Sophia of trying "to repress the publication" of Thoreau's manuscripts. See Fields, *Biographical Notes and Personal Sketches* (Boston: Houghton Mifflin Co., 1882), p. 101; and Higginson, *Carlyle's Laugh and Other Surprises* (Boston: Houghton Mifflin Co., 1909), pp. 68–69.

4. *The Journals of Ralph Waldo Emerson,* ed. E. W. Emerson and W. F. Forbes (Boston: Houghton Mifflin Co., 1909–14), 9: 311. A. Bronson Alcott, *Concord Days* (Boston: Roberts Brothers, 1872), p. 264.

This suggestion was not lost on Sophia, who in 1873 saw the appearance of Channing's *Thoreau, the Poet-Naturalist*, a garbled pastiche of biography, criticism, and unauthorized manuscript quotations. She sold the Concord home that year and moved to Maine, determined that the papers would go to a responsible editor after her death.

The three trunks she left under Alcott's immediate care, with explicit restrictions as to their contents:

> I am to hold them sacred from all but Thoreau's friends, allow none to take them away for perusal, subject to his sister's pleasure during her lifetime, and if I survive her, then they become mine for quotation and publishing.[5]

Actually, Sophia had other plans. After interviewing T. W. Higginson, who now declined her offer, she decided in June 1874 that the best available editor was Harrison Blake, Thoreau's longtime friend and correspondent from Worcester. Visiting Concord to announce this decision, she discovered with alarm that Alcott had permitted Sanborn to take the *Journal* trunk into his home—where Channing was a frequent guest. Accordingly, in early 1875 she asked Alcott to deposit the manuscripts at the town library, under the trusteeship of Emerson, her newly chosen executor. Alcott readily agreed to this arrangement, and Emerson tactfully appeased Sanborn by suggesting that Sophia had feared only that Channing would have unauthorized access to the papers.[6]

Sophia died shortly thereafter, in October 1876, and the terms of her will directed that Blake should receive the two wooden trunks. Sanborn was bitterly disappointed by this decision, because Emerson had promised to recommend him for the honor. In later years Sanborn always attributed his loss to the bad feelings between Sophia and Channing. The leather trunk, filled mostly with surveys, maps, and assorted

---

5. *The Journals of Bronson Alcott*, ed. O. Shepard (Boston: Little, Brown Co., 1938), p. 431.

6. Ibid., pp. 431–33, 450–51; H. Hoeltje, "Thoreau in Concord Church and Town Records," *New England Quarterly* 12 (1939): 359; F. B. Sanborn, "A Concord Notebook," repr. *Transcendental Epilogue*, ed. K. W. Cameron (Hartford, Conn.: Transcendental Books, 1965), 3:13.

manuscript fragments, remained at the town library, where it survives today. In December 1876 Emerson sent the two wooden trunks to Blake by express. With characteristic absent-mindedness, Emerson forgot to include the keys, thus requiring the risk of a separate mailing: "I shall be anxious about the arrival of trunks & keys until I hear from you that the entire precious property is safely in your possession." [7]

Ironically, the Thoreau papers were to suffer from considerable mishandling while Blake retained them. His first major effort, attempting to sort and classify the various notebook volumes, proved to be most damaging. On the front of each notebook he pasted a label, giving a volume number, date, and title for the supposed contents. The labels still survive: many of Blake's titles are misleading, most of his dates are inaccurate, and none of his numbers correspond to Thoreau's original sequences. Yet with the passage of time Blake's mistakes have attained legitimacy, for curators and even some scholars have come to assume that the labels are Thoreau's own.

Blake was also careless in his editing of the manuscripts. After considerable discussion with others,[8] he adopted a plan somewhat analogous to Alcott's earlier suggestion, selecting passages from the *Journal* and arranging them in seasonal order. Working at a leisurely pace, Blake completed this four-volume cycle in eleven years: *Early Spring in Massachusetts* (1881), *Summer* (1884), *Winter* (1888), and *Autumn* (1892). While editing his books, he browsed freely through the manuscripts, marking boldly with blue pencil any passages to be copied from the *Journal* and casually dipping into other papers, such as those for *Walden* or *Cape Cod*, when the need arose. He did not scruple to follow Thoreau's text closely, supplying his own words or marks of punctuation whenever convenient.

---

7. Pierpont Morgan Library (MA 1768). Two days later Emerson wrote a second letter, now in the Abernethy Collection of the Middlebury College Library.

8. *The Journals of Bronson Alcott*, pp. 450–51, 471–73. Blake outlined his editorial plan in a letter to C. M. Skinner on 17 October 1877. See the fall 1971 catalogue for The Current Company, Bristol, R. I., p. 31. I thank Professor Walter Harding for calling this item to my attention.

As F. H. Allen later pointed out, Blake also confused dates and misread more of Thoreau's handwriting "than one might have expected from a correspondent of many years." [9]

We must also assume that Blake did not try to preserve the manuscripts' order, because at some time during his trusteeship the original ribbon and pin fasteners began to disappear, throwing the unbound leaves into considerable disarray. Indeed, evidence indicates that in his confusion Blake mislaid two entire volumes of the *Journal*, from 1840 and 1846, which he copied in the "calendar" books but did not pass on to his inheritor, Elias Harlowe Russell. [10]

E. H. Russell, principal of the Worcester State Normal School, became owner of the Thoreau papers when Blake died in 1898. The terms of Blake's will directed that Russell might dispose of the manuscripts in a "proper and suitable" manner, but that any income from Thoreau's writings must go to "the benefit of the relatives of said Thoreau who may need such assistance." [11] Russell, only a marginal acquaintance of Thoreau, seems to have been interested mostly in self-assistance. According to Sanborn, Russell never carefully examined the papers; certainly, he never tried to reclassify the leaves that Blake had rather badly scrambled. [12]

As early as 1900 Russell entertained proposals for publishing the *Journal*, especially from the Houghton Mifflin Company, for whom Horace Scudder had produced the "Riverside Edition" of Thoreau's writings in 1893. Scudder had no luck with Russell, but his successor, Bliss Perry, tried again in 1902 with better results. A fascinating series of letters from Perry to Russell survives in the Houghton Mifflin Letter Books, now in the Houghton Library at Harvard University. The outcome of their transactions, amusingly similar to shrewd Yankee horse-trading, was that the company would

---

9. "Thoreau's Editors: History and Reminiscence," *Thoreau Society Booklet* 7 (1950): 11–12.

10. P. Miller, *Consciousness in Concord* (Boston: Houghton Mifflin Co., 1958), p. 6–7.

11. E. Schofield, "The Will of H. G. O. Blake," *Thoreau Society Bulletin* 68 (Summer, 1959): 2.

12. Letter to W. K. Bixby, Olin Library, Washington University.

pay Russell $3,000 for publication rights to the *Journal* and an undisclosed amount for the purchase of certain "bundles of loose manuscript, already used by printers in making some of Thoreau's earliest volumes." Houghton Mifflin planned to bind these leaves into a deluxe version of the new Thoreau edition, similar to their autograph editions of Hawthorne (1900) and Emerson (1903).[13]

But before Russell could close this deal, he had to contend in court with the Thoreau heirs. Although Blake's will seemed in their favor, Russell successfully obtained a decree in April 1903 awarding him absolute ownership of the manuscripts, full power to publish their contents, and the right to all proceeds "free from any trust."[14] At that time he apparently intended to profit only from the sale of publication rights. According to George Mifflin, Russell had stated that the *Journal* manuscript itself "could not be purchased either for love or money," and that after publication it would go either to Harvard University or the Boston Public Library.[15]

By September 1904, however, Russell had mastered this generous impulse and sold all his manuscripts, plus an option on the *Journal*, to George S. Hellman, a prominent New York dealer. Hellman's expert knowledge of the collecting market brought him a handsome return in barely three years' time. After removing one of the wooden chests to his office, he spent several weeks sorting the loose manuscripts into groups of published and unpublished text, early drafts, and late copy.[16] Unfortunately, several of these groupings were quite inaccurate, an error Hellman compounded by ordering them to be custom-bound. To this day, some mounted fragments of *A Week* rest between sumptuous leather boards, stamped in brilliant gold leaf, "The Maine Woods."[17] But

---

13. Houghton-Mifflin Company Letter Books, Houghton Library, Harvard University; "Editorial" volumes 21 (pp. 355, 377), 26 (p. 98), and 28 (pp. 201, 316–18, 355–55a, 384).

14. Schofield, "The Will of H. G. O. Blake," pp. 2–3.

15. Letter Books, "Private" volume 12, p. 26.

16. Letter Books, "Editorial" volume 31, p. 77r; G. S. Hellman, *Lanes of Memory* (New York: A. A. Knopf, 1927), pp. 31–32.

17. See item D5a within.

if the dealer had no instinct for accuracy, he at least knew
how to promote swift sales. Hellman's first customer was
William Augustus White, a New York furrier, who in late
1904 purchased almost four hundred miscellaneous leaves,
containing fragments of all the Thoreau books, most of the
essays, and even some portions of the early *Journal*.[18]

The second customer was William Keeney Bixby, a wealthy
St. Louis manufacturer, who in August 1905 bought all of
Hellman's unconsigned manuscripts. This massive group of
papers contained all the extract books, the "nature notes,"
and complete drafts of Thoreau's poems, translations, lectures,
essays, and books, especially *Walden*. Bixby hired F. B. Sanborn, since Sophia's death the reigning authority on Thoreau,
to examine, identify, and transcribe these manuscripts. Bixby's
intentions were of the best sort, but he could hardly have
selected a more unreliable adviser. Sanborn dashed through
the papers with careless dispatch, hazarding wild guesses as
to dates or identity, and frequently inking his own notes over
Thoreau's text. Occasionally he even rolled manuscript leaves
into his typewriter to rap out a lengthy comment! [19] Nor did
he confine his abuse to the papers alone. His air of expertise
persuaded Bixby to finance the notorious "Bibliophile" editions of *The First and Last Journeys of Thoreau* (1905)
and *Walden* (1909), in which Sanborn mingled barbarously
"paraphrased" excerpts of the manuscripts with his own commentary and Thoreau's original text.

The third block of Hellman's manuscripts went, as previously arranged, to Houghton Mifflin in 1906 for their "Manuscript Edition." The company prepared six hundred sets of
this twenty-volume edition, each set with a single manuscript
leaf (or half-leaf) tipped into volume 1. Because half-leaves
were used, the total number of leaves distributed in this
manner probably came to between three and four hundred.
Locating and identifying these fugitive leaves remains, even

18. A note describing White's purchase appears in MS Am 278.5.20,
Folder 1; Houghton Library, Harvard University.
19. Letters to W. K. Bixby and H. R. Harper, Olin Library, Washington University. Most of Sanborn's notations appear on manuscripts
now in the Huntington Library.

sixty-five years later, a frustrating and seemingly endless task. A full list of the manuscripts has not survived, although one is mentioned in the company letter books; [20] but present records identify most of the leaves as belonging to drafts of Thoreau's late essays, especially those published posthumously in the *Atlantic Monthly*. A few leaves of *Walden* were also scattered in this fashion, and undoubtedly other valuable papers await future discovery. At least one reviewer of the Manuscript Edition charged the publishers with "vandalism" for breaking up Thoreau's manuscripts, but to the editors this seemed a "legitimate" means of disposal, especially for fragments of text long since published. [21]

The final group of manuscripts, Russell's most valuable, belonged to the *Journal*. Early in 1905, when the notebooks were only just transcribed, he asked for their return, apparently because Hellman had an interested buyer waiting. The editors refused, arguing that both copy and proof had to be carefully checked against the originals. Not until late 1906, after publication, did they return the notebooks to Russell's custody. [22] In March 1907, expressing reluctance "to part with a treasure, for a consideration so much below its value," Russell sent the *Journal* trunk and its entire contents (sans two early volumes, still missing) to Hellman, who sold it at once to Stephen H. Wakeman, a New York collector. Wakeman kept the *Journal* a few years in his impressive library of Americana, then sold the chest and another large group of papers to J. Pierpont Morgan in 1916. According to Hellman, who also arranged this sale, Morgan was persuaded to buy the Wakeman collection because it contained the manuscript of his favorite poem, Longfellow's "The Children's Hour"! [23]

The Thoreau trunk that Morgan bought contained all of the *Journal* manuscripts that had been published in the 1906

---

20. "Editorial" volume 35, p. 274.

21. Letter Books, "Editorial" volume 35, p. 394. Later, F. H. Allen conceded that some of the manuscripts added "materially to the value of the sets." See *Bibliography of Henry David Thoreau* (Boston: Houghton Mifflin Co., 1908), p. 53.

22. Letter Books, "Editorial" volume 32, p. 881.

23. Letter of E. H. Russell to G. S. Hellman, Pierpont Morgan Library (RV Autog. Misc. Am.); *Lanes of Memory*, pp. 42–47.

edition. Numerous fragments of some early, mutilated volumes, however, were scattered throughout the White and Bixby purchases. Sanborn edited some of these papers in 1905 and identified others for Bixby in 1907, but their full extent remained unknown until very recent times.[24] The two missing volumes, from 1840 and 1846, appeared for sale in 1912, apparently not from Russell's hands. Wakeman bought them, discussed their contents with an expert, and kept them for his collection instead of selling to Morgan. When the Wakeman library was sold in 1924, Warren H. Colson bought the two volumes, and for the next thirty years he protected them so zealously from examination that legends arose about their "secret" contents. Not until 1958 did both volumes finally come to rest in public collections, thus restoring the *Journal* trunk to its original capacity.[25]

E. H. Russell died in 1917, and during the next two decades most of his Thoreau manuscripts descended to public collections. William A. White presented his manuscripts to Harvard University in 1919, in 1923 Julian Willis Abernethy bequeathed a sizeable group of poetry and prose fragments to Middlebury College, and the library of J. P. Morgan became a public institution in 1924. Henry E. Huntington purchased several Thoreau items at the famous Wakeman sale in 1924, as did Warren H. Colson and W. T. H. Howe, president of the American Book Company.[26] Shortly after publication of *The Moon* (Boston: Houghton Mifflin Co., 1927), Houghton Mifflin Company released for sale a series of lecture fragments, mostly left over from their 1906 consignment. Many of these items went either to Howe or to Middlebury. The Huntington Library also went public in 1927, and after Bixby's death in 1931 his heirs broke up the manuscript col-

24. Letter to W. K. Bixby, Olin Library, Washington University. See also section E, within.

25. Wakeman's "expert" was F. H. Allen, one of the *Journal* editors. See the *Thoreau Society Bulletin* 50 (Fall, 1954): 2; *Consciousness in Concord*, p. 7; and footnote 26, Item 982. The *Journal* volumes are now housed in individual slipcases and no longer fit the trunk.

26. *The Stephen H. Wakeman Collection . . . of Nineteenth Century American Writers* (New York: American Art Association, 1924). Partially reprinted in K. W. Cameron, *Transcendentalists and Minerva* (Hartford, Conn.: Transcendental Books, 1958) 2: 389–414.

lection, donating a few poems to Washington University before selling the rest to the Morgan Library, the Huntington Library, and Howe. A few items also went to Middlebury and lesser collections before the public auction of 1934.[27]

In 1940 Dr. Albert A. Berg of New York acquired the Howe collection for his own great library of English and American literature, which he presented to the New York Public Library that same year.[28] After World War II several manuscripts gravitated to the fast-growing collections of Charles Feinberg, Albert Lownes, and C. Waller Barrett. The last great sale of Thoreau manuscripts occurred in 1958, dispersing the collection of Warren H. Colson.[29] Sales went principally to dealers, who in turn sold various items to the Morgan Library, the Berg Collection, the University of Texas, and to Messrs. Barrett, Feinberg, and Lownes.

By the late 1960s the latter three collections had passed into public repositories: Barrett to the University of Virginia, Feinberg to Southern Illinois University, and Lownes to Brown University. With the end of that decade most of Thoreau's manuscripts had finally come to rest, no longer to be traded on the open market. Scattered fragments are still in private hands and some Manuscript Editions remain unlocated, but virtually 95 percent of Thoreau's papers are now available for study by qualified researchers. No one can calculate the present value of these manuscripts; they have simply acquired that special degree of rarity, pricelessness, that seems an appropriate fate for Thoreau's legacy.

The Calendar

The preceding history clearly establishes our need for a reference volume of this sort. Once a unified and orderly set of papers, Thoreau's manuscripts are now widely scattered

27. None of the Thoreau manuscripts are listed in the auction catalogue, *First Editions and Manuscripts, Collected by the Late Mr. and Mrs. William K. Bixby* (New York: American Art Association, 1934).

28. A brief history and description of the Berg Collection is available from its curator, Mrs. Lola S. Szladits.

29. A reprint of the Parke-Bernet catalogue, with annotations, appears in the *Thoreau Society Bulletin* 65 (Summer, 1958).

across the length and breadth of America. Few scholars have the patience, cash, or desire to visit these collections personally; fewer still are the curators and collectors who welcome repeated questions about their papers. This book's primary function, then, is to reassemble Thoreau's manuscripts as they were in May 1862, providing an entry on the location, description, and identification of each surviving group. But the calendar also has a secondary function, which I can best describe by recounting its development.

In the fall of 1967 I first examined some *Journal* and extract books in the Morgan Library, hoping to find physical clues about Thoreau's writing habits. Following the example set by J. Lyndon Shanley in *The Making of Walden* (Chicago: University of Chicago Press, 1957), I measured leaves, noted their color and substance (wove or laid), and checked for stationer's marks. I also collated the bound gatherings according to established bibliographical formulas.[30] My notes soon verified the presence of identical paper and gatherings in successive *Journal* and extract volumes, indicating Thoreau had bought pairs of notebooks, one for each series, and written in them at about the same time. Although that conclusion now seems perfectly unremarkable, at the time no one had ever noticed the similarities or accurately dated the extract books. If simple comparisons could produce this sort of data, then all of Thoreau's manuscripts begged for similar inspection. An opportunity to pursue this task appeared in the form of Calendars of American Literary Manuscripts (CALM), whose Editorial Board approved my proposal for this volume in early 1968.

For the next two years I examined manuscript collections in twenty states, compiling several files of notes on the physical condition of Thoreau's papers. The notes revealed, not surprisingly, that he developed certain methodical—and frugal —writing habits early in his career, modifying them only slightly thereafter. He worked on his compositions slowly, first taking preliminary notes or writing outlines on scrap paper (usually the versos of his father's old business letters), then

---

30. See Fredson Bowers, *Principles of Bibliographical Description* (Princeton: Princeton University Press, 1949).

drafting paragraphs into the *Journal* for later reference, and finally composing several drafts, half-copied, half-original, of his basic text. Two or three drafts might develop for a single lecture, each draft containing leaves from its predecessors. He repeated this process when converting lectures to essays: notes, *Journal*, drafts; this time moving forward lecture sheets that required no drastic revision. An essay might also require several drafts, each retaining fragments of its predecessors. If the essay became part of a book, as in *The Maine Woods* or *Cape Cod*, Thoreau traveled the same route once again, moving forward early leaves and inserting new pages of revision when necessary. His final manuscripts, those preceding his fair copy for the printers, might contain leaves written over a considerable number of years—even a full decade, as in the case of *A Week* or *Walden*.

Because of this incremental method, consistent with Thoreau's aesthetics but confusing to later eyes, most scholars have agreed that his writings cannot be dated precisely. Walter Harding, concluding that "no final order of composition of Thoreau's works can be established," lists them according to their dates of final revision.[31] But the manuscripts themselves do contain certain detectable patterns left by Thoreau's working habits. Never one to waste resources, he bought packets of inexpensive writing paper, using each packet for several purposes—transcription, spot revision, fair copy— until it was exhausted. He then bought a new packet, taking whatever size and color the stationer offered at a convenient price.

Enough physical differences exist between the various papers to constitute definite "types," and the types conform to quite limited periods of time. Despite the great variety of paper appearing in Thoreau's manuscripts, various types clearly measure the stages of his writing process, and in fact provide a reliable means of dating those stages accurately. Two tables at the end of this volume describe the various paper types and record their chronological sequence.[32] Establishing these tables

---

31. *A Thoreau Handbook* (New York: New York University Press, 1959), p. 41.
32. See pp. 376–82, below.

took considerable time, as each manuscript had to be analyzed according to paper, identity of text, and known history of composition. Thoreau's letters and *Journal* provided most of the historical data, with the frequent aid of Walter Harding's biographical works.[33]

The Calendar itself follows a generally chronological arrangement, both within and between its eight sections. Most of the manuscripts appear according to date of composition, but in several instances the date of final revision or publication has determined their order. Several items that came to light while this volume was in production have been placed in their correct chronological position and identified with a superior figure "one" following the item number. The format and terminology of entries closely resemble those used by Kenneth Lohf in *The Literary Manuscripts of Hart Crane* (Columbus: Ohio State University Press, 1967) and by Ronald Gottesman and Charles L. P. Silet in *The Literary Manuscripts of Upton Sinclair* (Columbus: Ohio State University Press, 1973), with several necessary modifications. Each of the entries contains the following information: [34]

Citation: Title, whether published, unpublished, or conjectured; type of manuscript; number of written sides; writing medium (ink, pencil, crayon) and purpose (composition, revision, deletion, notation, pagination); location symbol and call number.

Title: An exact transcription, following Thoreau's spelling, punctuation, capitals, superscripts, underscorings, and line endings.

First line: An exact transcription of the first line or, if very brief, lines, in an attempt to establish a context, but with no indication of line endings in the case of prose. Most transcriptions are of the original, unrevised text.

---

33. "A Checklist of Thoreau's Lectures," *BNYPL* 70 (1948): 78–87. *A Thoreau Handbook*, pp. viii–xi, 1–96; *The Last Days of Henry Thoreau* (New York: Alfred Knopf, 1965), passim.

34. For symbols and abbreviations, see pp. xxxiii–xxxvii, below.

Collation: Number of leaves, color, substance (wove or laid), paper type (see Tables); dimensions, maximum length and width; pagination, conjectured and original; and other details on physical condition. Collation by signatures appears for bound volumes.

Date: Conjectured or specific, with most conjectures resting on paper type, state of text, and historical evidence.

Contents: Type of manuscript (notes, draft, copy, and so on); number of stanzas and lines (poetry); relation of text to published versions; location of facsimiles; cross references to other entries.

Note: Additional comment on any of the above; location of other descriptions.

The absence of any category means that the information is either inapplicable or unavailable for that particular item. Notes appear before each of the sections to introduce their contents and to explain other changes in format or terminology. Two indexes record each item according to title and location, allowing readers to find all related manuscripts and all manuscripts within a given collection.

ABBREVIATIONS

References

AL   *American Literature*

BBr   *Books at Brown*

BNYPL   *Bulletin of the New York Public Library*

CC   *Consciousness in Concord. The Text of Thoreau's Hitherto "Lost Journal" (1840–1841) Together with Notes and a Commentary by Perry Miller.* Boston: Houghton Mifflin Co., 1958.

Corr.   *The Correspondence of Henry David Thoreau.* Edited by Walter Harding and Carl Bode. New York: New York University Press, 1958.

CP   *Collected Poems of Henry Thoreau.* Edited by Carl Bode. Baltimore: Johns Hopkins University Press, 1964.

ESQ   *Emerson Society Quarterly*

FLJ   *The First and Last Journeys of Thoreau.* Edited by F. B. Sanborn. Boston: Bibliophile Society, 1905.

HDT   F. B. Sanborn. *Henry David Thoreau.* Boston: Houghton Mifflin Co., 1889.

HLQ   *Huntington Library Quarterly*

Hovde   Carl Hovde. "The Writing of Henry D. Thoreau's *A Week on the Concord and Merrimack Rivers*" (Princeton University, Ph.D. diss., 1956).

J	*The Journal of Henry D. Thoreau.* Edited by Bradford Torrey [and Francis H. Allen]. 14 vols. Boston: Houghton Mifflin Co., 1906.
Kern	*Two Fragments from the Journal.* Edited by Alexander Kern. Iowa City, Iowa: Windhover Press, University of Iowa, 1969.
LHDT	F. B. Sanborn. *The Life of Henry David Thoreau. Including Many Essays Hitherto Unpublished.* . . . Boston: Houghton Mifflin Co., 1917.
MR	*Massachusetts Review*
NEQ	*New England Quarterly*
PT	F. B. Sanborn. *The Personality of Thoreau.* Boston: C. E. Goodspeed, 1901.
SWR	*Sir Walter Raleigh.* Introduction by F. B. Sanborn, edited by Henry A. Metcalf. Boston: Bibliophile Society, 1905.
Shanley	J. Lyndon Shanley. *The Making of Walden.* Chicago: University of Chicago Press, 1957.
Stoller	*Henry David Thoreau 1817–1862. Books, Manuscripts, and Association Items in Detroit and Ann Arbor.* [Edited by Leo Stoller] Detroit: Wayne State University Libraries, 1962.
TC	Kenneth W. Cameron. *Transcendental Climate.* Hartford, Conn.: Transcendental Books, 1963.
THC	Kenneth W. Cameron. *Thoreau and his Harvard Classmates.* Hartford, Conn.: Transcendental Books, 1965.
THY	Kenneth W. Cameron. *Thoreau's Harvard Years.* Hartford, Conn.: Transcendental Books, 1966.
TM	Kenneth W. Cameron. *The Transcendentalists and Minerva.* 3 vols. Hartford, Conn.: Transcendental Books, 1958.
TS	*The Service.* Edited by F. B. Sanborn. Boston: C. E. Goodspeed, 1902.
TSB	*Thoreau Society Bulletin*
URLB	*University of Rochester Library Bulletin*

W   *The Writings of Henry D. Thoreau.* 6 vols.
                     Boston: Houghton Mifflin Co., 1906.

Manuscript Abbreviations

a.l.s   Autograph letter signed
a.ms.   Autograph manuscript
a.n.s.   Autograph note signed
(anom.)   Anomalous paper, origin not Thoreau
(c)   Composition
(d)   Deletion, a vertical line through the text
(n)   Notation
(p)   Pagination
r   Recto
(r)   Revision
t.n.s.   Typed note signed
ts.   Typescript
(type)   Paper type (see Tables)
v   Verso

Manuscript Symbols

*   Not in Thoreau's hand
| Line ends
[ ]   Conjectured title, signature, page, or date.
π^2 Leaves preceding first signature
$+2$ Leaves following last signature
$[A\text{-}G]^8$ Seven unsigned gatherings, each of eight leaves
$[A\text{-}G]^{16/8}$ Seven unsigned gatherings, alternately sixteen
                     and eight leaves (Collation alphabet has 25
                     letters, A-H J-Z)
$ Any or all signatures

Library Symbols

CALIFORNIA
CSmH   Henry E. Huntington Library and Art Gallery,
                     San Marino
CSdS   San Diego State College, San Diego
CU-S   University of California, San Diego

CONNECTICUT

CtLkH   Edsel Ford Memorial Library, The Hotchkiss School, Lakeville

CtY   Beinecke Rare Book Library, Yale University, New Haven

DISTRICT OF COLUMBIA

DLC   Manuscript Division, The Library of Congress

IOWA

IaU   Iowa University, Iowa City

ILLINOIS

ICarbS   Morris Library, Southern Illinois University, Carbondale

IElP   Brooks Library, Principia College, Elsah

INDIANA

InU   Lilly Library, Indiana University, Bloomington

MASSACHUSETTS

MA   Amherst College, Amherst

MB   Boston Public Library, Boston

MCon   Concord Free Public Library, Concord

MConA   Concord Antiquarian Society, Concord

MConL   The Thoreau Lyceum, Concord

MEd   Edgartown Public Library, Edgartown

MH   Houghton Library, Harvard University, Cambridge

MH-UA   Harvard University Archives, Cambridge

MH-W   Hilles Library, Radcliffe College, Cambridge

MH-Z   Agassiz Museum of Comparative Zoology, Harvard University, Cambridge

MHarF   Fruitlands Museum, Harvard

MWelHS   Wellfleet Historical Society, Wellfleet

MWor   Worcester Public Library, Worcester

MICHIGAN

MiDW   Wayne State University, Detroit

MiU   University of Michigan, Ann Arbor

MINNESOTA

MnM   Minneapolis Public Library, Minneapolis

MISSOURI

MoSW   Olin Library, Washington University, St. Louis

NEW HAMPSHIRE
NhExA   Exeter Academy, Exeter
NhU   University of New Hampshire, Durham

NEW JERSEY
NjP   Firestone Library, Princeton University,
             Princeton
NjPentS   The Pennington School, Pennington

NEW YORK
NBu   Buffalo and Erie County Public Library, Buffalo
NNC   Columbia University, New York
NNCoC   City College of New York, New York
NNPf   Carl H. Pforzheimer Library, New York
NNPM   Pierpont Morgan Library, New York
NRRI   Rochester Institute of Technology, Rochester
NSchU   Schaffer Library, Union College, Schenectady
NYPL   New York Public Library, New York

PENNSYLVANIA
PPiU   Hillman Library, University of Pittsburgh,
             Pittsburgh

RHODE ISLAND
RPB   John Hay Library, Brown University,
             Providence

TEXAS
TxU   Miriam Lutcher Stark Library, University of
             Texas, Austin

VERMONT
VtMiM   Starr Library, Middlebury College, Middlebury

VIRGINIA
ViU   Alderman Library, University of Virginia,
             Charlottesville

WASHINGTON
WaSpH   Whitworth College, Spokane

CANADA
CaAEU   The Cameron Library, University of Alberta,
             Edmonton
CaNBFU   Harriet Irving Library, University of
             New Brunswick, Fredericton

A.

STUDENT WRITINGS, 1828–1837

The earliest of Thoreau's surviving manuscripts are his school papers, almost all written during his undergraduate years at Harvard. The college compositions are mostly of two types, Themes and Forensics. They were assigned by Professor Edward Tyrrel Channing on an annual basis, with every student required to complete a set quota before Commencement. Kenneth W. Cameron has explained Channing's system for assigning and marking these papers, thus confirming their dates of composition.[1] In the following descriptions the entry for "Date" gives the Theme or Forensic number, the date assigned, and the date submitted. Thoreau rarely dated his papers, but he often marked down their assigned numbers.

Other items in this section pertain to Harvard, including Thoreau's Exhibition part, two senior essays, a Class Book entry, and his Commencement part. A large series of his college notes and notebooks also survive, the latter containing some original book reviews; but see section F for their descriptions. Those papers are not listed here because their dates and contents extend well beyond Thoreau's Harvard years. F. B. Sanborn's texts of the college papers are quite corrupt; they will soon be replaced by *Early Essays and Miscellanies* in *The Writings of Henry D. Thoreau* (Princeton University Press).

---

1. *THY* 2: 2–19.

A1.   Citation: "The Seasons" A.ms., 2 sides. Ink (c). MCon.

Title: The Seasons. | Why do the Seasons change? and why | Does Winter's stormy brow appear? | It is the word of him on high, | Who rules the changing varied year.

First line: There are four Seasons in a year, Spring, Summer, Autumn, and Winter.

Collation: 1 leaf of white wove, 23.9 x 19.9 cm., pp. [1–2]; tipped in Henry S. Salt, *The Life of Henry David Thoreau* (London: W. Scott, Ltd., 1896). 2 vols., extended by Alfred W. Hosmer; leaf precedes p. 23.

Date: [1828–1829].

Contents: Fair copy of school exercise; text in Walter Harding, *The Days of Henry Thoreau* (New York: A. Knopf, 1965), p. 27. For other contents see B1.

Note: The signature "Henry David Thoreau" is a form of his name Thoreau did not adopt until 1837.

A2.   Citation: [College Theme] A.ms., 4 sides. Ink (c) Pencil (n*). CSmH (HM 934).

Title: Give your idea of the anxieties and Delights of a | Discoverer of whatever class, Columbus, Herschel, | Newton.

First line: It almost invariably happens, that the lives of most distinguished characters are chequered with trials and disappointments,

Collation: 2 leaves of white wove (type 15), 24.5 x 20.1 cm., pp. [1–4], paged "11–13"; mounted and bound, with ts. copy.

Date: [Theme No. 6, 15 November to 6 December 1834].

Contents: Fair copy of class exercise; varies from text published as "Anxieties and Delights of a Discoverer" in *LHDT*, pp. 68-69.

A3.   Citation: [College Theme] A.ms., 4 sides. Ink (c). ViU (6345-e).

Title: The different ideas we form of men whose pursuit is | money, power, distinction, domestic happiness, | public good.

First line: Each one is, for the most part, under the influence of some ruling passion,

Collation: 2 leaves of white wove (type 15), 24.3 x 20 cm., pp. [1-4].

Date: [Theme No. 7, 6-20 December 1834].
Contents: Fair copy of class exercise; varies from text published as "The Varying Pursuits of Men" in *LHDT*, pp. 76-78.

A4.   Citation: [College Theme] A.ms., 4 sides. Ink (c) Pencil (n*). CSmH (HM 934).

Title: Of keeping a private journal or record of our thoughts, feelings, | studies, and daily experience, ——containing abstracts of books, | and the opinions we formed of them on first reading them. [underscored after last line]

First line: As those pieces which the painter sketches for his own amusement in his leisure hours,

Collation: 2 leaves of white wove (type 15), 24.5 x 19.9 cm., pp. 1-3 [4]; mounted and bound, with ts. copy.

Date: [Theme No. 8, 20 December 1834 to 17 January 1835].

Contents: Fair copy of class exercise; varies from text published as "Shall We Keep Journals?" in *LHDT*, pp. 73–74.

A5.   Citation: [College Theme] A.ms., 3 sides. Ink (c) Pencil (n*). CSmH (HM 934).

Title: We are apt to become what others, (however erroneously) | think us to be; hence another motive to guard against the | power of others' unfavourable opinion

First line: We find, on looking around us, even within the small circle of our acquaintances, many who, though not at all deficient in understanding,

Collation: 2 leaves of white wove (type 15), 24.5 x 20 cm., pp. [1–4], paged "17–18"; mounted and bound, with ts. copy.

Date: [Theme No. 9, 17–31 January 1835].

Contents: Fair copy of class exercise; varies from text published as "Following the Fashion" in *LHDT*, pp. 66–67.

A6.   Citation: [College Theme] A.ms., 4 sides. Ink (c,r) Pencil (n*). RPB.

Title: On what grounds may the forms, ceremonies, and | restraints of polite society be objected to? | Speak of some of them. | What purposes are they intended to answer?

First line: In a primitive state of society, where man is buried in ignorance,

Collation: 2 leaves of white wove (type 15), 24.6 x 20.3 cm., pp. [1–4].

Date: [Theme No. 10, 31 January to 14 February 1835].

Contents: Late draft of class exercise; varies from text published as "Social Forms and Restraints" in *LHDT*, pp. 166–69.

A7.   Citation: [College Theme] A.ms., 4 sides. Ink (c) Pencil (n*). CSmH (HM 934).

Title: Explain the phrases,——a man of business, a man of | pleasure, a man of the world.

First line: To say of one that he is a man of business, according to the general acceptation of the phrase,

Collation: 2 leaves of white wove (type 15), 24.5 x 20.1 cm., pp. [1–4], paged "14–16"; mounted and bound, with ts. copy.

Date: [Theme No. 11, 14–28 February 1835].

Contents: Fair copy of class exercise; varies from text published as "Mankind Classified" in *LHDT*, pp. 164–66.

A8.   Citation: [College Theme] A.ms., 4 sides. Ink (c) Pencil (n*). CSmH (HM 934).

Title: "One of a cold and of a constant mind, | Not quickened into ardent action soon, | Not prompt for petty enterprise; yet bold. | Fierce where need is, and capable of all things." | [paragraph] Distinguish between this and other kinds of energetic character—— | and speak of one or more in History, who answer to the above description.

First line: Energy is a quality common to various characters, which to the eye of the careless observer appear to have no resemblance.

Collation: 2 leaves of white wove (type 15), 24.5 x 19.9 cm., pp. [1–4], paged "8–11"; mounted and bound, with ts. copy.

Date: [Theme No. 16, 9–23 May 1835].

Contents: Fair copy of class exercise; varies from text published as "An Essay on Variety of Energy in Men" in *LHDT*, pp. 70–73.

A9. Citation: [Exhibition Part] A.ms., 3 sides. Ink (c). MH-UA.

Title: Διαλογς. | Δεχιος ——— Clarke, Manlius S. | κατων ——— Thoreau, David H.

First line: Δεχιος Oᶜ Καισαρ σε Χαιρειν διαχλευεται.

Collation: 2 leaves of white wove, 23.1 x 19.4 cm., pp. [1–4]; bound in *Exhibition and Commencement Performances, 1834–1835*.

Date: 13 July 1835.

Contents: Fair copy of dialogue in Greek. Text and facsimile in *THC*, pp. 78–81. The text is translated and annotated.

A10. Citation: [College Theme] A.ms., 4 sides. Ink (c) Pencil (n*). NNPM (MA 920).

Title: "I live like a prince, not indeed in the pomp | of greatness, but in the pride of liberty; master of | my books, master of my time." | [paragraph] Speak of the privileges and plea | sures of a literary man.

First line: "Scriptorum chorus omnis amat nessus, et fugit urbes." This is as true of the literary man of the present day,

Collation: 2 leaves of white wove (type 15), 24.4 x 19.9 cm., pp. [1–4]; mounted and bound.

Date: [Theme No. 20, 4–18 September 1835].

Contents: Fair copy of class exercise; varies from text published as "The Literary Life" in *LHDT*, pp. 85–87.

A11. Citation: [College Forensic] A.ms., 4 sides. Ink (c, r). TxU.

Title: The comparative moral policy of severe and mild pun-|ishments.

First line: The end of all punishment is the welfare of the state,——the good of community at large,—— not the suffering of an individual.

Collation: 2 leaves of white wove (type 3), 25.4 x 20.3 cm., pp. [1–4].

Date: [Forensic No. 2, September 1835].

Contents: Late draft of class exercise; varies from text published as "The Comparative Moral Policy of Severe and Mild Punishments" in *LHDT*, pp. 79–82. A facsimile of the first leaf appears in *ESQ*, No. 13 (1958), p. 99.

A12. Citation: [College Theme] A.ms., 4 sides. Ink (c). NNPM (MA 920).

Title: The ways in which a man's style may be said to | offend against simplicity.

First line: If we would aim at perfection in any- thing, simplicity must not be overlooked.

Collation: 2 leaves of white wove (type 3), 25.3 x 20.1 cm., pp. [1–4]; mounted and bound.

Date: [Theme No. 25, 13–27 November 1835].

Contents: Fair copy of class exercise; varies from text published as "The Simple Style" in *LHDT*, pp. 90–92.

A13. Citation: [College Forensic] A.ms., 4 sides. Ink (c). NNPM (MA 2392).

Title: Advantages and disadvantages of foreign in | fluence on American Literature.

First line: The nations of the old world have each a literature peculiarly its own.

Collation: 2 leaves of white wove (type 3), 25.2 x 20.1 cm., pp. [1–4]; mounted, with ts. copy.

Date: [Forensic No. 7, April 1836].

Contents: Fair copy of class exercise; varies from text published as "American Literature" in *LHDT*, pp. 130–34.

A14.   Citation: [College Forensic] A.ms., 2 sides. Ink (c) Pencil (n*). CSmH (HM 934).

First line: Our respect for what is foreign has a tendency, on the other hand, to render us blind to native merit,

Collation: 1 leaf of white wove (type 3), 25.2 x 20.1 cm., pp. [5–6], paged "29–30"; mounted and bound, with ts. copy.

Date: [Forensic No. 7, April 1836].

Contents: Fair copy of class exercise; varies from text published as the final three paragraphs of "American Literature" in *LHDT*, pp. 133–34.

A15.   Citation: [College Forensic] A.ms., 4 sides. Ink (c). CSmH (HM 934).

Title: Whether the Cultivation of the Imagination conduce | to the Happiness of the Individual.

First line: Man is an intellectual being. Without the least hesitation, as well as from the most careful investigation,

Collation: 2 leaves of white wove (type 3), 25.3 x 20.1 cm., pp. [1–4], paged "4–7"; mounted and bound, with ts. copy.

Date: [Forensic No. 10, September 1836].

Contents: Fair copy of class exercise; varies from text published as "Imagination as an Element of Happiness" in *LHDT*, pp. 114–17.

A16. Citation: [College Theme] A.ms., 4 sides. Ink (c). NNPM (MA 920).

Title: The Love of Stories, real or fabulous, in young | and old. Account for it, and show what good | use it may serve.

First line: One thing can hardly be called more curious than another, yet all are not equally the objects of our curiosity.

Collation: 2 leaves of white wove (type 3), 25.3 x 20 cm., pp. [1–4]; mounted and bound.

Date: [Theme No. 39, 16–30 September 1836].

Contents: Fair copy of class exercise; varies from text published as "The Story-Telling Faculty" in *LHDT*, pp. 117–20.

A17. Citation: [College Essay] A.ms., 10 sides. Ink (c) Pencil (n*). CSmH (HM 934).

Title: Introductions | to | The Study | of the | Greek Classic Poets. | by | Henry Nelson Coleridge, Esqr. M.A. | Late Fellow of King's College, Cambridge. Part 1.

First line: "My wish" says the author, "Is to enable the youthful student to form a more just and liberal judgment of the characters and merits of the Greek Poets,

Collation: 5 leaves of white wove (type 3), 25.2 x 20.1 cm., pp. [1–10], paged "19–28"; mounted and bound, with ts. copy.

Date: 1 October 1836.

Contents: Fair copy of class exercise; text in Carl Bode, "A New College Manuscript of Thoreau's", *AL* 21 (1949): 311–20. For similar essays see F1a, F2d.

A18.   Citation: [College Forensic] A.ms., 4 sides. Ink (c). DLC (Literary Miscellany).

Title: Whether the Government ought to educate the | children of those parents, who refuse to do it them | selves——

First line: I maintain that the Government ought to provide for the education of all children who would otherwise be brought up, or rather grow up, in ignorance.

Collation: 2 leaves of white wove (type 3), 25.2 x 19.9 cm., pp. [1–4]; mounted and bound, with ts. copy.

Date: [Forensic No. 11, October 1836].

Contents: Fair copy of class exercise; varies from text published as "Compulsory Education" in *LHDT*, pp. 178–79. A facsimile is in *United States Library of Congress Quarterly Journal of Acquisitions* 6 (1949): 102–6.

A19.   Citation: [College Theme] A.ms., 4 sides. Ink (c) Pencil (n*). VtMiM.

Title: What is the meaning of "Fate," in the an- | cient use of the word? | What its popular significa- tion now?

First line: No language is so meagre, or so imper- fect, as not to contain a term very nearly, if not exactly, synonymous with our word Fate.

Collation: 2 leaves of white wove (type 3), 25.3 x 20.1 cm., pp. [1–4].

Date: [Theme No. 41, 14–28 October 1836].

Contents: Fair copy of class exercise; varies from text published as "Fate Among the Ancients" in *LHDT*, pp. 175–78.

A20. Citation: [College Theme] A.ms., 2 sides. Ink (c) Pencil (n*). MH (*AC 85.St 317).

First line: The travelling author lands on our shores with all the prejudices of the old country fresh in his mind,

Collation: 1 leaf of white wove (type 3), 25.2 x 20.1 cm., pp. [1–2]; tipped in E. C. Steadman, *Poets of America* (Cambridge, Mass.: Houghton Mifflin Co., 1885), 2: facing p. 340.

Date: [Theme No. 42, 28 October to 11 November 1836].

Contents: Fair copy of college exercise; varies from text published as the conclusion of "Various Means of Public Influence" in *LHDT*, pp. 161–62.

Note: The assigned topic for this theme was as follows: "State some of the causes of differing and imperfect accounts of countries given by travellers and by native authors". See *THY*, p. 12.

A21. Citation: [College Theme] A.ms., 9 sides. Ink (c). NNPM (MA 920).

Title: Show how it is that a writer's nationality and indi | vidual genius may be fully manifested in a Play or other | Literary work upon a Foreign or Ancient subject —— | and yet full justice be done to the subject.

First line: Man has been called a bundle of habits. This truth, I imagine, was the discovery of a philosopher—

Collation: 5 leaves of white wove (type 3), 25.2 x 20.1 cm., pp. [1–10], rectos foliated* "a–e"; mounted and bound.

Date: [Theme No. 44, 25 November to 16 December 1836].

Contents: Fair copy of class exercise; varies from text published as "National and Individual Genius" in *LHDT*, pp. 106–13.

A22.   Citation: [College Essay] A.ms., 14 sides. Ink (c,r) Pencil (r*). VtMiM.

Title: [on 7v] L'Allegro & Il Penseroso

First line: bright spot in the student's history, [a cloud] by day, a pillar of fire by night, shedding a grateful lustre over long years of toil,

Collation: 7 leaves (including fragments) of gray wove (type 4), 24.7 x 19.8 cm., pp. [1–14], paged "5–8, 11–15".

Date: January 1837.

Contents: Late draft, incomplete, of class exercise; text in Edwin Moser, "The Order of Fragments of Thoreau's Essay on 'L'Allegro' and 'Il Penseroso' ", *TSB* 101 (1968):1–2. A facsimile is in *TM* 1:170–82.

A23.   Citation: [College Theme] A.ms., 6 sides. Ink (c) Pencil (n*). MH (MS Am 278.5.5*).

Title: Point out particulars in the speeches of Moloch & the | rest, P. L. II, which appear to you characteristic.

First line: "After short silence then, And summons read, the great consult began." [paragraph] Satan, Moloch, Belial, Mammon, and Beëlzebubb,

Collation: 3 leaves of gray wove (type 4), 24.5 x 19.5 cm., pp. [1–6]; bound.

Date: [Theme No. 45, 16 December 1836 to 20 January 1837].

Contents: Fair copy of class exercise; varies from text published as "Characteristics of Milton's Poesy" in *LHDT*, pp. 93–97. A facsimile is in *TM* 1:184–87.

A24.   Citation: [College Theme] A.ms., 4 sides. Ink (c,r) Pencil (r). VtMiM.

Title: Speak of the characteristics which, either humorously or reproach- | fully, we are in the habit of ascribing to the people of dif- | ferent sections of our own country. [underscored after last line]

First line: A nationality is not necessarily, nor strictly speaking, an agregate of individualities, any further than words are concerned.

Collation: 2 leaves of gray wove (type 4), 24.6 x 19.8 cm., pp. [1–4].

Date: [Theme No. 47, 3–17 February 1837].

Contents: Late draft of class exercise; varies from text published as "Provincial Americans" in *LHDT*, pp. 155–57.

A25.   Citation: [College Theme] A.ms., 2 sides. Ink (c) Pencil (n*). VtMiM.

Title: Compare some of the Methods of gaining or exerci- | sing public Influence: as | Lectures, the Pulpit Associations, the Press, | Political Office.

First line: Inveterate custom, as well as the respect with which most men regard his sacred office, secure to the preacher

Collation: 1 leaf of gray wove (type 4), 24.6 x 19.8 cm., pp. [1–2], verso paged "20".

Date: [Theme No. 48, 17 February to 3 March 1837].

Contents: Late draft, incomplete, of class exercise; varies from text published as initial portion of "Various Means of Public Influence" in *LHDT*, pp. 159–61.

A26.   Citation: [College Theme] A.ms., 7 sides. Ink (c,r). NjPentS.

Title: Name, and speak of, Titles of Books, either as | pertinent to the matter, or merely ingenious and attractive.

First line: When at length, after infinite toil and anxiety, an author has fairly completed his work,

Collation: 4 leaves of gray wove (type 4), 24.6 x 19.8 cm., pp. [1–8].

Date: [Theme No. 49, 3–17 March 1837].

Contents: Late draft of class exercise; text and facsimile in R. B. Shuman, "Thoreau's *Of Books and their Titles*: A New Edition", *ESQ*, No. 18 (1960), pp. 26–34.

A27.   Citation: [College Theme] A.ms., 10 sides. Ink (c,r) Pencil (n*). MH (MS Am 278.5.5*).

Title: "The thunder's roar, the Lightning's flash, the | billows' roar, the earthquake's shock, all derive their | dread sublimity from Death." | "The Inheritance." chapter. 55. | Examine this theory.

First line: "Whatever," says Burke, "is fitted in any sort to excite the ideas of pain, and danger, that is to say, whatever is in any sort terrible

Collation: 5 leaves of gray wove (type 4), 24.5 x 19.5 cm., pp. [1–10]; bound.

Date: [Theme No. 50, 17–31 March 1837].

Contents: Late draft of class exercise; varies from text published as "The Sublimity of Death" in *LHDT*, pp. 142–48.

A28.   Citation: [College Forensic] A.ms., 4 sides. Ink (c).
         RPB.

         Title: The opinions of Dymond and Mrs. Opie re-
         specting | the general obligation to tell the truth
         [four words underscored]; are they | sound and
         applicable? | [paragraph] Vide Dymond's "Essays on
         Morality" and Mrs. Opie's | "Illustrations of Lying."

         First line: I shall confine myself to the examination
         of Mr. Dymond's opinions without pretending to
         offer any of my own.

         Collation: 2 leaves of gray wove (type 4), 24.8 x 19.9
         cm., pp. [1–4]; with ts. note by F. B. Sanborn.

         Date: [Forensic No. 16, 28 April 1837].

         Contents: Fair copy of class exercise; varies from
         text published as "The Morality of Lying" in LHDT,
         pp. 171–73. For another description see B. L. St.
         Armand, "Thoreau Comes to Brown", BBr 22 (1968):
         126–27.

A29.   Citation: [College Theme] A.ms., 7 sides. Ink (c)
         Pencil (n*). VtMiM.

         Title: Paley in his Nat. Theology, Chap 23 speaks |
         of minds utterly averse to "the flatness [underscored]
         of being con- | tent with common reasons"—and con-
         siders the high- | est minds "most liable to this re-
         pugnancy." | [paragraph] See the passage, and ex-
         plain the moral or in- | tellectual defect.

         First line: Turgot has said, "He that has never
         doubted the existence of matter, may be assured he
         has no aptitude for metaphysical inquiries."

         Collation: 4 leaves of gray wove (type 4), 24.7 x
         19.7 cm., pp. [1–8].

         Date: [Theme No. 51, 31 March to 5 May 1837].

         Contents: Late draft of class exercise; varies from
         text published as "The Superior and the Common
         Man" in LHDT, pp. 137–40.

A30.   Citation: [College Theme] A.ms., 4 sides. Ink (c, r) Pencil (n*). VtMiM.

Title: "The clock sends me to bed at ten, and makes me | rise at eight. I go to bed awake, and arise asleep; but | I have ever held conformity one of the best arts of life, | and though I might choose my own hours, I think | it proper to follow theirs" | E. Montagu's Letters. | [paragraph] Speak of the duty, inconvenience and dangers | of conformity [underscored], in little things and great.

First line: Neither natural nor revealed religion affords any rules by which we may determine the comparative enormity of different vices,

Collation: 2 leaves of gray wove (type 4), 24.7 x 19.8 cm., pp. [1–4].

Date: [Theme No. 52, 5–19 May 1837].

Contents: Late draft of class exercise; varies from text published as "Conformity in Things Unessential" in LHDT, pp. 150–52.

A31.   Citation: [College Forensic] A.ms., 4 sides. Ink (c,r). VtMiM.

Title: Whether Moral Excellence tend directly to increase | Intellectual Power?

First line: First, what is moral excellence? Not, surely, the mere acknowledgement of the divine origin of the Scriptures, and obedience to their dictates as such;

Collation: 2 leaves of gray wove (type 4), 24.7 x 19.8 cm., pp. [1–4].

Date: [Forensic No. 17, 26 May 1837].

Contents: Fair copy of class exercise; text in Reginald L. Cook, The Concord Saunterer (Middlebury, Vt.: Middlebury College Press, 1940), pp. 60–61.

A32.   Citation: [College Theme] A.ms., 4 sides. Ink (c,r)
        Pencil (n*). VtMiM.

        Title: The mark or standard by which a nation is
        judged | to be barbarous or civilized. | Barbarities of
        Civilized States.

        First line: The justice of a nation's claim to be re-
        garded as civilized, seems to depend, mainly, upon
        the degree in which Art has triumphed over Nature.

        Collation: 2 leaves of gray wove (type 4), 24.7 x
        19.7 cm., pp. [1–4].

        Date: [Theme No. 53, 19 May to 2 June 1837].

        Contents: Late draft of class exercise; varies from
        text published as "Barbarism and Civilization" in
        LHDT, pp. 180–83.

A33.   Citation: [College Theme: see Section H].

A34.   Citation: [Class Book Entry] A.ms., 2 sides. Ink (c).
        MH-UA.

        Title: David Henry Thoreau

        First line: I am of French extract, my ancestors
        having taken refuge in the isle of Jersey, on the
        revocation of the edict of Nantes, by Lewis 14th, in
        the year 1685.

        Collation: 2 leaves of white wove, 34.3 x 23.1 cm.,
        pp. [1–4]; bound in the Class Book of 1837.

        Date: [Before 30 August 1837].

        Contents: Fair copy of an autobiographical sketch;
        text and facsimile in TM, 1:224–25.

A35.   Citation: [Commencement Part] A.ms., 6 sides. Ink
        (c). MH-UA.

Title: "The commercial Spirit of modern times considered | in its influence on the Political, Moral, and | Literary character of a Nation."

First line: The history of the world, it has been justly observed, is the history of the progress of humanity;

Collation: 4 leaves of gray wove (type 4), 24.7 x 19.9 cm., pp. [1–8]; bound in *Exhibition and Commencement Performances, 1836–1837.*

Date: [30 August 1837].

Contents: Fair copy of commencement oration; varies from text published in *W* 6:8–10. See also *TM* 1:233–35.

B.

POEMS AND TRANSLATIONS, 1828–1860

Thoreau's earliest literary ambition, planted and nurtured by Emerson, was to become a major Transcendental poet. As a student he wrote a few poems, but once settled in Concord he became a devoted versifier, translating or copying excerpts of ancient and modern poetry for his commonplace books (1836–1843) and drafting his own efforts into the early *Journal* (1837–1841). These he later copied and revised, either as single poems for *The Dial* (1841–1844) or as set pieces for the drafts of *A Week* (1845–1848) and *Walden* (1845–1854). Thoreau wrote virtually 90 percent of his poems before 1850; in later years he found new interests to supplant that youthful vocation. But for more than a dozen years, he worked long and seriously to become a poet, as the following manuscripts will attest.

This section of the Calendar lists exactly 201 titles of poems and translations, comprising a total of 331 draft versions. Included here are 75 items that have appeared since Carl Bode's landmark edition *Collected Poems of Henry Thoreau* (Baltimore: Johns Hopkins University Press, 1964). Of these items, only 11 are poems new to the edition; 64 are additional drafts of titles already listed there. Readers will find the Bode edition an excellent source of information, especially on textual matters and publishing history. This listing supplements the *Collected Poems* by adjusting Thoreau's canon, deleting and adding a few poems; by correcting some readings; and by dating all poems according to paper, text, and known history of composition.

As a result the arrangement here differs considerably from the *Collected Poems*, which divides Thoreau's verse into three categories (published, unpublished, undated), each having a different chronology. Here the arrangement is unitary, following a single chronology of *dates of composition*, from 1828 to 1860. Poems existing in multiple drafts appear according to their earliest date of composition, regardless of Thoreau's subsequent revision or publication (see "Inspiration," B12a–l). Conversely, a history of previous publication has no bearing if the early drafts have not survived (see "Light-winged Smoke, Icarian bird," B189). The listing also ignores spurious dates, which appear on manuscripts Thoreau copied from earlier sources (see B50–B84, B94, B123–B124, B159–B160) or on postumous copies made by Sophia Thoreau (see B199–B201). Instead, these papers appear according to their date of transcription. Specific dates (day, month, year) precede general dates (year only), and groups of the latter sort (see B22–B31, B125–B137, B140–B158) follow the order of *Collected Poems.*

Note

An item of associational importance to this section is Thoreau's own set of *The Dial*, now at ICarbS. Each volume has his penciled annotations, which revise his own texts, indicate their source in the *Journal*, and identify other contributors.

B1. Citation: "Why do the seasons change? and why"
A.ms., 1 side. Ink (c). MCon.

Title: The Seasons

First line: Why do the Seasons change? and why

Collation: 1 leaf of white wove 23.9 x 19.9 cm., pp.
[1–2]; tipped in H. S. Salt, *The Life of Henry David
Thoreau* (London: W. Scott, Ltd., 1896).

Date: [1828–1829].

Contents: Fair copy of 4 lines; text in *CP*, pp. 243,
336. For other contents see A1.

Note: Although printed in *CP*, the quatrain is probably not original. Similar inscriptions appear in the
college themes and forensics.

B2. Citation: "To the Comet" A.ms., 2 sides. Ink (c,r,d)
Pencil (r,d,n*). RPB.

Title: To The Comet.

First line: Reserved traveller what thy race?

Collation: 1 leaf of white wove (type 3), 25.2 x
20.5 cm., pp. [1–2].

Date: [1835–1836].

Contents: Early draft of 6 stanzas, 44 lines; text in
CP, pp. 88, 302–3.

Note: Probably inspired by Halley's Comet, which
appeared in 1835.

B3. Citation: "Speech of a Saxon Ealderman" A.ms., 2
sides. Ink (c). NNPM (MA 920).

Title: Speech of a Saxon Ealderman.

First line: This life, O king, of men on earth,

Collation: 1 leaf of gray wove (type 4), 24.5 x 19.6
cm., pp. [1–2]; mounted and bound.

Date: 1 July 1837.

Contents: Fair copy of 8 stanzas, 34 lines; text in
CP, pp. 213–14, 327. A facsimile is in TM 1:226–27.

B4.   Citation: "Life is a summer's day" A.ms., 2 sides. Ink
(c,r). ICarbS.

Title: Sic Vita. [partly erased]

First line: Life is a summer's day,

Collation: 1 leaf of white wove (type 9), 24.7 x
19.9 cm., pp. [1–2].

Date: 2 July 1837.

Contents: Late draft of 11 stanzas, 33 lines; text in
CP, pp. 382, 400.

B5a.   Citation: "The morning in our prime" [see Section
H].

B5b.   Citation: "I love a careless streamlet" [see Section
H].

B6.   Citation: "Friends! that parting tear reserve it" A.ms.,
1 side. Ink (c). MH-UA.

First line: "Friends! that parting tear reserve it

Collation: 1 leaf of white wove, 34.3 x 23.1 cm., pp.
[1–2]; bound in Class Book of 1837.

Date: [Before 18 July 1837].

Contents: Fair copy of 4 lines; text in CP, pp. 244,
336. A facsimile is in TM 1:224–25.

B7.   Citation: "Pens to mend, and hands to guide" A.ms.,
1 side. Ink (c). NYPL (Berg).

First line: Pens to mend, and hands to guide

Collation: 1 leaf of white wove, 24 x 18.4 cm., pp. [1-2].

Date: 13 October 1837.

Contents: Fair copy of 2 lines; text in *Corr.*, p. 13.

B8.   Citation: ["Methinks that time has reached his prime"] A.ms., 1 side. Pencil (c,r,d). Prof. R. Adams, Chapel Hill, N.C.

First line: Methinks that time has reached his prime

Collation: 1 leaf of white wove (type 9), 25 x 20 cm., pp. [1-2].

Date: [Before 22 October 1837].

Contents: Early draft of 3 stanzas, 17 lines; unpublished. For a later parallel text see *CP*, p. 126.

B9.   Citation: ["Twa Merrit Wemen"] A.ms., 1 side. Pencil (c). ViU (6345).

Title: Extract from conclusion of Dunbar's "Twa Merrit | Wemen", 1530. Anglo Saxon.

First line: "While that the Day did up Dawn

Collation: 1 leaf of white wove (type 1), 32 x 19.9 cm., pp. [1-2]; bound, with ts. copy.

Date: [1837–1838].

Contents: Fair copy of 6 lines; unpublished.

B10a.   Citation: "The Fall of the Leaf" A.ms., 4 sides. Pencil (c,r,d). CSmH (HM 13201: 2, 4r, 10r).

First line: (2) September rides upon the gale
        (4) The cricket chirps beneath the sod
        (10) I hear the crickets slumbrous lay

Collation: 3 leaves of white wove (type 9), 24.8 x 19.7 cm., pp. [1–6].

Date: [After 24 February 1838].

Contents: Early draft of 5 stanzas, 32 lines; text in CP, pp. 236–38, 253–55, 258 (as lines 9–12, 29–40, 49–64). For other contents see B13b, B14a, B16b, E1b–c.

B10b.   Citation: "The Fall of the Leaf" A.ms., 2 sides. Pencil (c,r). CSmH (HM 13201:6).

First line: Far in the woods these golden days

Collation: 1 fragment of gray wove (type 1), 12.7 x 20.1 cm., pp. [1–2].

Date: [After June 1840].

Contents: Early draft of 12 lines; text in CP, pp. 237–38, 256 (as lines 41–48).

Note: Verso contains two prose sentences that were the basis for these lines.

B10c.   Citation: "The Fall of the Leaf" A.ms., 1 side. Pencil (c). CSmH (HM 13201:5r).

First line: And greatness now need walk alone

Collation: 1 leaf of white wove, 21 x 15.5 cm., pp. [1–2].

Date: [1840].

Contents: Early draft of 5 stanzas, 20 lines; text in CP, pp. 255–56. For other contents see F2b.

B10d.   Citation: "The Fall of the Leaf" A.ms., 2 sides. Pencil (c,r). CSmH (HM 13201: 1r, 3v).

First line: (1) The evening of the year draws on
          (3) So in mid-summer I have seen

Collation: 2 leaves of white wove (type 2), 31.1 x
19.1 cm., pp. [1–4].

Date: 6 September [1841].

Contents: Early draft of 23 lines; text in *CP*, pp.
236–38; 251; 254 (as lines 17–24, 27–28). For other
contents see B11a.

B10e.   Citation: "The Fall of the Leaf" A.ms., 4 sides. Ink
(c) Pencil (r,d). NYPL (Berg).

Title: The Fall of the Leaf.

First line: The evening of the year draws on,

Collation: 2 leaves of gray wove (type 3), 24.9 x
20.1 cm., pp. [1–4], 11 paged* "342" and original
paging "105–6" erased.

Date: [1842].

Contents: Late draft of 21 stanzas, 84 lines; text
varies considerably from *CP*, pp. 236–38.

B10f.   Citation: "The Fall of the Leaf" A.ms., 7 sides. Ink
(c,r) Pencil (r). NYPL (Berg).

Title: The Fall of the Leaf.

First line: Grown tired of the rank summer's wealth,

Collation: 4 leaves of blue wove (type 1), 25.2 x 20
cm., pp. [1–8].

Date: [1847].

Contents: Late draft of 42 stanzas, 168 lines; text
varies considerably from *CP*, pp. 236–38.

B10g.   Citation: "The Fall of the Leaf" A.ms., 1 side. Ink
(c) Pencil (d). CSmH (HM 13182:III, 4r).

First line: The thread bare trees so poor & thin,

Collation: 1 leaf of blue wove (type 1), 25.2 x 20 cm., pp. [1–2], paged "369".

Date: [1847].

Contents: Fair copy of 2 stanzas, 8 lines; text in *CP*, pp. 238, 334–35 (as lines 57–60). For other contents see B13i, D9b.

B11a. Citation: "Friendship" A.ms., 2 sides. Ink (c,r). CSmH (HM 13201:3v).

First line: That Love of which I purposed to sing,

Collation: 1 leaf of white wove (type 2), 31.1 x 19.1 cm., pp. [1–2].

Date: 8 April 1838.

Contents: Early draft of 3 stanzas, 15 lines; text in *CP*, pp. 90–91, 303. For other contents see B10d.

B11b. Citation: "Friendship" A.ms., 3 sides. Ink (c) Pencil (d). NNPM (MA 1302:1).

Title: Friendship.

First line: I think awhile of Love, and while I think,

Collation: 2 leaves of white wove (type 25), 11.2 x 9.3 cm., pp. [1–4], paged "65–67"; bound in [vol. 1] of the *Journal*.

Date: [November 1841], dated "April 8 1838".

Contents: Fair copy of 11 stanzas, 55 lines; text in *CP*, pp. 89–91, 303.

B12. Citation: "The Cliffs & Springs" A.ms., 2 sides. Pencil (c) Ink (traces pencil). NYPL (Berg).

Title: The Cliffs & Springs.

First line: When breathless noon hath paused on hill and side

Collation: 1 leaf of white wove (type 9), 24.9 x 19.8 cm., pp. [1–2]; in folder marked "Miscellaneous Holograph Notes".

Date: 25 April 1838.

Contents: Fair copy of 22 lines; text in *CP*, p. 92. For contents of the verso see B13a, B14b.

B13a.   Citation: "Inspiration" A.ms., 1 side. Pencil (c). NYPL (Berg).

First line: No fame can tempt the bard

Collation: 1 leaf of white wove (type 9), 24.9 x 19.8 cm., pp. [1–2].

Date: [After 25 April 1838].

Contents: Early draft of 23 lines; text varies considerably from *CP*, p. 233. For other contents see B12, B14b.

B13b.   Citation: "Inspiration" A.ms., 6 sides. Pencil (c,r,d). CSmH (HM 13201: 10, 12, 13).

First line: (10) Always the general show of things
             (12) My memory I'll educate
             (13) Whose clear and ancient harmony

Collation: 3 leaves of white wove (type 9), 24.7 x 19.8 cm., pp. [1–6].

Date: [After 8 July 1838].

Contents: Early draft of 73 lines; text in *CP*, pp. 230–33 (as lines 1–4, 17–28, 33–64, 69–80). See also *CP*, pp. 258–63. For other contents see B10a, B16b, E1c.

B13c.   Citation: "Inspiration" A.ms., 2 sides. Pencil (c,r,d). Prof. R. Adams, Chapel Hill, N.C.

First line: If with light head erect I sing

Collation: 1 leaf of gray wove (type 1), 25 x 19.5
cm., pp. [1–2].

Date: [After 8 September 1841].

Contents: Intermediate draft of 3 stanzas, 12 lines;
text varies from CP, pp. 230–33, 259. For other contents see B46a.

B13d.   Citation: "Inspiration" A.ms., 2 sides. Ink (c). MH
(MS Am 278.5.20[1]).

Title: Inspiration.

First line: I hearing yet who had but ears,

Collation: 1 leaf of gray wove (type 1), 25.1 x 19.9
cm., pp. [1–2]; mounted.

Date: [1842–1843].

Contents: Fair copy of 4 lines; text varies from CP,
p. 231 (lines 25–28).

B13e.   Citation: "Inspiration" A.ms., 2 sides. Ink (c) Pencil
(r,d). VtMiM.

Title: Inspiration.

First line: I hearing get who had but ears,

Collation: 1 fragment of gray wove (type 1), 20.4 x
20.1 cm., pp. [1–2]; in folder marked "Fragments".

Date: [1842–1843].

Contents: Intermediate draft of 4 lines; text in CP,
pp. 231, 333–34.

B13f.   Citation: "Inspiration" A.ms., 1 side. Pencil (c,r,d).
CSmH (HM 13201:11r).

First line: I hear beyond the range of sound

Collation: 1 fragment of gray wove (type 1), 16 x
19.5 cm., pp. [1–2].

Date: [1842–1843].

Contents: Early draft of 9 lines; text in *CP*, pp. 231–32, 260.

B13g.   Citation: "Inspiration" A.ms., 1 side. Ink (c*,r*). MH (bMS Am 1280 H [46]).

Title: Henry T's lines which pleased me so | well were

First line: "I hearing get, who had but ears,

Collation: 1 leaf of white wove (anom.), pp. [1–2], paged "127"; bound in R. W. Emerson's *Notebook U*.

Date: [1843].

Contents: Fair copy of 4 lines, in Emerson's hand; text in *CP*, p. 234.

B13h.   Citation: "Inspiration" A.ms., 2 sides. Ink (c). ICarbS.

Title: Inspiration.

First line: If thou wilt but stand by my ear,

Collation: 1 leaf of blue wove (type 1), 25.1 x 20.2 cm., pp. [1–2]; formerly laid in Thoreau's copy of *The Dial*.

Date: [1847].

Contents: Fair copy of 4 lines; text in *CP*, p. 234.

B13i.   Citation: "Inspiration" A.ms., 1 side. Ink (c) Pencil (d). CSmH (HM 13182: III, 4r).

First line: I moments live, who lived but years

Collation: 1 leaf of blue wove (type 1), 25.2 x 20 cm., pp. [1–2], paged "369".

Date: [1847].

Contents: Late draft of 4 lines; text in *CP*, pp. 231, 333. For other contents see B10g, D9b.

B13j.   Citation: "Inspiration" A.ms., 3 sides. Ink (c).
         NNPM (MA 925).

         Title: Inspiration.

         First line: Always the general show of things.

         Collation: 2 leaves of blue wove, 24.6 x 20.1 cm.,
         pp. [1–4]; mounted and bound as fifty-first leaf in
         "Mrs. Field's Album"; with a.n.s. Sophia E. Thoreau.

         Date: [1848].

         Contents: Fair copy of 16 stanzas, 64 lines; text in
         CP, pp. 230–33, 333–34.

B13k.   Citation: "Inspiration" A.ms., 1 side. Ink (c)*. MH
         (bMS Am 1280 H [59]).

         First line: "I hearing get, who had but ears,

         Collation: 1 leaf of white wove (anom.), pp. [1–2];
         bound in R. W. Emerson's Notebook AZ.

         Date: 1 November 1849.

         Contents: Fair copy of 4 lines, in Emerson's hand;
         text in CP, p. 234.

         Note: The quatrain serves as Emerson's motto for
         his notebook.

B13l.   Citation: "Inspiration" A.ms., 3 sides. Ink (c)* Pen-
         cil (n)*. MH (bMS Am 1280 H [117]).

         Title: Inspiration. By H. D. Thoreau. [line under-
         scored]

         First line: If with light head erect I sing,

         Collation: 2 leaves of white wove (anom.), pp.
         [1–4], paged "51–53"; bound in R. W. Emerson's
         Notebook HT, "Miscellaneous Notes on H. D. Tho-
         reau".

         Date: July 1864.

Contents: Fair copy of 12 stanzas, 48 lines, in Emerson's hand; text in *CP*, pp. 231–34.

B14a.   Citation: "The Bluebirds" A.ms., 1 side. Ink (c) Pencil (r,d). CSmH (HM 13201:2v).

First line: Meanwhile old earth jogged steadily on

Collation: 1 leaf of white wove (type 9), 24.8 x 19.7 cm., pp. [1–2].

Date: [26 April 1838].

Contents: Early draft of 20 lines; text in *CP*, pp. 94, 252–53. For other contents see B10a.

B14b.   Citation: "The Bluebirds" A.ms., 1 side. Pencil (c). NYPL (Berg).

First line: Many a bird of shorter wing

Collation: 1 leaf of white wove (type 9), 24.9 x 19.8 cm., pp. [1–2]; in folder marked "Miscellaneous Holograph Notes".

Date: [26 April 1838].

Contents: Early draft of 8 lines; not in text of *CP*, pp. 93–96. For other contents see B12, B13a.

B14c.   Citation: "The Bluebirds" A.ms., 4 sides. Ink (c). NNPM (MA 1302:1).

Title: The Bluebirds

First line: In the midst of the poplar that stands by our door,

Collation: 2 leaves of white wove (type 25), 11.2 x 9.3 cm., pp. [1–4], paged "69–72"; bound in [vol. 1] of the *Journal*.

Date: [November 1841], dated "April 26 1838".

Contents: Fair copy of 20 stanzas, 80 lines; text in
CP, pp. 93–96.

B15.   Citation: "I knew a man by sight" A.ms., 2 sides.
Ink (c). VtMiM.

First line: I knew a man by sight,

Collation: 1 leaf of gray wove (type 3), 24.8 x 19.9
cm., pp. [1–2]; in folder marked "Fragments".

Date: 17 June 1838.

Contents: Fair copy of 6 stanzas, 30 lines; text in
CP, pp. 102–3.

B16a.   Citation: "Upon the bank at early dawn" A.ms., 1
side. Pencil (c,r). CSmH (HM 13201:7r).

First line: When in my bed at early dawn

Collation: 1 fragment of white wove (type 10),
12.1 x 20.2 cm., pp. [1–2].

Date: [1838].

Contents: Early draft of 3 stanzas, 12 lines; text in
CP, pp. 203, 257. For contents of verso see F4c.

B16b.   Citation: "Upon the bank at early dawn" A.ms., 4
sides. Pencil (c,r,d). CSmH (HM 13201:10r, 13r).

First line: The stars with held their shining not

Collation: 2 leaves of white wove (type 9), 24.9 x
19.8 cm., pp. [1–4].

Date: [1838].

Contents: Early draft of 12 lines; text in *CP*, pp.
203–4, 258. For other contents see B10a, B13b, E1c.

B16c.   Citation: "Upon the bank at early dawn" A.ms., 3
sides. Ink (c) Pencil (r,d). NYPL (Berg).

Title: Cock-crowing.

First line: Upon my bed at early dawn

Collation: 2 leaves of gray wove (type 3), 24.9 x 20.1 cm., pp. [1–4], paged* "333".

Date: [Before 31 August 1839].

Contents: Intermediate draft of 15 stanzas, 62 lines; text varies from CP, p. 203.

B16d.   Citation: "Upon the bank at early dawn" A.ms., 1 side. Pencil (c) Ink (d). NNPM (MA 920).

First line: The stars withold their shining not

Collation: 1 leaf of white wove (type 21), 20.3 x 16 cm., pp. [1–2]; mounted and bound.

Date: [1840].

Contents: Late draft of 5 stanzas, 20 lines; text in CP, pp. 203–4; 326. For contents of recto see B18a.

B16e.   Citation: "Upon the bank at early dawn" A.ms., 1 side. Ink (c). CSmH (HM 13195).

First line: Upon the bank at early dawn

Collation: 1 leaf of white wove (type 11), 24.6 x 19.3 cm., pp. [11–12]; in folder marked "Monday".

Date: [1843–1844].

Contents: Fair copy of 9 stanzas, 36 lines; text in CP, pp. 203–4, 326. For other contents see D5c.

B17a.   Citation: "The Promethus Bound of Aeschylus" A.ms., 46 sides. Ink (c,r,d) Pencil (r,d). CSmH (HM 926).

First line: Kratos | We are come to the far-bounded plain of earth,

Collation: 23 leaves,
17 of blue wove (type 2), 25 x 20.2 cm.,
3 of white wove (type 9), 24.9 x 20 cm.,
2 of white wove (type 3), 25.4 x 20.1 cm.,
1 of white wove (type 21), 20.2 x 15.9 cm.,
pp. [1–46]; mounted and bound with leaves of the
Riverside Edition (1893).

Date: [1838–1840 (c), 1840–1842 (r)].

Contents: Early draft of 1,068 lines; text varies from
W 5:337–75. For other contents see B40c, C4b, D5e,
D6e, D23m, E1d. For corrections to the text see
L. M. Kaiser, "Remarks on Thoreau's Translation of
the Prometheus", *Classical Weekly* 56 (1953):69–70.

B17b.   Citation: "The Promethus Bound of Aeschylus"
A.ms., 44 sides. Ink (c) Pencil (r). MH (Ms.
278.5.15).

Title: Promethus Bound; | Of AEschylus

First line: Kr. We are come to the far-bounding
plain of earth,

Collation: 22 leaves of white wove (type 11), 24.7 x
19.7 cm., pp. 1 [2–44].

Date: [1842].

Contents: Intermediate draft of 1,060 lines; text
varies from W 5:337–75.

B18a.   Citation: "The Peal of the Bells" A.ms., 1 side. Ink
(c). NNPM (MA 920).

First line: And the metal goes round 't a single
bound,

Collation: 1 leaf of white wove (type 21), 20.3 x 16
cm., pp. [1–2]; mounted and bound.

Date: [After 10 February 1839].

Contents: Early draft of 4 stanzas, 16 lines; text in
CP, pp. 111, 306. For contents of verso see B16d.

B18b.   Citation: "The Peal of the Bells" A.ms., 2 sides. Ink
(c). NNPM (MA 1302:1).

Title: The Peal of the Bells.

First line: When the world grows old by the chimney side,

Collation: 2 leaves of white wove (type 25), 11.2 x
9.3 cm., pp. [1–4], paged "115–18", bound in [vol.
1] of the *Journal*.

Date: [November 1841], dated "February 10 1839".

Contents: Early draft of 4 stanzas, 22 lines; text in
CP, pp. 111, 306.

B18c.   Citation: "The Peal of the Bells" A.ms., 2 sides. Ink
(c). CSmH (HM 924:A).

First line: Now up they go, ding,

Collation: 2 leaves of blue wove (type 1), 25.1 x
19.9 cm., pp. [125–28], paged "²69/81".

Date: [1846–1847].

Contents: Early draft of 3 stanzas, 12 lines; text in
CP, p. 111 and Shanley, p. 162.

B18d.   Citation: "The Peal of the Bells" A.ms., 1 side. Ink
(c). CSmH (HM 924:E).

First line: Now up they go, ding,

Collation: 1 leaf of blue wove (type 8), 24.6 x 19.3
cm., pp. [23–24].

Date: [1853].

Contents: Intermediate draft of 3 lines; text in CP,
p. 111.

B18e.   Citation: "The Peal of the Bells" A.ms., 1 side. Ink
(c) Pencil (r,d). CSmH (HM 924:F).

First line: Now up they go, ding, then down again,
dong

Collation: 1 leaf of white wove (type 19), 23.7 x 19.2 cm., pp. [27–28].

Date: [1853–1854].

Contents: Late draft of 10 lines; text in *CP*, p. 111.

B19a.   Citation: "The Assabet" A.ms., 1 side. Pencil (c). CSmH (HM 13186:v).

First line: Rivers from the mountains flow

Collation: 1 leaf of white wove (type 9), 24.9 x 20 cm., pp. [1–2].

Date: [18 July 1839].

Contents: Early draft of 2 stanzas, 10 lines; text in *CP*, pp. 113–15, 307. For contents of recto see B24a.

B19b.   Citation: "The Assabet" A.ms., 3 sides. Ink (c) Pencil (d). NNPM (MA 1302:1).

Title: The Assabet.

First line: Up this pleasant stream let's row

Collation: 2 leaves of white wove (type 25), 11.2 x 9.3 cm., pp. [1–4], paged "133–36"; bound in [vol. 1] of the *Journal*.

Date: [November 1841], dated "July 18 1839".

Contents: Fair copy of 12 stanzas, 60 lines; text in *CP*, pp. 113–15, 307.

B19c.   Citation: "The Assabet" A.ms., 1 side. Ink (c). CSmH (HM 13195).

First line: In each dew drop of the morning

Collation: 1 leaf of white wove (type 11), 24.5 x 19.4 cm., pp. [1–2]; in folder marked "Sunday".

Date: [1843–1844].

Contents: Late draft of 2 lines; text in *CP*, pp. 113–14. For other contents see D4a.

Note: A second copy of this couplet is owned by Mr. C. B. Hansen, Westfield, N.J.

B19d. Citation: "The Assabet" A.ms., 1 side. Ink (c). CSmH (HM 13195).

First line: Ply the oars! away! away!

Collation: 1 leaf of blue wove (type 5), 24.6 x 19.9 cm., pp. [1–2]; in folder marked "Tuesday".

Date: [1848].

Contents: Fair copy of 3 lines; text in *CP*, pp. 113–14. For other contents see D6b.

Note: A posthumous copy of this poem, by Sophia Thoreau, is in the collection of Miss Grace Davenport, Glendale, Calif.

B20a. Citation: "The Fisher's Son" A.ms., 4 sides. Ink (c) Pencil (r). VtMiM.

Title: The Fisher's Son.

First line: I know the world where land and water meet,

Collation: 2 leaves of gray wove (type 2), 25.1 x 19.7 cm., pp. 1–4.

Date: [After 10 January 1840].

Contents: Late draft of 17 stanzas, 68 lines; text in *CP*, pp. 121–23, 308–9.

B20b. Citation: "The Fisher's Son" A.ms., 4 sides. Ink (c) Pencil (d). NNPM (MA 1302:2).

Title: The Fisher's Son.

First line: I know the world where land and water meet,

Collation: 2 leaves of white wove (type 25), 11.2 x 9.3 cm., pp. [1–4,] paged "19–22"; bound in [vol. 2] of the *Journal*.

Date: [November 1841], dated "January 10 1840".

Contents: Fair copy of 19 stanzas, 76 lines; text in *CP*, pp. 121–23, 308–9.

B21a.   Citation: "Godfrey of Boulogne" A.ms., 2 sides. Ink (c) Pencil (r,d). MH (bMS Am 278.5 [4,G]).

First line: Oh ye proud days of Europes middle age

Collation: 1 leaf of white wove, 24 x 19.5 cm., pp. [1–2], paged "161–62".

Date: [Before June 1840].

Contents: Early draft of 4 stanzas, 42 lines; text in *CP*, pp. 192–93, 323–24.

B21b.   Citation: "Godfrey of Boulogne" A.ms., 2 sides. Ink (c) Pencil (r). CSmH (HM 13197).

Title: Godfrey of Boulogne.

First line: The moon hung low o'er Provence vales,

Collation: 1 leaf of white wove, 25 x 19.5 cm., pp. [1–2].

Date: [September 1842].

Contents: Late draft of 4 stanzas, 48 lines; text in *CP*, pp. 192–93, 323–24.

B22a.   Citation: "Each more melodious note I hear" A.ms., 1 side. Ink (c). NNPM (MA 607).

First line: Each more melodious note I hear

Collation: 1 leaf of gray wove (type 3), 24.8 x 19.9 cm., pp. [9–10].

Date: July 1840.

Contents: Fair copy of 4 lines; text in *CP*, pp. 119, 308. For other contents see C2.

B22b.   Citation: "Each more melodious note I hear" A.ms., 1 side. Ink (c) Pencil (d). NNPM (MA 1302:2).

First line: Each more melodious note I hear

Collation: 1 leaf of white wove (type 25), 11.2 x 9.3 cm., pp. [1–2], paged "7"; bound in [vol. 2] of the *Journal.*

Date: [November 1841], originally ca. December 1839.

Contents: Fair copy of 4 lines; text in *CP*, pp. 119, 308.

B22c.   Citation: "Each more melodious note I hear" A.ms., 2 sides. Ink (c). MH (bMS Am 278.5 [2. 8r]).

First line: Each more melodious note I hear

Collation: 1 leaf of white wove (type 14), 24.5 x 18.9 cm., pp. [1–2]; in folder.

Date: [1846].

Contents: Late draft of 4 lines; text varies considerably from *CP*, p. 119.

B23a.   Citation: "Great God, I ask thee for no meaner pelf" A.ms., 2 sides. Pencil (c,d). Prof. R. Adams, Chapel Hill, N.C.

First line: Great God, I ask thee for no meaner pelf

Collation: 1 leaf of white wove (type 9), 25 x 20 cm., pp. [1–2].

Date: [Ca. 1840].

Contents: Early draft of 4 stanzas, 23 lines; text varies considerably from CP, p. 10.

B23b.   Citation: "Great God, I ask thee for no meaner pelf" A.ms., 2 sides. Ink (c). ICarbS.

Title: Prayer.

First line: Great God, I ask thee for no meaner pelf

Collation: 1 leaf of white wove (type 7), 25.1 x 20.2 cm., pp. [1–2]; formerly laid in Thoreau's copy of *The Dial*.

Date: [Before July 1842].

Contents: Fair copy of 2 stanzas, 10 lines; text in CP, p. 10.

Note: A fair copy in Sophia Thoreau's hand is at MConA.

B24a.   Citation: "Independence" A.ms., 2 sides. Ink (c). CSmH (HM 13186:r).

Title: Independence.

First line:: Ye princes keep your realms

Collation: 1 leaf of white wove (type 9), 24.9 x 20 cm., pp. [1–2].

Date: [1840].

Contents: Early draft of 4 stanzas, 16 lines; text in CP, pp. 132, 310. For contents of verso see B19a.

B24b.   Citation: "Independence" A.ms., 2 sides. Ink (c). CtY.

Title: Independence.

First line: My life more civil is and free

Collation: 1 leaf of blue wove (type 2), 25 x 19.7 cm., pp. [1–2].

Date: 30 July 1841.

Contents: Fair copy of 8 stanzas, 29 lines; text in CP, pp. 132–33, 310.

B24c. Citation: "Independence" A.ms., 1 side. Ink (c) Pencil (r). MH (bMS Am 278.5 [18]).

First line: Be sure your fate

Collation: 1 leaf of white wove (type 11), 24.7 x 19.5 cm., pp. [1–2].

Date: [1844 (c), 1848 (r)].

Contents: Late draft of 14 lines; text in CP, pp. 132, 310. For other contents see C10a.

B25a. Citation: "Our Country" A.ms., 2 sides. Ink (c). ViU (6345-e).

Title: Our Country.

First line: It is a noble country where we dwell,

Collation: 1 leaf of white wove (type 7), 24.9 x 19.5 cm., pp. [1–2]; with ts. copy and notes by F. B. Sanborn.

Date: [1840].

Contents: Fair copy of 47 lines; text varies from CP, pp. 134–35.

B25b. Citation: "Our Country" A.ms., 2 sides. Ink (c) Pencil (r,d). MoSW.

Title: Our Country.

First line: It is a noble country where we dwell,
Collation: 1 leaf of green wove, 25 x 19.6 cm., pp. [1–2]; with ts. copy.
Date: [1841].
Contents: Late draft of 52 lines; text varies from *CP*, p. 134.

B25c. Citation: "Our Country" A.ms., 1 side. Ink (c) Pencil (d). CSmH (HM 13182:III, 2v).
First line: It is a glorious country where we dwell,
Collation: 1 leaf of blue wove (type 1), 25.2 x 20 cm., pp. [1–2].
Date: [1847].
Contents: Fair copy of 20 lines; text varies from *CP*, pp. 134–35.

B26a. Citation: "My friends, why should we live" A.ms., 1 side. Ink (c). MoSW.
First line: Tell me why should I live?
Collation: 1 leaf of white wove (type 9), 24.9 x 20 cm., pp. [1–2]; with ts. copy.
Date: [1840].
Contents: Early draft of 4 stanzas, 17 lines; text varies considerably from *CP*, p. 137.

B26b. Citation: "My friends, why should we live" A.ms., 1 side. Ink (c). NNPM (MA 1303).
First line: My friends why should we live
Collation: 1 leaf of white wove (type 1a), 31.9 x 19.8 cm., pp. [1–2], paged "83–84"; bound.
Date: [1845].

Contents: Fair copy of 3 stanzas, 12 lines; text in *CP*, pp. 137, 311.

B26c. Citation: "My friends, why should we live" A.ms., 1 side. Ink (c). NNPM (MA 920:11).

First line: Life is an idle war —— a toilsome peace

Collation: 1 leaf of blue wove (type 1), 25 x 20 cm., pp. [1–2]; mounted and bound.

Date: [1847].

Contents: Fair copy of 1 line; text in *CP*, pp. 137, 311. For other contents see B150, B154.

B27a. Citation: "Wait not till I invite thee, but observe" A.ms., 1 side. Ink (c) Pencil (r,d). VtMiM.

Title: Short Flights

First line: Wait not till I invite thee, but observe

Collation: 1 fragment of gray wove (type 3), 20.4 x 20.1 cm., pp. [1–2]; in folder marked "Fragments".

Date: [1840].

Contents: Early draft of 2 lines; text in *CP*, p. 185.

B27b. Citation: "Wait not till I invite thee, but observe" A.ms., 1 side. Ink (c) Pencil (d) Blue pencil (d). NNPM (MA 1302:4).

First line: Wait not till I invite thee, but observe

Collation: 1 leaf of white wove, 18.4 x 15.2 cm., pp. [1–2], paged "67–68"; bound in [vol. 4] of the *Journal*.

Date: 7 February 1841.

Contents: Fair copy of 2 lines; text in *CP*, pp. 185, 321.

Note: A prose version of this couplet appears in
W 1:289.

B28a.   Citation: "Who equallest the coward's haste" A.ms.,
1 side. Pencil (c,r). CSmH (HM 13201:13r).
First line: Who equallest the coward's haste
Collation: 1 leaf of white wove (type 9), 24.9 x 19.8
cm., pp. [1–2].
Date: [Ca. 1840].
Contents: Early draft of 4 lines; text in *CP*, p. 194.

B28b.   Citation: "Who equallest the coward's haste" A.ms.,
2 sides. Ink (c). ICarbS.
Title: Omnipresence.
First line: Who equalleth the cowards haste,
Collation: 1 leaf of white wove (type 10), 25.1 x
20.2 cm., pp. [1–2]; formerly laid in Thoreau's copy
of *The Dial*.
Date: [1843].
Contents: Fair copy of 4 lines; text in *CP*, pp. 194,
324.

B29a.   Citation: "Ive searched my faculties around" A.ms.,
1 side. Pencil (c). CSmH (HM 13201:13v).
First line: Ive searched my faculties around
Collation: 1 leaf of white wove (type 9), 24.9 x
19.8 cm., pp. [1–2].
Date: [Ca. 1840].
Contents: Early draft of 4 lines; text in *CP*, p. 195.

B29b.   Citation: "Ive searched my faculties around" A.ms.,
2 sides. Ink (c). ICarbS.

Title: Mission.

First line: I've searched my faculties around

Collation: 1 leaf of white wove (type 10), 25.1 x 20.2 cm., pp. [1–2]; formerly laid in Thoreau's copy of *The Dial.*

Date: [1843].

Contents: Fair copy of 4 lines; text in *CP*, pp. 195, 324.

B30a.   Citation: "Delay" A.ms., 1 side. Pencil (c,r,d). CSmH (HM 13201:11r).

First line: No act of duty can delay

Collation: 1 fragment of gray wove (type 2), 16 x 19.5 cm., pp. [1–2].

Date: [1840].

Contents: Early draft of 4 lines; text varies from *CP*, pp. 235, 259.

B30b.   Citation: "Delay" A.ms., 2 sides. Ink (c). ICarbS.

Title: Delay.

First line: No generous action can delay,

Collation: 1 leaf of blue wove (type 10), 25.1 x 20.2 cm., pp. [1–2]; formerly laid in Thoreau's copy of *The Dial.*

Date: [1843].

Contents: Fair copy of 4 lines; text in *CP*, p. 235.

B31.   Citation: "The tidy night with cooler feet" A.ms., 2 sides. Pencil (c). CSmH (HM 13201:9).

First line: The tidy night with cooler feet

Collation: 1 leaf of white wove (type 21), 20 x 15.7 cm., pp. [1–2].

Date: [1840].

Contents: Fair copy of 4 stanzas, 16 lines; text in CP, pp. 257–58. For other contents see F2c.

B32.   Citation: "The Freshet" A.ms., 2 sides. Ink (c) Pencil (r). TxU.

Title: The Freshet.

First line: 'Tis now the twenty-third of March,

Collation: 1 leaf of white wove (type 7), 25.1 x 20.1 cm., pp. [1–2], paged* "337".

Date: [Before 22 March 1841].

Contents: Late draft of 7 stanzas, 26 lines; text varies from CP, pp. 8–9.

Note: Verso contains memoranda on personal debts, 1840–1841.

B33.   Citation: "Friendship" A.ms., 1 side. Ink (c). NNPM (MA 1302:5).

Title: Friendship ——

First line: Now we are partners in such legal trade,

Collation: 1 leaf of white wove, 21.6 x 16.5 cm., pp. 1–2; bound in [vol. 5] of the *Journal*.

Date: 30 March 1841.

Contents: Fair copy of 4 lines; text in CP, p. 125.

B34.   Citation: "On the Sun Coming out in the Afternoon" A.ms., 1 side. Ink (c) Pencil (d). NNPM (MA 1302:5).

Title: On the Sun coming out in the afternoon. [partially underscored]

First line: Methinks all things have travelled since you shined,

Collation: 1 leaf of white wove, 21.6 x 16.5 cm., pp. 1–2; bound in [vol. 5] of the *Journal*.

Date: 1 April 1841.

Contents: Fair copy of 4 lines; text in *CP*, p. 126.

B35. Citation: "They who prepare my evening meal below" A.ms., 1 side. Ink (c). NNPM (MA 1302:5).

First line: They who prepare my evening meal below

Collation: 1 leaf of white wove, 21.6 x 16.5 cm., pp. [1–2], paged "3–4"; bound in [vol. 5] of the *Journal*.

Date: 4 April 1841.

Contents: Fair copy of 2 stanzas, 12 lines; text in *CP*, p. 127.

B36a. Citation: "My ground is high" A.ms., 1 side. Ink (c) Pencil (d). NNPM (MA 1302:5).

First line: My ground is high,

Collation: 1 leaf of white wove, 21.6 x 16.5 cm., pp. [1–2], paged "5–6"; bound in [vol. 5] of the *Journal*.

Date: 7 April 1841.

Contents: Fair copy of 8 lines; text in *CP*, p. 128.

B36b. Citation: "My ground is high" A.ms., 1 side. Ink (c). CSmH (HM 13182:III, 10r).

First line: My ground is high,

Collation: 1 leaf of white wove (type 12), 24.5 x 19.6 cm., pp. [1–2].

Date: [1853–1854].

Contents: Fair copy of 4 lines; text in *CP*, pp. 128, 309. For other contents see B37b.

Note: This leaf may belong to draft D of *Walden*.

B37a.   Citation: "If from your price ye will not swerve"
A.ms., 1 side. Ink (c) Pencil (r,d). NNPM (MA
1302:5).

First line: If from your price ye will not swerve,

Collation: 1 leaf of white wove, 21.6 x 16.5 cm.,
pp. [1–2], paged "5–6"; bound in [vol. 5] of the
Journal.

Date: 7 April 1841.

Contents: Late draft of 10 lines; text in *CP*, pp. 129,
310.

B37b.   Citation: "If from your price ye will not swerve"
A.ms., 1 side. Ink (c). CSmH (HM 13182:III, 10r).

First line: If from your price ye will not swerve,

Collation: 1 leaf of white wove (type 12), 24.5 x
19.6 cm., pp. [1–2].

Date: [1853–1854].

Contents: Fair copy of 10 lines; text in *CP*, pp. 129,
310. For other contents see B36b.

Note: This leaf may belong to draft D of *Walden.*

B38a.   Citation: "Friendship's Steadfastness" A.ms., 2 sides.
Ink (c) Pencil (d). NNPM (MA 1302:5).

Title: Friendship's Steadfastness [partially under-
scored]

First line: True friendship is so firm a league

Collation: 1 leaf of white wove, 21.6 x 16.5 cm.,
pp. [1–2], paged "11–12"; bound in [vol. 5] of the
Journal.

Date: 11 April 1841.

Contents: Fair copy of 4 stanzas, 16 lines; text in
CP, pp. 130, 310.

B38b.   Citation: "Friendship's Steadfastness" A.ms., 2 sides. Ink (c,r) Pencil (r,d). MH (bMS Am 278.5 [15.D]).

First line: If I would safely keep this new got pelf

Collation: 1 leaf of blue wove (type 1), 25.1 x 20 cm., pp. [13–14],paged "352–53".

Date: [1847].

Contents: Late draft of 3 stanzas, 12 lines; text in CP, pp. 130, 310. For other stanzas see B74c.

B39.   Citation: "Death cannot come too soon" A.ms., 1 side. Ink (c) Pencil (d). NNPM (MA 1302:5).

First line: Death cannot come too soon

Collation: 1 leaf of white wove, 21.6 x 16.5 cm., pp. [1–2], paged "11–12"; bound in [vol. 5] of the Journal.

Date: 11 April 1841.

Contents: Fair copy of 4 lines; text in CP, p. 131.

B40a.   Citation: "With frontier strength ye stand your ground" A.ms., 1 side. Ink (c) Pencil (d). NNPM (MA 1302:5).

Title: Wachusett [partially underscored]

First line: Especial — I remember thee,

Collation: 1 leaf of white wove, 21.6 x 16.5 cm., pp. [1–2], paged "25–26"; bound in [vol. 5] of the Journal.

Date: 2 May 1841.

Contents: Fair copy of 19 lines; text in CP, pp. 49–50, 292–93.

B40b.   Citation: "With frontier strength ye stand your ground" A.ms., 3 sides. Ink (c,r). NYPL (Berg).

First line: With grand content ye circle round

Collation: 2 leaves of white wove (type 1), 32 x 19.9 cm., pp. [1–2]; in early draft of "A Walk to Wachusett"; bound in album used by John, Henry, and Sophia Thoreau.

Date: [October 1842].

Contents: Early draft of 75 lines; text in CP, pp. 47–50. For other contents see C4a.

B40c.   Citation: "With frontier strength ye stand your ground" A.ms., 1 side. Pencil (c). CSmH (HM 926: 14v).

Title: The Mountains in the Horizon.

First line: With grand content ye circle round,

Collation: 1 leaf of gray wove, 25 x 20 cm., pp. [1–2].

Date: [1842–1843].

Contents: Early draft of 8 lines, text varies from CP, p. 47. For other contents see B17a.

Note: Over this pencil draft Thoreau wrote, in ink, part of his translation of the Prometheus Bound.

B40d.   Citation: "With frontier strength ye stand your ground" A.ms., 6 sides. Ink (c). MH (MS Am 1280.214.1[2]).

Title: The Mountains in the Horizon [partially underscored]

First line: With frontier strength ye stand your ground —

Collation: 3 leaves of gray wove (type 2), 25.1 x 19.7 cm., pp. [1–6].

Date: [1843].

Contents: Fair copy of 10 stanzas, 157 lines; text varies from *CP*, pp. 47–50, 292–93.

B40e. Citation: "With frontier strength ye stand your ground" A.ms., 1 side. Ink (c). CSmH (HM 13201:11v).

Title: The Mountains in the Horizon [partially underscored]

First line: The confines of the sky and ground —

Collation: 1 fragment of gray wove (type 2), 16 x 19.5 cm., pp. [1–2].

Date: [1843].

Contents: Fair copy of 12 lines; text in *CP*, pp. 47, 260, 293.

B41a. Citation: "The needles of the pine" A.ms., 1 side. Ink (c) Pencil (d). NNPM (MA 1302:5).

Title: Westward-ho! [partially underscored]

First line: The needles of the pine

Collation: 1 leaf of white wove, 21.6 x 16.5 cm., pp. [1–2], paged "29–30"; bound in [vol. 5] of the *Journal*.

Date: 9 May 1841.

Contents: Fair copy of a couplet; text in *CP*, p. 22.

B41b. Citation: "The needles of the pine" A.ms., 1 side. Ink (c). NYPL (Berg).

First line: The needles of the pine

Collation: 1 leaf of white wove (type 1), 32 x 19.9 cm., pp. [1–2]; bound in album used by John, Henry, and Sophia Thoreau.

Date: [October 1842].

Contents: Fair copy of a couplet; text in *CP*, pp. 22, 287. For other contents see C4a.

B42.   Citation: "Dong, sounds the brass in the east" A.ms., 1 side. Ink (c) Pencil. NNPM (MA 1302:5).

Title: The Echo of the Sabbath bell — | heard in the Woods. [partially underscored]

First line: Dong—sounds the brass in the east—

Collation: 1 leaf of white wove, 21.6 x 16.5 cm., pp. [1–2], paged "31–32"; bound in [vol. 5] of the *Journal*.

Date: 9 May 1841.

Contents: Fair copy of 4 stanzas, 16 lines; text in *CP*, pp. 40, 291.

B43a.   Citation: "My life has been the poem I would have writ" A.ms., 1 side. Ink (c) Pencil (d). NNPM (MA 1302:5).

First line: My life hath been the poem I would have writ,

Collation: 1 leaf of white wove, 21.6 x 16.5 cm., pp. [1–2], paged "81–82"; bound in [vol. 5] of the *Journal*.

Date: 28 August 1841.

Contents: Early draft of 2 lines; text in *CP*, pp. 85, 301.

B43b.   Citation: "My life has been the poem I would have writ" A.ms., 1 side. Ink (c) Pencil (r,d). VtMiM.

Title: Short Flights.

First line: My life has been the poem I would have writ

Collation: 1 fragment of gray wove (type 1), 20.4 x 20.1 cm., pp. [1–2]; in folder marked "Fragments".

Date: [1842–1843].

Contents: Late draft of 2 lines; text in *CP*, p. 85.

B43c.   Citation: "My life has been the poem I would have writ" A.ms., 1 side. Ink (c). MH (MS Am 278.5 [20.1]).

Title: Short Flights.

First line: My life has been the poem I would have writ

Collation: 1 leaf of gray wove (type 1), 25.1 x 19.9 cm., pp. [1–2]; mounted.

Date: [1842–1843].

Contents: Fair copy of 2 lines; text in *CP*, p. 85.

B44a.   Citation: "To the Mountains" A.ms., 1 side. Ink (c). CSmH (HM 13183).

Title: To the Mountains

First line: And when the sun puts out his lamp

Collation: 1 fragment of white wove (type 9), 12.5 x 20 cm., pp. [1–2].

Date: August 1841.

Contents: Fair copy of 3 stanzas, 22 lines; text in *CP*, p. 200. A facsimile is in *FLJ* 1:122.

B44b.   Citation: "To the Mountains" A.ms., 1 side. Ink (c,r). NYPL (Berg).

Title: To the Mountains

First line: Trusting to His inveterate skill

Collation: 1 leaf of white wove (type 1a), 32 x 19.9 cm., pp. [1–2]; bound.

Date: [1845].

Contents: Early draft of 6 lines; text in *CP*, pp. 200, 325.

B45.   Citation: "Greater is the depth of sadness" A.ms., 1 side. Ink (c) Pencil (d). NNPM (MA 1302:5).

First line: Greater is the depth of sadness

Collation: 1 leaf of white wove, 21.6 x 16.5 cm., pp. [1–2], paged "97–98"; bound in [vol. 5] of the *Journal*.

Date: 5 September 1841.

Contents: Fair copy of 2 lines; text in *CP*, p. 185.

B46a.   Citation: "Upon the lofty elm tree sprays" A.ms., 2 sides. Pencil (c,r,d). Prof. R. Adams, Chapel Hill, N.C.

First line: With minstrel sound these trivial days

Collation: 1 leaf of gray wove (type 2), 25 x 19.5 cm., pp. [1–2].

Date: [After 8 September 1841].

Contents: Early draft of 3 stanzas, 12 lines; text varies considerably from *CP*, p. 6. For other contents see B13c.

Note: Recto contains early draft of an a.l.s.; text varies from *Corr.*, p. 46.

B46b.   Citation: "Upon the lofty elm tree sprays" A.ms., 2 sides. Ink (c). ICarbS.

Title: The Vireo.

First line: Upon the lofty elm tree sprays

Collation: 1 leaf of white wove (type 7), 25.1 x 20.2 cm., pp. [1–2]; formerly laid in Thoreau's copy of *The Dial.*

Date: [Before July 1842].

Contents: Fair copy of 4 lines, text in *CP*, pp. 6, 282.

B47a.   Citation: "Where I have been" A.ms., 1 side. Ink (c) Pencil (d). NNPM (MA 1302:5).

First line: Where I have been

Collation: 1 leaf of white wove, 21.6 x 16.5 cm., pp. [1–2], paged "111–12"; bound in [vol. 5] of the *Journal.*

Date: 12 September 1841.

Contents: Fair copy of 2 lines; text in *CP*, p. 186.

B47b.   Citation: "Where I have been" A.ms., 1 side. Ink (c). MH (MS Am 278.5 [20.1]).

Title: Short Flights.

First line: Where I have been

Collation: 1 leaf of gray wove (type 1), 25.1 x 19.9 cm., pp. [1–2]; mounted.

Date: [1842–1843].

Contents: Fair copy of 2 lines; text in *CP*, p. 186.

B48a.   Citation: "Better wait" A.ms., 1 side. Ink (c). NNPM (MA 1302:5).

First line: Better wait

Collation: 1 leaf of white wove, 21.6 x 16.5 cm., pp. [1–2], paged "115–16"; bound in [vol. 5] of the *Journal.*

Date: 30 September 1841.

Contents: Fair copy of 2 lines; text in *CP*, p. 186.

B48b. Citation: "Better wait" A.ms., 1 side. Ink (c). MH (MS Am 278.5 [20.1]).

Title: Short Flights.

First line: Better wait

Collation: 1 leaf of gray wove (type 1), 25.1 x 19.9 cm., pp. [1–2]; mounted.

Date: [1842–1843].

Contents: Fair copy of 2 lines; text in *CP*, p. 186.

B49. Citation: "To Edith" A.ms., 1 side. Ink (c*). MH (MS Am 137 [OP]).

First line: Thou little bud of being, Edith named

Collation: 1 leaf of white wove (anom.), pp. [1–2], paged "95".

Date: [After 22 November 1841].

Contents: Fair copy of 16 lines, in Emerson's hand; text in *CP*, p. 396. A facsimile is in K. W. Cameron, "A New Thoreau Poem . . . ", *ESQ*, No. 22 (1960), pp. 40–41.

B50. Citation: "The Inward Morning" A.ms., 1 side. Ink (c) Pencil (d) Blue pencil (d). NNPM (MA 1302:6).

First line: Packed in my mind lie all the clothes

Collation: 1 leaf of white wove, 20.7 x 17.5 cm., pp. [1–2], paged "8–9"; bound in [vol. 6] of the *Journal*.

Date: [After 30 November 1841].

Contents: Fair copy of 6 stanzas, 24 lines; text in CP, pp. 74–75, 298–99. For related verses, which CP treats as a later version, see B85.

B51.   Citation: "Each summer sound" A.ms., 2 sides. Ink (c) Pencil (d). NNPM (MA 1302:1).

First line: Each summer sound

Collation: 2 leaves of white wove (type 25), 11.2 x 9.3 cm., pp. [1–4], paged "47–48, 153–54"; bound in [vol. 1] of the Journal.

Date: [November 1841], dated "February 19 1838" and "February 27 1838".

Contents: Fair copies of couplet; text in CP, p. 22.

B52.   Citation: "May Morning" A.ms., 1 side. Ink (c). NNPM (MA 1302:1).

Title: May Morning.

First line: So mild the air a pleasure t'was to breathe,

Collation: 1 leaf of white wove (type 25), 11.2 x 9.3 cm., pp. [1–2], paged "78"; bound in [vol. 1] of the Journal.

Date: [November 1841], dated "May 21 1838".

Contents: Fair copy of 4 stanzas, 16 lines; text in CP, p. 97.

B53a.   Citation: "Walden" A.ms., 2 sides. Ink (c) Pencil (r,d) Blue pencil (d). NNPM (MA 1302:1).

Title: Walden.

First line: —True, our converse a stranger is to speech,

Collation: 1 leaf of white wove (type 25), 11.2 x 9.3 cm., pp. [1–2], paged "79–80"; bound in [vol. 1] of the Journal.

Date: [November 1841], dated "June 3 1838".

Contents: Late draft of 2 stanzas, 27 lines; text in CP, pp. 98-99, 304.

B53b.   Citation: "Walden" A.ms., 2 sides. Ink (c,r) Pencil (r,d). MH (bMS Am 278.5 [15.U]).

First line: O River tell me what

Collation: 1 leaf of white wove (type 14), 24.6 x 19.1 cm., pp. [1-2].

Date: [1846].

Contents: Early draft of 16 lines; text in CP, pp. 98-99, 304.

B54.   Citation: "Strange that so many fickle gods, as fickle as the weather" A.ms., 1 side. Ink (c). NNPM (MA 1302:1).

First line: Strange that so many fickle gods, as fickle as the weather,

Collation: 1 leaf of white wove (type 25), 11.2 x 9.3 cm., pp. [1-2], paged "79-80"; bound in [vol. 1] of the Journal.

Date: [November 1841], dated "June 14 1838".

Contents: Fair copy of 2 lines; text in CP, p. 185.

B55.   Citation: "Truth—Goodness—Beauty—those celestial thrins" A.ms., 1 side. Ink (c) Pencil (d). NNPM (MA 1302:1).

First line: Truth—Goodness—Beauty—those celestial thrins,

Collation: 1 leaf of white wove (type 25), 11.2 x 9.3 cm., pp. [1-2], paged "79-80"; bound in [vol. 1] of the Journal.

Date: [November 1841], dated "June 14 1838".

Contents: Fair copy of 1 stanza, 4 lines; text in *CP*, p. 100.

B56.   Citation: "In the busy streets, domain of trade" A.ms., 1 side. Ink (c) Pencil (d). NNPM (MA 1302:1).

First line: In the busy streets, domain of trade,

Collation: 1 leaf of white wove (type 25), 11.2 x 9.3 cm., pp. [1–2], paged "79–80"; bound in [vol. 1] of the *Journal*.

Date: [November 1841], dated "June 16 1838".

Contents: Fair copy of 4 lines; text in *CP*, p. 101.

B57.   Citation: "Cliffs" A.ms., 1 side. Ink (c) Pencil (d) Blue pencil (d). NNPM (MA 1302:1).

Title: Cliffs

First line: The loudest sound that burdens here the breeze

Collation: 1 leaf of white wove (type 25), 11.2 x 9.3 cm., pp. [1–2], paged "81–82"; bound in [vol. 1] of the *Journal*.

Date: [November 1841], dated "July 8 1838".

Contents: Fair copy of 8 lines; text in *CP*, p. 104.

B58.   Citation: "My Boots" A.ms., 1 side. Ink (c). NNPM (MA 1302:1).

Title: My Boots [last word underscored]

First line: Anon with gaping fearlessness they quaff

Collation: 1 leaf of white wove (type 25), 11.2 x 9.3 cm., pp. [1–2], paged "153–54"; bound in [vol. 1] of the *Journal*.

Date: [November 1841], "October 16 1838".

Contents: Fair copy of 10 lines; text in *CP*, p. 105.

B59. Citation: "Noon" A.ms., 1 side. Ink (c) Pencil (d). NNPM (MA 1302:1).

Title: Noon. [underscored]

First line: —Straightway dissolved, | Like to the morning mist, —or rather like the | subtler mists of noon—

Collation: 1 leaf of white wove (type 25), 11.2 x 9.3 cm pp. [1–2], paged "153–54"; bound in [vol. 1] of the *Journal*.

Date: [November 1841], dated "October 16 1838".

Contents: Fair copy of 2 stanzas, 11 lines; text in *CP*, pp. 106, 305.

B60a. Citation: "When Winter fringes every bough" A.ms., 3 sides. Ink (c) Pencil (d). NNPM (MA 1302:1).

Title: Fair-Haven

First line: When winter fringes every bough

Collation: 2 leaves of white wove (type 25), 11.2 x 9.3 cm., pp. [1–4], paged "99–102"; bound in [vol. 1] of the *Journal*.

Date: [November 1841], dated "December 15 1838".

Contents: Fair copy of 11 stanzas, 44 lines; text in *CP*, pp. 14–15, 283–84.

B60b. Citation: "When Winter fringes every bough" A.ms., 2 sides. Ink (c). VtMiM.

First line: When winter fringes every bough

Collation: 1 leaf of white wove (type 11), 24.7 x 19.7 cm., pp. [1–2], paged "27–28"; mounted, in folder marked "Fragments".

Date: [July 1843].

Contents: Fair copy of 10 stanzas, 40 lines; text varies from *CP*, p. 14. For other contents see C6c.

B61a.   Citation: ["Anacreontics"] A.ms., 2 sides. Ink (c) Pencil (r,d). NNPM (MA 1302:1).

Title: Anacreon's Ode to the Cicada.

First line: We pronounce thee happy, cicada,

Collation: 1 leaf of white wove (type 25), 11.2 x 9.3 cm., pp. [1–2], paged "105–6"; bound in [vol. 1] of the *Journal*.

Date: [November 1841], dated [after] "December 15 1838."

Contents: Late draft of 17 lines; text in *J* 1:66–67.

B61b.   Citation: "Anacreontics" A.ms., 2 sides. Ink (c) Pencil (c). NNPM (MA 1302:1).

Title: Anacreontics | Return of Spring

First line: Behold, how Spring appearing

Collation: 1 leaf of white wove (type 25), 11.2 x 9.3 cm., pp. [1–2], paged "111–12"; bound in [vol. 1] of the *Journal*.

Date: [November 1841], dated "December 23 1838".

Contents: Fair copy of 14 lines; text in *J* 1:69.

B61c.   Citation: "Anacreontics" A.ms., 2 sides. Ink (c) Pencil (d). NNPM (MA 1302:1).

Title: Anacreontics | Cupid Wounded

First line: Love, once among roses

Collation: 1 leaf of white wove (type 25), 11.2 x 9.3 cm., pp. [1–2], paged "111–12"; bound in [vol. 1] of the *Journal*.

Date: [November 1841], dated "December 23 1838".

Contents: Fair copy of 16 lines; text in *J* 1:70.

B62a.   Citation: "The Thaw" A.ms., 2 sides. Ink (c) Pencil (d). NNPM (MA 1302:1).

Title: The Thaw.

First line: I saw the civil sun drying earth's tears—

Collation: 2 leaves of white wove (type 25), 11.2 x 9.3 cm., pp. [1–4], paged "111–12"; bound in [vol. 1] of the *Journal*.

Date: [November 1841], dated "January 11 1839".

Contents: Fair copy of 3 stanzas, 10 lines; text in *CP*, pp. 107, 305.

B62b.   Citation: "The Thaw" A.ms., 1 side. Ink (c). NNPM (MA 1303).

First line: I fain would stretch me by the highway side,

Collation: 1 leaf of white wove (type 1a), 31.9 x 19.8 cm., pp. [1–2], paged "197–98"; bound.

Date: [1845].

Contents: Fair copy of 2 stanzas, 8 lines; text in *CP*, p. 107, 305.

B63.   Citation: "Last night as I lay gazing with shut eyes" A.ms., 2 sides. Ink (c) Pencil (r,d). NNPM (MA 1302:1).

Title: The Dream Valley. | The prospect of our river valley from Ta- | natanan Cliff—appeared to me again in | my dreams.

First line: Last night as I lay gazing with shut eyes

Collation: 1 leaf of white wove (type 25), 11.2 x 9.3 cm., pp. [1–2], paged "113–14"; bound in [vol. 1] of the *Journal*.

Date: [November 1841], dated "January 20 1839".

Contents: Late draft of 3 stanzas, 14 lines; text in *CP*, pp. 108, 306.

B64.   Citation: "Love" A.ms., 1 side. Ink (c) Pencil (r). NNPM (MA 1302:1).

Title: Love.

First line: We two that planets erst had been

Collation: 1 leaf of white wove (type 25), 11.2 x 9.3 cm., pp. [1–2], paged "113–14"; bound in [vol. 1] of the *Journal*.

Date: [November 1841; originally before 3 February 1839].

Contents: Fair copy of 2 stanzas, 8 lines, text in *CP*, pp. 109, 306.

B65.   Citation: "The deeds of king and meanest hedger" A.ms., 1 side. Ink (c). NNPM (MA 1302:1).

First line: The deeds of king and meanest hedger

Collation: 1 leaf of white wove (type 25), 11.2 x 9.3 cm., pp. [1–2], paged "113–14", bound in [vol. 1] of the *Journal*.

Date: [November 1841], dated "February 3 1839".

Contents: Fair copy of couplet; text in *CP*, p. 185.

B66.   Citation: "The western wind came lumbering in" A.ms., 1 side. Ink (c) Pencil (d). NNPM (MA 1302:1).

Title: The Evening Wind.

First line: The eastern mail comes lumbering in

Collation: 1 leaf of white wove (type 25), 11.2 x 9.3 cm., pp. [1–2], paged "115–16"; bound in [vol. 1] of the *Journal*.

Date: [November 1841], dated "February 3 1839".

Contents: Fair copy of 8 lines, text in *CP*, pp. 52, 294.

B67.   Citation: " 'Twill soon appear if we but look" A.ms., 1 side. Ink (c) Pencil (d). NNPM (MA 1302:1).

First line: 'Twill soon appear if we but look

Collation: 1 leaf of white wove (type 25), 11.2 x 9.3 cm., pp. [1–2], paged "115–16"; bound in [vol. 1] of the *Journal*.

Date: [November 1841], dated "February 3 1839".

Contents: Fair copy of 4 lines; text in *CP*, p. 110.

B68.   Citation: "His steady sails he never furls" A.ms., 1 side. Ink (c) Pencil (r) NNPM (MA 1302:1).

Title: The Shrike

First line: Hark—hark—from out the thickest fog

Collation: 1 leaf of white wove (type 25), 11.2 x 9.3 cm., pp. [1–2], paged "117–18"; bound in [vol. 1] of the *Journal*.

Date: [November 1841], dated "February 25 1839".

Contents: Fair copy of 2 stanzas, 8 lines; text in *CP*, pp. 4, 281.

B69.   Citation: "Lately, alas, I knew a gentle boy" A.ms., 3 sides. Ink (c). NNPM (MA 1302:1).

Title: Sympathy

First line: Lately alas I knew a gentle boy,

Collation: 2 leaves of white wove (type 25), 11.2 x 9.3 cm., pp. [1–4], paged "131–34"; bound in [vol. 1] of the *Journal*.

Date: [November 1841], dated "June 24 1839".

Contents: Fair copy of 13 stanzas, 52 lines; text in *CP*, pp. 64–66, 297.

B70.   Citation: "The 'Book of Gems' " A.ms., 2 sides. Ink (c) Pencil (r,d). NNPM (MA 1302:1).

Title: The "Book of Gems"

First line: —With cunning plates the polished leaves were decked,

Collation: 2 leaves of white wove (type 25), 11.2 x 9.3 cm., pp. [1–2], paged "127–30"; bound in [vol. 1] of the *Journal*.

Date: [November 1841], dated "July 4 1839".

Contents: Late draft of 2 stanzas, 16 lines; text in *CP*, pp. 112, 307.

B71.   Citation: "The Breeze's Invitation" A.ms., 2 sides. Ink (c). NNPM (MA 1302:1).

Title: The Breeze's Invitation.

First line: Come let's roam the breezy pastures,

Collation: 1 leaf of white wove (type 25), 11.2 x 9.3 cm., pp. [1–2], paged "137–38"; bound in [vol. 1] of the *Journal*.

Date: [November 1841], dated "July 20 1839".

Contents: Fair copy of 6 stanzas, 30 lines; text in *CP*, pp. 116–17, 308.

B72.   Citation: "Nature doth have her dawn each day"
A.ms., 1 side. Ink (c). NNPM (MA 1302:1).

First line: Nature doth have her dawn each day,

Collation: 1 leaf of white wove (type 25), 11.2 x
9.3 cm., pp. [1–2], paged "139–40"; bound in [vol.
1] of the *Journal.*

Date: [November 1841], dated "July 24 1839".

Contents: Fair copy of 5 stanzas, 20 lines; text in
CP, pp. 70, 297.

B73a.   Citation: "Loves Farewell" A.ms., 1 side. Ink (c)
Pencil (d) Blue pencil (d). NNPM (MA 1302:1).

Title: Farewell

First line: —Light-hearted, thoughtless, shall I take
my way,

Collation: 1 leaf of white wove (type 25), 11.2 x
9.3 cm., pp. [1–2], paged "149–50"; bound in [vol.
1] of the *Journal.*

Date: [November 1841], dated "November 19 1839."

Contents: Fair copy of 4 lines; text in *CP*, pp. 118,
308.

B73b.   Citation: "Loves Farewell" A.ms., 2 sides. Ink (c).
MH (MS Am 278.5.20[1]).

Title: Loves' Farewell

First line: Light hearted, thoughtless, shall I take
my way,

Collation: 1 leaf of gray wove (type 1), 25.1 x 19.9
cm., pp. [1–2]; mounted.

Date: [1842–1843].

Contents: Intermediate draft of 4 lines; varies from
text in *CP*, pp. 118, 308.

B73c. Citation: "Loves Farewell" A.ms., 2 sides. Ink (c)
Pencil (r,d). VtMiM.

Title: Loves Farewell.

First line: Light hearted, careless, shall I take my
way,

Collation: 1 fragment of gray wove (type 1), 20.4
x 20.1 cm., pp. [1–2]; in folder marked "Fragments".

Date: [1842–1843].

Contents: Late draft of 4 lines; text in *CP*, pp. 118,
308.

B74a. Citation: "Let such pure hate still underprop" A.ms.,
1 side. Ink (c) Pencil (r,d). NNPM (MA 1302:2).

First line: By a strong liking we prevail

Collation: 1 leaf of white wove (type 25), 11.2 x
9.3 cm., pp. [1–2], paged "23–24"; bound in [vol. 2]
of the *Journal*.

Date: [November 1841], dated "January 19 1840".

Contents: Late draft of 4 lines; text in *CP*, pp. 71–
73, 298.

B74b. Citation: "Let such pure hate still underprop" A.ms.,
4 sides. Ink (c). MH (MS Am 278.5.10).

Title: Friendship | "Friends — Romans — Country-
men — and Lovers"

First line: Let such pure hate still underprop

Collation: 2 leaves of white wove (type 10), 24.8
x 20.6 cm., pp. [1–4]; bound.

Date: [1843].

Contents: Fair copy of 17 stanzas, 80 lines; text in
CP, pp. 71–73, 298.

B74c.   Citation: "Let such pure hate still underprop" A.ms., 2 sides. Ink (c,r) Pencil (r,d) MH (bMS Am 278.5 [15.L]).

Title: Friendship | "Friends—Romans—Countrymen —and Lovers."

First line: Let such pure hate still underprop

Collation: 1 leaf of blue wove (type 1), 25.1 x 20 cm., pp. [1–2].

Date: [1847].

Contents: Late draft of 15 stanzas, 78 lines; text in CP, pp. 71–73, 298. For stanzas, 3, 7, and 8 see B38b.

B75a.   Citation: "The river swelleth more and more" A.ms., 3 sides. Ink (c) Pencil (d). NNPM (MA 1302:2).

Title: The Freshet.

First line: — — A stir is on the Worc'ter hills,

Collation: 2 leaves of white wove (type 25), 11.2 x 9.3 cm., pp. [1–4], paged "39–42"; bound in [vol. 2] of the Journal.

Date: [November 1841], dated "February 24 1840".

Contents: Fair copy of 6 stanzas, 48 lines; text in CP, pp. 8–9, 282.

B75b.   Citation: "The river swelleth more and more" A.ms., 1 side. Ink (c). NNPM (MA 1303).

First line: A stir is on the Wooster hills,

Collation: 1 leaf of white wove (type 1a), 31.9 x 19.8 cm., pp. [1–2], paged "197–98"; bound.

Date: [1845].

Contents: Fair copy of 6 lines, text in CP, pp. 8–9, 282.

B76.   Citation: "The Poet's Delay" A.ms., 1 side. Ink (c) Pencil (d) NNPM (MA 1302:2).

First line: Two years and twenty now have flown—

Collation: 1 leaf of white wove (type 25), 11.2 x 9.3 cm., pp. [1–2], paged "48–49"; bound in [vol. 2] of the *Journal*.

Date: [November 1841], dated [after] "March 8 1840".

Contents: Fair copy of 5 stanzas, 20 lines; text in *CP*, pp. 78, 299–300.

B77a.   Citation: "Who sleeps by day and walks by night" A.ms., 1 side. Ink (c) Pencil (d). NNPM (MA 1718).

First line: Who sleeps by day and walks by night,

Collation: 1 leaf of white wove, 10.4 x 8.5 cm., pp. 1–2; bound in [vol. 3] of the *Journal*.

Date: [November 1841], dated "July 1840".

Contents: Early draft of a couplet; text in *CP*, p. 84.

B77b.   Citation: "Who sleeps by day and walks by night" A.ms., 1 side. Ink (c). VtMiM.

Title: Short Flights.

First Line: Who sleeps by day and walks by night

Collation: 1 fragment of gray wove (type 1), 20.4 x 20.1 cm., pp. [1–2]; in folder marked "Fragments".

Date: [1842–1843].

Contents: Late draft of 2 lines; text in *CP*, p. 84.

B77c.   Citation: "Who sleeps by day and walks by night" A.ms., 1 side. Ink (c,r). NYPL (Berg).

First line: Who sleeps by day and walks by night

Collation: 1 leaf of white wove (type 11), 24.7 x 19.5 cm., pp. [1–2], paged* "39–40".

Date: [1843–1844].

Contents: Late draft of 2 lines; text in *CP*, p. 84.

B77d. Citation: "Who sleeps by day and walks by night" A.ms., 1 side. Ink (c). NNPM (MA 1303).

First line: Who sleeps by day and walks by night,

Collation: 1 leaf of white wove (type 1a), 31.9 x 19.9 cm., pp. [1–2], paged "33–34"; bound.

Date: [1845].

Contents: Fair copy of 2 lines; text in *CP*, pp. 84, 301.

B78. Citation: "I've heard my neighbor's pump at night" A.ms., 1 side. Ink (c) Pencil (r,d). NNPM (MA 1718).

First line: I've heard my neighbor's pump at night,

Collation: 1 leaf of white wove, 10.4 x 8.5 cm., pp. 1–2; bound in [vol. 3] of the *Journal*.

Date: [November 1841], dated "July 30 1840".

Contents: Late draft of 6 lines; text in *CP*, p. 384.

B79. Citation: "When with pale cheek and sunken eye I sang" A.ms., 1 side. Ink (c) Pencil (d). NNPM (MA 1718).

First line: When with pale cheek and sunken eye I sang

Collation: 1 leaf of white wove, 10.4 x 8.5 cm., pp. [1–2], paged "17–18"; bound in [vol. 3] of the *Journal*.

Date: [November 1841], dated "August 12 1840".

Contents: Fair copy of 4 stanzas, 16 lines; text in CP, p. 385.

B80.   Citation: "I arose before light" A.ms., 2 sides. Ink (c) Pencil (d). NNPM (MA 1718).

First line: I arose before light

Collation: 2 leaves of white wove, 10.4 x 8.5 cm., pp. [1–4], paged "55–58"; bound in [vol. 3] of the Journal.

Date: [November 1841], dated "October 14 1840".

Contents: Fair copy of 3 stanzas, 16 lines; text in CP, p. 386.

B81.   Citation: "I'm guided in the darkest night" A.ms., 2 sides. Ink (c) Pencil (d). NNPM (MA 1718).

First line: —I'm guided in the darkest night

Collation: 1 leaf of white wove, 10.4 x 8.5 cm., pp. [1–2], paged "69–70"; bound in [vol. 3] of the Journal.

Date: [November 1841], dated "November 7 1840".

Contents: Fair copy of 4 stanzas, 28 lines; text in CC, p. 181.

B82.   Citation: "Who hears the parson" A.ms., 1 side. Ink (c) Pencil (d). NNPM (MA 1718).

Title: The church bell is not a natural sound | to the church goer.

First line: Who hears the parson

Collation: 1 leaf of white wove, 10.4 x 8.5 cm., pp. [1–2], paged "119–20"; bound in [vol. 3] of the Journal.

Date: [November 1841], dated "January 10 1841".

Contents: Fair copy of 2 stanzas, 8 lines; text in CP, pp. 390, 403.

B83.   Citation: "Friends" A.ms., 2 sides. Ink (c) Pencil (d). NNPM (MA 1718).

Title: Friendship —— in The Dial [underscored] Dec 28th 1840

First line: Friends — | They cannot help,

Collation: 1 leaf of white wove, 10.4 x 8.5 cm., pp. [1–2], paged "109–10"; bound in [vol. 3] of the Journal.

Date: [November 1841], dated "January 1841".

Contents: Fair copy of 6 stanzas, 30 lines; text in CP, p. 391.

B84.   Citation: "When in some cove I lie" A.ms., 1 side. Ink (c) Pencil (d). NNPM (MA 1718).

First line: When in some cove I lie,

Collation: 1 leaf of white wove, 10.4 x 8.5 cm., pp. [1–2], paged "111–12"; bound in [vol. 3] of the Journal.

Date: [November 1841], dated "January 1841".

Contents: Fair copy of 10 lines; text in CP, p. 393.

B85.   Citation: "The Inward Morning" A.ms., 1 side. Ink (c) Pencil (d) Blue pencil (d). NNPM (MA 1302:6).

First line: What is it gilds the trees and clouds

Collation: 1 leaf of white wove, 20.7 x 17.5 cm., pp. [1–2], paged "11–12"; bound in [vol. 6] of the Journal.

Date: 12 [December] 1841.

Contents: Fair copy of 4 stanzas, 16 lines; text in *CP*, pp. 74–75, 298–99. For related verses, which *CP* treats as an earlier version, see B50.

B86.   Citation: "Within the circuit of this plodding life" A.ms., 2 sides. Ink (c) Pencil (d) Blue pencil (d). NNPM (MA 1302:6).

First line: Within the circuit of this plodding life

Collation: 1 leaf of white wove, 20.7 x 17.5 cm., pp. [1–2], paged "31–32"; bound in [vol. 6] of the *Journal*.

Date: 30 December 1841.

Contents: Fair copy of 16 lines; text in *CP*, pp. 3, 281.

B87a.   Citation: "I was made erect and lone" A.ms., 1 side. Ink (c) Pencil (c,r). CSmH (HM 13182:III, 11v).

First line: I was made erect and lone

Collation: 1 fragment of white wove (type 21), 20.2 x 13.1, pp. [1–2].

Date: [1841].

Contents: Early draft of 9 lines; text in *CP*, pp. 197, 325. A facsimile is in *FLJ* 1:136. For other contents see D9d.

B87b.   Citation: "Delay in Friendship" [see Section H].

B88.   Citation: "Thou dusky spirit of the wood" A.ms., 1 side. Ink (c,r) Pencil (d). MHarF.

First line: From wood to wood, from hill to hill

Collation: 1 leaf of white wove (type 7), 25.1 x 19.5 cm., pp. [1–2].

Date: [May 1842].

Contents: Fair copy of 10 lines; text varies from *CP*, p. 7. For other contents see C3.

B89a.   Citation: "The Funeral Bell" A.ms., 2 sides. Ink (c). MH (bMS Am 278.5 [4,E]).

First line: One more is gone

Collation: 1 leaf of white wove (type 17a), 24 x 19.5 cm., pp. [1–2], paged "91–92".

Date: 18 July 1842.

Contents: Early draft of 8 lines; text in *CP*, pp. 211, 327.

B89b.   Citation: "The Funeral Bell" A.ms., 2 sides. Brown ink (c) Black ink (r) Pencil (r). CSmH (HM 13185).

Title: The Funeral Bell.

First line: One more is gone | Out of the busy throng

Collation: 1 leaf of white wove (type 5), 25 x 20 cm., pp. [1–2].
Date: [1848].

Contents: Late draft of 4 stanzas, 24 lines; text in *CP*, pp. 211, 327.

B89c.   Citation: "The Funeral Bell" A.ms., 1 side. Ink (c)*. CSmH (HM 13190).

First line: One more is gone

Collation: 1 leaf of white wove, 23.7 x 19.7 cm., pp. [1–2].

Date: [1863].

Contents: Fair copy of 5 stanzas, 30 lines; text in *CP*, pp. 211, 327.

Note: Copied in the hand of Sophia Thoreau.

B90. Citation: "Not unconcerned Wachusett rears his head" A.ms., 1 side. Ink (c). NYPL (Berg).

First line: Not unconcerned Wachusett rears his head

Collation: 1 leaf of white wove (type 1), 32 x 19.9 cm., pp. [1–2]; bound in album used by John, Henry, and Sophia Thoreau.

Date: [After 19 July 1842].

Contents: Fair copy of 4 lines; text in *CP*, pp. 16, 284. For other contents see C4a.

B91a. Citation: "The Virgin" A.ms., 2 sides. Ink (c). MH (bMS Am 278.5 [4,G]).

First line: In some withdrawn untraversed mead

Collation: 1 leaf of white wove (type 17a), 24 x 19.5 cm., pp. [1–2], paged "151–52".

Date: [September 1842].

Contents: Early draft of 6 lines; text varies considerably from *CP*, p. 212.

Note: Thoreau later split this draft into two poems. See B92a.

B91b. Citation: "The Virgin" A.ms., 1 side. Ink (c,r,d) Pencil (r,d). CSmH (HM 13187).

Title: The Virgin

First line: With her calm aspiring eyes

Collation: 1 fragment of white wove (type 2), 9.5 x 19.5 cm., pp. [1–2].

Date: [1843].

Contents: Intermediate draft of 2 stanzas, 8 lines; text in *CP*, pp. 212, 327. For other contents see B96a.

B92a. Citation: "Nature" A.ms., 2 sides. Ink (c,r). MH (bMS Am 278.5 [4.G]).

First line: In some withdrawn untraversed mead

Collation: 1 leaf of white wove (type 17a), 24 x 19.4 cm., pp. [1–2], paged "151–52".

Date: [September 1842].

Contents: Early draft of 6 lines; text varies considerably from *CP*, pp. 216, 329. For other contents see B91a.

B92b. Citation: "Nature" A.ms., 1 side. Ink (c). NNPM (MA 920:2r).

Title: Nature.

First line: O nature I do not aspire

Collation: 2 leaves of blue wove (type 1), 25 x 20 cm., pp. [1–4]; mounted and bound.

Date: [Ca. 1847].

Contents: Fair copy of 20 lines; text in *CP*, pp. 216, 329. For other contents see B122b, B143, B151, B156a.

B93a. Citation: "A Winter and Spring Scene" A.ms., 4 sides. Ink (c) Pencil (d). CSmH (HM 13182:III, 6v–8r).

First line: Sun melts the snow

Collation: 3 leaves of white wove (type 17a), 24 x 19.2 cm., pp. [1–6], paged "193–98".

Date: 14 October 1842.

Contents: Intermediate draft of 20 stanzas, 82 lines; text in *CP*, pp. 239–42, 263–65, 335–36.

Note: This draft may be two versions, 42 and 40 lines each, of the same poem.

B93b.   Citation: "A Winter and Spring Scene" A.ms., 1 side. Ink (c) Pencil (r,n). ICarbS.

First line: The rabbit leaps | The mouse outcreeps

Collation: 1 fragment of white wove (type 17a), 14 x 19.5 cm., pp. [1–2].

Date: [1843].

Contents: Late draft of 8 stanzas, 32 lines; text varies from *CP*, pp. 239–42, 263–64, 335–36. for other contents see E10b. A facsimile is in Stoller, p. 6.

B94.   Citation: "Fair Haven" A.ms., 3 sides. Ink (c) Pencil (r). NNPf.

Title: Fair Haven. [flourish; underscored]

First line: When little hills like lambs did skip,

Collation: 2 leaves of white wove (type 11), 24.6 x 19.7 cm., pp. [1–4].

Date: [1842], dated "May 27 1837".

Contents: Fair copy of 7 stanzas, 28 lines; text varies from *CP*, p. 381.

Note: A fair copy of 4 stanzas, written on hickory leaves in Sophia Thoreau's hand, is at MConA.

B95a.   Citation: "An early unconverted saint" A.ms., 2 sides. Ink (c) Pencil (d). MoSW.

Title: Some streaks of Morning | methinks I could translate into the fair light | of May.

First line: Thou front of evening

Collation: 1 fragment of green wove (type 1), 13 x 20 cm., pp. [1–2]; with ts. copy.

Date: [1842].

Contents: Early draft of 2 stanzas, 22 lines; text much longer than CP, p. 37.

B95b.   Citation: "An early unconverted Saint" A.ms., 1 side. Ink (c) CSmH (HM 13188:v).

Title: Morning.

First line: Heathen without reproach

Collation: 2 leaves of white wove, 24.9 x 20 cm., pp. [1–2].

Date: [1843].

Contents: Late draft of 8 lines; text in CP, pp. 37, 290. For contents of recto see B164.

B95c.   Citation: "An early unconverted Saint" A.ms., 1 side. Ink (c) CSmH (HM 13195).

Title: Morning.

First line: Thou early unconverted saint

Collation: 1 leaf of white wove (type 11), 24.5 x 19.4 cm., pp. [1–2]; in folder marked "Sunday".

Date: [1844].

Contents: Fair copy of 10 lines; text in CP, pp. 37, 290. For other contents see D4a.

B96a.   Citation: "No earnest work that will expand the frame" A.ms., 1 side. Pencil (r,d). CSmH (HM 13187).

First line: Hell were not quite so hard to face

Collation: 1 fragment of white wove (type 2), 9.5 x 19.5 cm., pp. [1–2].

Date: [1842].

Contents: Early draft of 5 lines; text in *CP*, pp. 191, 323. For other contents see B91b.

B96b. Citation: "No earnest work that will expand the frame" A.ms., 2 sides. Ink (c). MH (bMS Am 278.5 [20.C]).

First line: No earnest work that will expand the frame

Collation: 1 leaf of white wove (type 5), 25.1 x 20.1 cm., pp. [1–2].

Date: [1848].

Contents: Fair copy of 2 stanzas, 12 lines; text in *CP*, p. 191.

B97a. Citation: "Such near aspects had we" A.ms., 1 side. Ink (c). MH (MS Am 278.5 [20.1]).

Title: Short Flights

First line: Such near aspects had we

Collation: 1 leaf of gray wove (type 1), 25.1 x 19.9 cm., pp. [1–2]; mounted.

Date: [1842–1843].

Contents: Fair copy of 2 lines; text in *CP*, p. 85.

B97b. Citation: "Such near aspects had we" A.ms., 1 side. Ink (c). CSmH (HM 13195).

First line: Such near aspects had we

Collation: 1 leaf of white wove (type 1a), 31.9 x 19.3 cm., pp. [5–6]; in folder marked "Wednesday".

Date: [1845].

Contents: Fair copy of 2 lines; text in *CP*, p. 85.
For other contents see D7b.

B97c. Citation: "Such near aspects had we" A.ms., 2 sides.
Ink (c). MH (bMS Am 278.5 [15.0]).

First line: Such near aspects had we

Collation: 1 leaf of white wove (type 5), 25.1 x
19.9 cm., pp. [1–2], paged "341".

Date: [1848].

Contents: Fair copy of 2 lines; text in *CP*, p. 85.

B98a. Citation: "Expectation" A.ms., 2 sides. Ink (c) Pencil (r,d). VtMiM.

Title: Expectation

First line: No sound from my forge

Collation: 1 fragment of gray wove (type 1), 20.4 x
20.1 cm., pp. [1–2]; in folder marked "Fragments".

Date: [1842–1843].

Contents: Early draft of 4 lines; text in *CP*, p. 188.

B98b. Citation: "Expectation" A.ms., 2 sides. Ink (c). MH
(MS Am 278.5.20[1]).

Title: Expectation

First line: No sound from my forge

Collation: 1 leaf of gray wove (type 1), 25.1 x 19.9
cm., pp. [1–2]; mounted.

Date: [1842–1843].

Contents: Fair copy of 4 lines; text in *CP*, p. 188.

B99.   Citation: "The Centaur" A.ms., 1 side. Ink (c,r).
       MoSW.

       Title: The Centaur.

       First line: Alas, when will this roving head & breast

       Collation: 1 leaf of green wove (type 1), 25.4 x 20.2
       cm., pp. [1–2]; with ts. copy.

       Date: [1842–1843].

       Contents: Early draft of 23 lines; text in CP, pp.
       389, 402–3.

B100. Citation: "Fog" A.ms., 1 side. Ink (c,r) Pencil (r,d).
       CSmH (HM 13182:III, 9r).

       Title: Fog

       First line: Dull water spirit — and Protean god

       Collation: 1 leaf of white wove (type 17a), 24 x
       19.2 cm., pp. [1–2], paged "355".

       Date: 11 April 1843.

       Contents: Early draft of 10 lines; text in CP, pp.
       150, 314. For other contents see E9f.

B101. Citation: "The Departure" A.ms., 2 sides. Ink (c,r,d)
       Pencil (r,d). CSmH (HM 13184).

       Title: [The] Departure

       First line: In this roadstead I have ridden

       Collation: 1 leaf of white wove, 25 x 19.7 cm., pp.
       [1–2].

       Date: [Before May 1843].

       Contents: Intermediate draft of 10 stanzas, 45 lines;
       text in CP, pp. 209–10, 326–27.

       Note: A later copy of this poem, in Emerson's hand,
       is at MH (RWEMA).

B102a. Citation: "Brother where dost thou dwell" A.ms., 4 sides. Ink (c) Pencil (n*). VtMiM.

First line: Brother where dost thou dwell?

Collation: 2 leaves of gray wove, 25.3 x 20 cm., pp. [1–4].

Date: 23 May 1843.

Contents: Fair copy of 10 stanzas, 42 lines; in an a.l.s. [Castleton, Staten Island] to Helen Thoreau. Text in CP, pp. 151–52, 314–15.

B102b. Citation: "Brother where dost thou dwell" A.ms., 2 sides. Ink (c) Pencil (r). W. S. Thomas, Rochester, N.Y.

First line: Brother, where dost thou dwell?

Collation: 1 leaf of blue wove (type 1), 25.2 x 19.5 cm., pp. [1–2].

Date: [1847].

Contents: Late draft of 16 stanzas, 66 lines; text in CP, pp. 151–52, 314–15. For another description see W. S. Thomas, "Thoreau as His Own Editor", NEQ 15 (1942):101–3.

B102c. Citation: "Brother where dost thou dwell" A.ms., 1 side. Ink (c)*. CSmH (HM 7033).

First line: Brother, where dost thou dwell.

Collation: 2 leaves of white wove (anom.), pp. [1–4]; in an a.l.s. to D. Ricketson.

Date: 31 August [1862].

Contents: Fair copy, by Sophia Thoreau, of 10 stanzas, 42 lines; text in CP, p. 151.

B103. Citation: "Translations from Pindar" A.ms., 25 sides. Pencil (c,r,d). CSmH (HM 13204).

Title: Fragments of Pindar

First line: First at Artemisium | The children of the Athenians laid the shining | Foundation of freedom,

Collation: 14 leaves of white wove (type 11), 24.7 x 19.7 cm., pp. [1–28]; mounted with leaves of the Riverside edition (Cambridge, Mass.: Riverside Press, 1894).

Date: [July to November 1843].

Contents: Early draft of 474 lines; text varies from W 5:375, 377–82, 385–89, 390–92 (228 lines are unpublished).

B104. Citation: "Pray to what earth does this sweet cold belong" A.ms., 2 sides. Ink (c,n*). NNPM (MA 1719).

First line: Pray to what earth does this sweet cold belong,

Collation: 1 leaf of white wove (type 11), 24.6 x 19.6 cm., pp. [1–2], paged "41–42".

Date: [Before October 1843].

Contents: Fair copy of 17 lines, omitted by Emerson from "A Winter Walk"; text in CP, p. 228. A facsimile is in PT, p. 32. For other contents see C6d.

B105. Citation: "Epitaph on Pursy" A.ms., 1 side. Ink (c). CSmH (HM 13182:I).

First line: Traveller, this is no prison,

Collation: 1 leaf of white laid (type 4), 24.8 x 19.2 cm., pp. [1–2], paged "28".

Date: 22 [October 1843].

Contents: Fair copy of 2 stanzas, 8 lines; text in CP, pp. 153, 315. For other contents see B107a, B108a, B109a, E11d.

B106. Citation: "Epitaph on the World" A.ms., 1 side. Ink (c,r). CSmH (HM 13182:I).

Title: Ep on the World.

First line: Here lies the body of this world,

Collation: 1 leaf of white laid (type 4), 24.8 x 19.2 cm., pp. [1–2], paged "29".

Date: 22 [October 1843].

Contents: Early draft of 9 lines; text in CP, pp. 154, 315. For other contents see E11d.

B107a. Citation: "Epitaph on an Engraver" A.ms., 1 side. Ink (c). CSmH (HM 13182:I).

Title: Epitaph on an Engraver

First line: By Death's favor

Collation: 1 leaf of white laid (type 4), 24.8 x 19.2 cm., pp. [1–2], paged "28".

Date: 22 [October 1843].

Contents: Fair copy of 6 lines; text in CP, pp. 155, 315. For other contents see B105, B108a, B109a, E11d.

B107b. Citation: "Epitaph on an Engraver" A.ms., 1 side. Ink (c). W. S. Thomas, Rochester, N.Y.

Title: Epitaph on an Engraver.

First line: By deaths' favor

Collation: 1 fragment of white wove (type 1a), 27.8 x 19.4 cm., pp. [1–2].

Date: [1845].

Contents: Fair copy of 6 lines; text in CP, p. 155.

B108a. Citation: "On a good man" A.ms., 1 side. Ink (c) Pencil (c). CSmH (HM 13182:I).

Title: Ep—— on a good man

First line: There rises one

Collation: 1 leaf of white laid (type 4), 24.8 x 19.2 cm., pp. [1–2], paged "28".

Date: 22 [October 1843].

Contents: Early draft of 3 lines; text in *CP*, pp. 186, 322. For other contents see B105, B107a, B109a, E11d.

B108b. Citation: "On a good man" A.ms., 1 side. Ink (c). W. S. Thomas, Rochester, N.Y.

Title: On a good man

First line: Here lies——the world,

Collation: 1 fragment of white wove (type 1a), 27.8 x 19.4 cm., pp. [1–2].

Date: [1845].

Contents: Fair copy of 2 lines; text in *CP*, p. 186.

B109a. Citation: "Here lies an honest man" A.ms., 1 side. Ink (c) Pencil (r). CSmH (HM 13182:I).

First line: Here lies an honest man,

Collation: 1 leaf of white laid (type 4), 24.8 x 19.2 cm., pp. [1–2], paged "28".

Date: 22 [October 1843].

Contents: Early draft of 6 lines; text in *CP*, pp. 51, 294. For other contents see B105, B107a, B108a, E11d.

B109b. Citation: "Here lies an honest man" A.ms., 1 side. Ink (c). W. S. Thomas, Rochester, N.Y.

Title: Epitaph

First line: Here lies an honest man

Collation: 1 fragment of white wove (type 1a), 27.8 x 19.4 cm., pp. [1–2].

Date: [1845].

Contents: Fair copy of 6 lines; text in *CP*, pp. 51, 294.

B109c. Citation: "Here lies an honest man" A.ms., 2 sides. Ink (c) Pencil (r,d). MH (bMS Am 278.5 [15. J]).

First line: Here lies an Honest Man

Collation: 1 fragment of blue wove (type 5), 12.3 x 19.7 cm., pp. [1–2].

Date: [1848].

Contents: Late draft of 9 lines; text varies from *CP*, p. 51.

B110. Citation: "The Just Made Perfect" A.ms., 2 sides. Ink (c) Pencil (r,d). MoSW.

Title: The Just Made Perfect

First line: A stately music rises on my ear,

Collation: 1 leaf of green wove, 25 x 19.5 cm., pp. [1–2]; with ts. copy.

Date. [1843].

Contents: Early draft of 59 lines; text varies from *CP*, pp. 156–57.

B111. Citation: "The Seven Against Thebes" A.ms., 42 sides. Ink (c) Pencil (r). CSmH (HM 13193).

Title: The Seven Against Thebes

First line: Et. Citizens of Cadmus, it behooves that whenever the times require we should speak

Collation: 21 leaves,
   13 white wove (type 11) 24.7 x 19.7 cm.,
   6 of blue wove 25.4 x 20 cm.,
   2 of blue wove (type 2) 25 x 19.6 cm.,
pp. [1–42], paged "1–39".

Date: [1843].

Contents: Early draft of 1,078 lines; text (and 3 facsimiles) in L. M. Kaiser, "Thoreau's Translation of *The Seven Against Thebes*", *ESQ*, No. 17 (1959), pp. 3–28.

B112a. Citation: "Low-anchored cloud" A.ms., 2 sides. Ink (c) Pencil (r). CSmH (HM 956: 16v).

Title: Fog.

First line: Thru drifting meadows of the air

Collation: 1 leaf of white wove (type 11), 24.4 x 19.5 cm., pp. [1–2]; foliated* "16" in early draft of "Tuesday", *A Week*.

Date: [1843–1844].

Contents: Early draft of 16 lines; text in *CP*, pp. 56, 294. For other contents see D6a.

B112b. Citation: "Low-anchored cloud" A.ms., 1 side. Ink (c). NNPM (MA 1303).

Title: Fog.

First line: Those drifting meadows of the air

Collation: 1 leaf of white wove (type 1a), 31.9 x 19.8 cm., pp. [1–2], paged "119–20"; bound.

Date: [1845].

Contents: Late draft of 2 stanzas, 18 lines; text in *CP*, pp. 56, 294.

B112c. Citation: "Low-anchored cloud" A.ms., 1 side. Ink
(c) Pencil (r). ViU (6329–a).

Title: Fog.

First line: Low-anchored cloud, New foundland air,

Collation: 1 fragment of blue wove (type 9), 12.4 x
19 cm., pp. [1–2]; bound.

Date: [1845].

Contents: Late draft of 12 lines; text in CP, pp. 56,
294–95.

B113a. Citation: "The waves slowly beat" A.ms., 2 sides.
Ink (c). CSmH (HM 956: 26v).

First line: The waves slowly beat

Collation: 1 leaf of white wove (type 11), 24.4 x
19.2 cm., pp. [1–2]; foliated* "26" in early draft of
"Tuesday", A Week.

Date: [1843–1844].

Contents: Fair copy of 6 lines; text in CP, pp. 58,
295. For other contents see D6a.

B113b. Citation: "The waves slowly beat" A.ms., 2 sides.
Ink (c). NNPM (MA 1303).

First line: The waves slowly beat

Collation: 2 leaves of white wove (type 1a), 31.9 x
19.8 cm., pp. [1–4], paged "61–62, 115–16"; bound.

Date: [1845], dated "September 3 1842".

Contents: Fair copies of 6 lines and 4 lines (2 versions); text in CP, pp. 58, 295.

B114a. Citation: "Salmon Brook" A.ms., 2 sides. Ink (c)
Pencil (r). CSmH (HM 956).

First line: Salmon brook,

Collation: 1 leaf of white wove (type 11), 24.4 x 19.5 cm., pp. [1–2], foliated* "9"; bound.

Date: [1843–1844].

Contents: Early draft of 2 stanzas, 12 lines; text in *CP*, pp. 79, 300. For other contents see D5a.

B114b. Citation: "Salmon Brook" A.ms., 1 side. Ink (c). NNPM (MA 1303).

First line: Salmon Brook

Collation: 1 leaf of white wove (type 1a), 31.9 x 19.8 cm., pp. [1–2], paged "49–50"; bound.

Date: [1845], dated "September 1 1842".

Contents: Fair copy of 12 lines, text in *CP*, pp. 79, 300.

B114c. Citation: "Salmon Brook" A.ms., 1 side. Ink (c). CSmH (HM 13182: III, 5v).

First line: Salmon Brook,

Collation: 1 fragment of blue wove (type 9), pp. [1–2], paged "371–72".

Date: [1845].

Contents: Fair copy of 2 stanzas, 12 lines; text in *CP*, p. 79.

B114d. Citation: "Salmon Brook" A.ms., 1 side. Ink (c). MH (bMS Am 278.5 [15.O]).

First line: Salmon Brook

Collation: 1 leaf of blue wove (type 1), 25.1 x 20 cm., pp. [1–2], paged "322–23".

Date: [1847].

Contents: Fair copy of 2 stanzas, 12 lines; text in CP, p. 79.

B115a. Citation: "All things are current found" A.ms., 1 side. Ink (c,r). VtMiM.

First line: All things are current found

Collation: 1 leaf of white wove (type 11), 24.6 x 19.5 cm., pp. [1–2]; in folder marked "Fragments".

Date: [1843–1844].

Contents: Late draft of 4 stanzas, 16 lines; text in CP, pp. 83, 300–301. For other contents see D9f.

B115b. Citation: "All things are current found" A.ms., 1 side. Ink (c,r). NNPM (MA 1303).

First line: As oceans ebb and flow

Collation: 1 leaf of white wove (type 1a), 31.9 x 19.8 c., pp. [1–2], paged "125–26"; bound.

Date: [1845].

Contents: Late draft of 5 stanzas, 18 lines; text in CP, pp. 83, 300–301.

B116a. Citation: "I was born upon thy bank river" A.ms., 1 side. Ink (c,r) Pencil (d). NYPL (Berg).

First line: I was born upon thy bank, River,

Collation: 1 leaf of white wove (type 11), 24.7 x 19.5 cm., pp. [1–2], paged* "6–7".

Date: [1843–1844].

Contents: Late draft of 4 lines; text varies from CP, p. 120. For other contents see D1a.

B116b. Citation: "I was born upon thy bank river" A.ms., 1 side. Ink (c). NNPM (MA 1303).

First line: I was born upon thy bank river

Collation: 1 leaf of white wove (type 1a), 31.9 x 19.9 cm., pp. [1–2], paged "5–6"; bound.

Date: [1845].

Contents: Fair copy of 4 lines; text in CP, p. 120. For other contents see D1b.

B117a. Citation: "The moon now rises to her absolute rule" A.ms., 2 sides. Ink (c,r) Pencil (r,d). VtMiM.

First line: The moon no longer reflects the day

Collation: 1 leaf of white wove (type 11), 24.6 x 19.5 cm., pp. [1–2]; in folder marked "Fragments".

Date: [1843–1844].

Contents: Early draft of 34 lines; text varies considerably from CP, p. 136. For a prose version of these lines see W 1:404–5. For other contents see D9f.

B117b. Citation: "The moon now rises to her absolute rule" A.ms., 1 side. Ink (c,r) Pencil (r). NNPM (MA 1303).

First line: The moon now rises to her absolute rule

Collation: 1 leaf of white wove (type 1a), 31.9 x 19.3 cm., pp. [1–2], paged "61–62"; bound.

Date: [1845], dated "September 1 [1842]".

Contents: Late draft of 18 lines; text in CP, pp. 136, 311.

B118a. Citation: "Travelling" A.ms., 1 side. Ink (c,r) Pencil (r,d). CtY (Za 7).

Title: Travelling

First line: How little curious is man

Collation: 1 leaf of white wove (type 11), 24.7 x 19.7 cm., pp. [1–2].

Date: [1843–1844].

Contents: Early draft of 6 stanzas, 24 lines; text in CP, pp. 141, 132. For other contents see D8f.

B118b. Citation: "Travelling" A.ms., 1 side. Ink (c,r) Pencil (r). NNPM (MA 1303).

First line: How little curious is man

Collation: 1 leaf of white wove (type 1a), 31.9 x 19.8 cm., pp. [1–2], paged "121–22"; bound.

Date: [1845].

Contents: Early draft of 27 lines; text in CP, pp. 141, 312.

B118c. Citation: "Travelling" A.ms., 1 side. Ink (c,r) Pencil (d). CSmH (HM 13182:III, 13r).

First line: How little curious is man,

Collation: 1 leaf of green wove (type 1), 25.5 x 20 cm., pp. [1–2].

Date: [1846].

Contents: Intermediate draft of 25 lines; text in CP, pp. 141, 312. A facsimile is in FLJ 1:128.

B118d. Citation: "Travelling" A.ms., 1 side. Ink (c,r) Pencil (r,d). CSmH (HM 13182:III, 1v).

First line: How little curious is man

Collation: 1 leaf of blue wove (type 1), 25.2 x 20 cm., pp. [1–2].

Date: [1847].

Contents: Late draft of 13 lines; text in CP, pp. 141, 312.

B118e. Citation: "Travelling" A.ms., 1 side. Ink (c). MH
(MS Am 278.5 [16]).

First line: Our uninquiring corpses lie more low

Collation: 1 leaf of white wove (type 5), 25.1 x 20
cm., pp. [1–2].

Date: [1848].

Contents: Fair copy of 2 lines; text in *CP*, pp. 141,
312.

B119a. Citation: "On fields o'er which the reaper's hand
has passed" A.ms., 1 side. Ink (c,r). VtMiM.

First line: The field o'er which the reapers' hand has
passed,

Collation: 1 leaf of white wove (type 11), 24.6 x
19.5 cm., pp. [1–2]; in folder marked "Fragments".

Date: [1843–1844].

Contents: Early draft of 8 lines; text varies from *CP*,
p. 142. For other contents see D9f.

B119b. Citation: "On fields oer which the reaper's hand
has passed" A.ms., 1 side. Ink (c). NNPM (MA
1303).

First line: On fields oer which the reaper's hand has
passed

Collation: 1 leaf of white wove (type 1a), 31.9 x
19.8 cm., pp. [1–2], paged "135–36"; bound.

Date: [1845].

Contents: Fair copy of 8 lines; text in *CP*, p. 142.

B120. Citation: "My friends, my noble friends, know ye"
A.ms., 1 side. Ink (c). MH (bMS Am 278.5 [15.T]).

First line: My friends, my noble friends, know ye

Collation: 1 leaf of white wove (type 11), 24.5 x 19.4 cm., pp. [1–2].

Date: [1843–1844].

Contents: Fair copy of 3 lines; text in *CP*, p. 190.

B121a. Citation: "Between the traveller and the setting sun" A.ms., 1 side. Ink (c). CSmH (HM 13195).

First line: Between the traveller and the setting sun

Collation: 1 leaf of white wove (type 11), 24.4 x 19.5 cm., pp. [1–2]; in folder marked "Thursday".

Date: [1843–1844].

Contents: Late draft of 3 lines; Text in *CP*, pp. 205, 326. For other contents see D8a.

B121b. Citation: "Between the traveller and the setting sun" A.ms., 1 side. Ink (c). MH (bMS Am 278.5 [11]).

First line: Between the traveller and the setting sun

Collation: 1 leaf of blue wove (type 9), 24.7 x 19.5 cm., pp. [1–2].

Date: [1848].

Contents: Fair copy of 3 lines; text in *CP*, pp. 205, 326.

B122a. Citation: "Greece" A.ms., 1 side. Ink (c,r) Pencil (r). NNPM (MA 1302:12).

Title: Greece

First line: When life contracts in [torn]

Collation: 1 fragment of white wove (type 11), 24.4 x 9.9 cm., pp. [1–2]; laid in between pp. "136–37" of [vol. 6] of the *Journal*.

Date: [1843–1844 (c), 1851 (r)].

Contents: Early draft of 8 lines; text in *CP*, pp. 218, 329.

B122b.   Citation: "Greece" A.ms., 1 side. Ink (c). NNPM (MA 920:2v).

Title: Greece.

First line: When life contracts into a vulgar span

Collation: 2 leaves of blue wove (type 1), 25 x 20 cm., pp. [1–4]; mounted and bound.

Date: [Ca. 1847].

Contents: Late draft of 12 lines; text in *CP*, pp. 218, 329. For other contents see B92b, B143, B151, B156a.

B123.   Citation: "Where'er thou sail'st who sailed with me" A.ms., 1 side. Ink (c). NNPM (MA 1303).

First line: Where'er thou sail'st who sailed with me

Collation: 1 leaf of white wove (type 1a), 31.9 x 19.9 cm., paged "1–2"; bound.

Date: [1845], dated "August 31 1839".

Contents: Fair copy of 4 lines; text in *CP*, pp. 29, 289.

B124.   Citation: "I am the autumnal sun" A.ms., 2 sides. Ink (c). NNPM (MA 1303).

First line: I am the Autumnal sun,

Collation: 2 leaves of white wove (type 1a), 31.9 x 19.8 cm., pp. [1–2], paged "95–98"; bound.

Date: [1845], dated "October 7 1842".

Contents: Fair copy of 3 stanzas, 14 lines; text in *CP*, pp. 80, 300.

B125.   Citation: "I am bound, I am bound, for a distant shore" A.ms., 1 side. Ink (c). NNPM (MA 1303).

First line: By a lonely isle by a far Azore

Collation: 1 leaf of white wove (type 1a), 31.9 x 19.8 cm., pp. [1–2], paged "217–18"; bound.

Date: [1845].

Contents: Fair copy of 3 lines; text in CP, pp. 30, 289.

B126a. Citation: "I make ye an offer" A.ms., 1 side. Ink (c). MH (bMS Am 278.5 [15.R]).

First line: I'll be slave to no God

Collation: 1 leaf of blue wove (type 9), 24.2 x 19 cm., pp. [1–2].

Date: [1845].

Contents: Fair copy of 6 lines, text in CP, pp. 41, 292.

B126b. Citation: "I make ye an offer" A.ms., 1 side. Ink (c). NNPM (MA 1303).

Title: The Offer

First Line: I make ye an offer,

Collation: 1 leaf of white wove (type 1a), 31.9 x 19.8 cm., pp. [1–2], paged "161–62"; bound.

Date: [1845].

Contents: Fair copy of 16 lines; text in CP, pp. 41, 292.

B127.   Citation: "Where gleaming fields of haze" A.ms., 2 sides. Ink (c). NNPM (MA 1303).

First line: Far oer the bow

Collation: 2 leaves of white wove (type 1a), 31.9 x 19.8 cm., pp. [1–4], paged "115–18"; bound.

Date: [1845].

Contents: Fair copy of 9 stanzas, 54 lines; text in CP, pp. 60–61, 296.

B128a. Citation: "I mark the summer's swift decline" A.ms., 1 side. Ink (c) Pencil (n). NNPM (MA 1303).

First line: I mark the summer's swift decline

Collation: 1 leaf of white wove (type 1a), 31.9 x 19.8 cm., pp. [1–2], paged "93–94"; bound.

Date: [1845].

Contents: Fair copy of 6 lines; text in CP, p. 138.

B128b. Citation: "I mark the summer's swift decline" A.ms., 1 side. Ink (c). W. S. Thomas, Rochester, N.Y.

First line: I mark the summer's swift decline

Collation: 1 leaf of white wove (type 5), 25.1 x 20.1 cm., pp. [1–2].

Date: [1848].

Contents: Fair copy of 2 stanzas, 8 lines; text in CP, p. 138.

B129a. Citation: "Methinks that by a strict behavior" A.ms., 1 side. Ink (c). NNPM (MA 1303).

First line: Methinks that by a strict behavior

Collation: 1 leaf of white wove (type 1a), 31.9 x 19.8 cm., pp. [1–2], paged "117–18"; bound.

Date: [1845].

Contents: Fair copy of 3 lines; text in CP, p. 139.

B129b. Citation: "Methinks that by a strict behavior" (see section H]

B130a. Citation: "I have rolled near some other spirits path" A.ms., 1 side. Ink (c). NNPM (MA 1303).

First line: I have rolled near some other spirits path

Collation: 1 leaf of white wove (type 1a), 31.9 x 19.8 cm., pp. [1–2], paged "117–18"; bound.

Date: [1845].

Contents: Fair copy of 5 lines; text in *CP*, pp. 140, 311.

B130b. Citation: "I have rolled near some other spirits path" [see Section H]

B131. Citation: "To a Marsh Hawk in Spring" A.ms., 1 side. Ink (c). NNPM (MA 1303).

Title: To a marsh hawk | In Spring ——

First line: There is health in thy gray wing

Collation: 1 leaf of white wove (type 1a), 31.9 x 19.8 cm., pp. [1–2], paged "161–62"; bound.

Date: [1845].

Contents: Fair copy of 8 lines; text in *CP*, p. 143.

B132a. Citation: "Great Friend" A.ms., 2 sides. Ink (c,r). NNPM (MA 1303).

First line: Man walks in nature still alone,

Collation: 1 leaf of white wove (type 1a), 31.9 x 19.8 cm., pp. [1–2], paged "161–62"; bound.

Date: [1845].

Contents: Early draft of 6 stanzas, 25 lines; text in *CP*, pp. 144, 313.

B132b. Citation: "Great Friend" A.ms., 2 sides. Ink (c) Pencil (d). CSmH (HM 13182:III, 3).

First line: We walk in nature still alone,

Collation: 1 leaf of blue wove (type 1), 25.2 x 20 cm., pp. [1–2], paged "310–11".

Date: [1847].

Contents: Late draft of 3 stanzas, 23 lines; text in CP, pp. 144, 313.

B132c. Citation: "Great Friend" A.ms., 2 sides. Ink (c). MH (bMS Am 278.5 [15.0]).

Title: Great Friend

First line: (I walk in nature still alone

Collation: 1 leaf of white wove (type 5), 25.1 x 19.5 cm., pp. [1–2], paged "341".

Date: [1848].

Contents: Fair copy of 6 stanzas, 25 lines; text in CP, pp. 144, 313. For other contents see D7c.

B133. Citation: "Yet let us Thank the purblind race" A.ms., 1 side. Ink (c). NNPM (MA 1303).

First line: Yet let us Thank the purblind race,

Collation: 1 leaf of white wove (type 1a), 31.9 x 19.8 cm., pp. [1–2], paged "197–98"; bound.

Date: [1845].

Contents: Fair copy of 4 lines; text in CP, p. 145.

B134. Citation: "Ive seen ye, sisters, on the mountain-side" A.ms., 2 sides. Ink (c,r) Pencil (r). NNPM (MA 1303).

First line: Ive seen ye, sisters, on the mountain-side

Collation: 2 leaves of white wove (type 1a), 31.9 x
19.8 cm., pp. [1–4], paged "197–200"; bound.

Date: [1845].

Contents: Intermediate draft of 31 lines; text in CP,
pp. 146–47, 313.

B135.   Citation: "Ye do command me to all virtue ever"
A.ms., 1 side. Ink (c). NNPM (MA 1303).

First line: Ye do command me to all virtue ever

Collation: 1 leaf of white wove (type 1a), 31.9 x
19.8 cm., pp. [1–2], paged "201–2"; bound.

Date: [1845].

Contents: Fair copy of 5 lines; text in CP, p. 148.

Note: Items B134–B135 may be drafts of the same
poem.

B136a.   Citation: "Until at length the north winds blow"
A.ms., 1 side. Ink (c) Pencil (d). CSmH (HM
13182:III, 5r).

First line: Until at length the north winds blow,

Collation: 1 leaf of blue wove (type 9), 24.2 x 19
cm., pp. [1–2], paged "371–72".

Date: [1845].

Contents: Fair copy of 4 lines; text in CP, pp. 196,
325.

B136b.   Citation: "Until at length the north winds blow"
A.ms., 1 side. Ink (c) Pencil (d). MH (bMS Am
278.5 [15.Q]).

First line: Until at length the north winds blow

Collation: 1 leaf of blue wove (type 1), 25.2 x 20
cm., pp. [1–2], paged "417–18".

Date: [1847].

Contents: Late draft of 4 lines; text in CP, pp. 196, 325.

B137.   Citation: "Wait not till slaves pronounce the word" A.ms., 2 sides. Ink (c). CSmH (HM 13182:III, 12).

Title: Spes sibi quisque. | Each one his own hope.

First line: Wait not till slaves pronounce the word

Collation: 1 leaf of blue wove (type 9), 24.2 x 19 cm., pp. [1–2].

Date: [1845].

Contents: Fair copy of 11 stanzas, 44 lines; text in CP, pp. 198–99. A facsimile is in FLJ 1:136.

Note: For a possibly original couplet from the 1845 period, see D2a.

B138a.   Citation: "To a Stray Fowl" A.ms., 1 side. Ink (c). CSmH (HM 924:A, 63r).

First line: Poor bird! destined to lead thy life

Collation: 1 leaf of blue wove (type 1), 25.1 x 19.9 cm., pp. [125–26], paged "²69" in draft A of Walden.

Date: [1846–1847].

Contents: Late draft of 2 stanzas, 24 lines; text in CP, p. 12, and Shanley, pp. 160–61.

B138b.   Citation: "To a Stray Fowl" A.ms., 1 side. Ink (c). NNPM (MA 920).

First line: Poor bird! destined to lead thy life

Collation: 1 leaf of blue wove (type 9), 24.2 x 19.1 cm., pp. [1–2]; mounted and bound.

Date: [1849].

Contents: Fair copy of 2 stanzas, 24 lines; copied for inclusion in *Walden*; text in *CP*, pp. 12, 283.

Note: Written in hand of Henry, not Sophia, as conjectured in *CP*, p. 283.

B139a. Citation: "The good how can we trust" A.ms., 1 side. Ink (c,r) Pencil (r). MoSW.

First line: If love fails in strife with love

Collation: 1 leaf of blue wove (type 1), 25.2 x 20 cm., pp. [1–2].

Date: [Before 29 December 1847].

Contents: Early draft of 5 stanzas, 20 lines; text varies from *CP*, p. 69.

B139b. Citation: "The good how can we trust" A.ms., 1 side. Ink (c). NYPL (Berg).

First line: The good how can we trust?

Collation: 2 leaves of blue wove (type 1), 25.2 x 20.1 cm., pp. [1–4]; with ts. copy. Text appears on the top and bottom of p. [4]; the inner folds of an a.l.s. to R. W. Emerson.

Date: 29 December 1847.

Contents: Fair copy of 2 stanzas, 14 lines; text varies from *CP*, p. 69. For other contents see *Corr.*, pp. 199–201.

B140a. Citation: "Men say they know many things" A.ms., 1 side. Ink (c). CSmH (HM 924:A, 22r).

First line: Men say they know many things

Collation: 1 leaf of blue wove (type 1), 25.1 x 19.9 cm., pp. [43–44], paged "35" in draft A of *Walden*.

Date: [1847].

Contents: Early draft of 6 lines; text in Shanley, p. 124.

B140b. Citation: "Men say they know many things" A.ms., 1 side. Ink (c). CSmH (HM 924:D, 28r).

First line: Men say they know many things,

Collation: 1 leaf of white wove (type 18), 23.9 x 19.1 cm., pp. [55–56] in draft D of *Walden*.

Date: [1852].

Contents: Late draft of 6 lines; text in CP, pp. 24, 287.

B141. Citation: "Love equals swift and slow" A.ms., 1 side. Ink (c). CSmH (HM 13182:III, 3v).

First line: Love equals swift and slow,

Collation: 1 leaf of blue wove (type 1), 25.2 x 20 cm., pp. [1–2], paged "310–11".

Date: [1847].

Contents: Fair copy of 4 lines; text in CP, p. 23.

B142. Citation: "The respectable folks" A.ms., 2 sides. Ink (c) Pencil (d). CSmH (HM 13182:III, 2).

First line: The respectable folks,

Collation: 1 leaf of blue wove (type 1), 25.2 x 20 cm., pp. [1–2].

Date: [1847].

Contents: Early draft of 25 lines; text in CP, pp. 32, 289.

B143. Citation: "Though all the fates should prove unkind" A.ms., 1 side. Ink (c). NNPM (MA 920:2r).

Title: Travelling.

First line: If e'er our minds be ill at ease

Collation: 2 leaves of blue wove (type 1), 25 x 20 cm., pp. [1–4]; mounted and bound.

Date: [1847].

Contents: Early draft of 8 lines; text in CP, pp. 46, 292. For other contents see B92b, B122b, B151, B156a.

B144.   Citation: "Away! away! away! away!" A.ms., 2 sides. Ink (c). TxU.

First line: Away! away! away! away!

Collation: 1 leaf of blue wove (type 1), 25 x 19.9 cm., pp. [1–2].

Date: [1847].

Contents: Fair copy of 4 lines; text in CP, p. 54. For other contents see D50.

B145.   Citation: "My books I'd fain cast off, I cannot read" A.ms., 1 side. Ink (c) Pencil (n). CSmH (HM 1225).

First line: Tell Shakespeare to attend some leisure hour,

Collation: 1 leaf of blue wove (type 1), 25 x 17.9 cm., pp. [1–2]; bound.

Date: [1847].

Contents: Fair copy of 6 stanzas, 24 lines; text in CP, pp. 76–77, 299. For contents of verso see D8b.

B146a.   Citation: "The Hero" A.ms., 3 sides. Ink (c,r) Pencil (c,d). CSmH (HM 924:A, 67–69).

First line: What do we ask?

Collation: 3 leaves of blue wove (type 1), 25.1 x 19.9 cm., pp. [133–38], paged "² 81, 95, 85" in draft A of *Walden*.

Date: [1847].

Contents: Early draft of 34 lines; text in *CP*, pp. 161–63, 316–17, and in Shanley, pp. 165–66.

Note: *CP* prints the last four lines as a separate poem, "Must we still eat", p. 206.

B146b. Citation: "The Hero" A.ms., 5 sides. Ink (c,r) Pencil (r,d). NNPM (MA 1302:7).

Title: The Hero

First line: What doth he ask?

Collation: 3 leaves of white wove (type 22), 19.3 x 16.6 cm., pp. [1–6]; bound.

Date: [1847–1848].

Contents: Late draft of 12 stanzas, 125 lines; text in *CP*, pp. 161–63, 316–18.

B147a. Citation: "I seek the present time" A.ms., 3 sides. Ink (c) Pencil (r,d). CSmH (HM 924:A, 44-5).

First line: I seek the Present Time

Collation: 2 leaves of blue wove (type 1), 25.1 x 19.9 cm., pp. [87–90], paged "²11–13" in draft A of *Walden*.

Date: [1847].

Contents: Early draft of 85 lines; text in *CP*, pp. 165–67, 318–19, and Shanley, pp. 143–45.

B147b. Citation: "I seek the present time" A.ms., 4 sides. Ink (c,r) Pencil (r). NNPM (MA 1302:7).

First line: I seek the present time

Collation: 3 leaves of white wove (type 22), 19.3 x
16.6 cm., pp. [1–6].

Date: [1847–1848].

Contents: Late draft of 6 stanzas, 86 lines; text in
CP, pp. 165–67, 318–19.

B148a. Citation: "Canst thou love with thy mind" A.ms., 3
sides. Ink (c,r) Pencil (r). MoSW.

First line: With a tough tenderness

Collation: 2 leaves of blue wove (type 1), 25.2 x
20 cm., pp. [1–4].

Date: [1847].

Contents: Late draft of 6 stanzas, 62 lines; text varies
from CP, p. 180.

B148b. Citation: "Canst thou love with thy mind" A.ms.,
1 side. Ink (c). CSmH (HM 13196).

First line: Canst thou love with thy mind

Collation: 1 leaf of white wove (type 18), 23.8 x
19.1 cm., pp. [1–2].

Date: September 1852.

Contents: Fair copy of 2 stanzas, 8 lines; in an intermediate draft of the essay "Love". Text in CP, pp. 180,
321. For other contents see C12a.

B149a. Citation: "Indeed, indeed, I cannot tell" A.ms. 1 side.
Ink (c,r) Pencil (r). MoSW.

First line: If love fails in strife with love,

Collation: 1 leaf of blue wove (type 1), 25.2 x 20
cm., pp. [1–2].

Date: [1847].

Contents: Late draft of 15 lines; text varies from *CP*, p. 181.

B149b. Citation: "Indeed, indeed, I cannot tell" A.ms., 1 side. Ink (c). CSmH (HM 13196).

First line: Indeed indeed, I cannot tell

Collation: 1 leaf of white wove (type 18), 23.8 x 19.1 cm., pp. [1–2].

Date: September 1852.

Contents: Fair copy of 2 stanzas, 13 lines; in an intermediate draft of the essay "Love". Text in *CP*, pp. 181, 321. For other contents see C12a.

B150. Citation: "Guido's Aurora" A.ms., 1 side. Ink (c). NNPM (MA 920:1r).

Title: Guido's Aurora.

First line: The God of day rolls his car up the slopes,

Collation: 2 leaves of blue wove (type 1), 25 x 20 cm., pp. [1–4]; mounted and bound.

Date: [Ca. 1847].

Contents: Fair copy of 4 stanzas, 14 lines; text in *CP*, pp. 217, 329. For other contents see B92b, B122b.

B151. Citation: "Poverty" A.ms., 2 sides. Ink (c,n). NNPM (MA 920:1v-2r).

Title: Poverty

First line: If I am poor it is that I am proud,

Collation: 2 leaves of blue wove (type 1), 25 x 20 cm., pp. [1–4]; mounted and bound.

Date: [1847].

Contents: Late draft of 8 stanzas, 31 lines; text in CP, pp. 219–20, 330. For other contents see B26c, B92a, B122b, B143, B150, B152, B154, B155a, B156a.

B152.   Citation: "I'm not alone" A.ms., 1 side. Ink (c). NNPM (MA 920:1v).

First line: I'm not alone

Collation: 2 leaves of blue wove (type 1), 25 x 20 cm., pp. [1–4]; mounted and bound.

Date: [1847].

Contents: Late draft of 2 stanzas, 8 lines; text in CP, pp. 221, 330. For other contents see B26c, B150, B154, B155a.

B153.   Citation: "What sought they thus afar" A.ms., 1 side. Ink (c) Pencil (r). NNPM (MA 920).

First line: What sought they thus afar

Collation: 1 leaf of gray wove (type 6), 24.2 x 18.3 cm., pp. [1–2]; mounted and bound.

Date: [1847].

Contents: Early draft of 4 stanzas, 15 lines; text varies from CP, pp. 222, 330.

Note: Lines 14 and 17 of the CP version contain references to Jean Paul Richter (1763–1825), a German author and musical theorist. The lines should read "Richter on Music" and "after it. Richter". Joel Porte notes that the last two stanzas are quotations of the Caliph Ali and Richter, respectively. See *Emerson and Thoreau: Transcendentalists in Conflict* (Middletown, Conn.: Wesleyan University Press, 1966), p. 108.

B154.   Citation: "Music" A.ms., 1 side. Ink (c) Pencil (r,d). NNPM (MA 920:11r).

Title: Music.

First line: Ah, I have wandered many ways and lost

Collation: 2 leaves of blue wove (type 1), 25 x 19.5 cm., pp. [1–4]; mounted and bound.

Date: [1847].

Contents: Early draft of 2 stanzas, 29 lines; text in *CP*, pp. 223, 330–31. For other contents see B26c, B150, B152, B155a.

B155a. Citation: "I'm thankful that my life doth not deceive" A.ms., 1 side. Ink (c) Pencil (r,d). NNPM (MA 920:1v.

First line: I'm thankful that my life doth not deceive

Collation: 2 leaves of blue wove (type 1), 25 x 19.5 cm., pp. [1–4]; mounted and bound.

Date: [1847].

Contents: Early draft of 26 lines; text in *CP*, pp. 224, 331. For other contents see B26c, B150, B152, B154.

B155b. Citation: "I'm thankful that my life doth not deceive" A.ms., 2 sides. Ink (c) Pencil (d). TxU.

First line: I'm thankful that my life doth not deceive

Collation: 1 leaf of white wove (type 5), 25.2 x 19.9 cm., pp. [1–2].

Date: [1848].

Contents: Late draft of 13 lines; text varies from *CP*, pp. 224, 331. For other contents see B156b, B166b.

B156a. Citation: "Life" A.ms., 1 side. Ink (c) Pencil (r,d). NNPM (MA 920:2r).

First line: My life is like a stately warrior horse

Collation: 2 leaves of blue wove (type 1), 25 x 19.5 cm., pp. [1–4]; mounted and bound.

Date: [1847].

Contents: Early draft of 30 lines; text in *CP*, pp. 227, 332. A facsimile is in *Journal of American History* 3 (1909):596. For other contents see B92b, B122b, B143, B151.

B156b. Citation: "Life" A.ms., 2 sides. Ink (c,r) Pencil (n). TxU.

Title: Life.

First line: My life is like a stately warrior's horse,

Collation: 1 leaf of white wove (type 5), 25.2 x 19.9 cm., pp. [1–2], paged* "193" and "122".

Date: [1848].

Contents: Late draft of 26 lines; text in *CP*, pp. 227, 332. For other contents see B151b, B166b.

B157. Citation: "When the oaks are in the gray" A.ms., 1 side. Ink (c). CSmH (HM 924:A, 119).

First line: When the oaks are in the gray

Collation: 1 leaf of blue wove (type 1), 25.1 x 19.9 cm., pp. [237–38], paged "235".

Date: [1847].

Contents: Early draft of 2 lines; text in *CP*, p. 229, and Shanley, p. 208.

B158. Citation: "By his good genius prompted or the power" A.ms., 1 side. Ink (c). NNPM (MA 1302:9).

First line: By his good genius prompted or the power

Collation: 1 fragment of blue wove (type 5), 2 x 24.5 cm.; the stub appearing between pp. "142" and "151" of [vol. 3] of the *Journal*.

Date: [1847].

Contents: Fair copy of 2 lines; text in *CP*, p. 247.

B159. Citation: "Tell me ye wise ones if ye can" A.ms., 2 sides. Ink (c). NNPM (MA 1302:8).

First line: Tell me ye wise ones if ye can

Collation: 1 leaf of white wove (type 22), 19.1 x 16.5 cm., pp. [1–2], paged "30"; bound.

Date: [1847–1848], dated "July 14 1845".

Contents: Fair copy of 47 lines; text in *CP*, pp. 158–59, 316.

B160. Citation: "This is my Carnac, whose unmeasured Dome" A.ms., 1 side. Ink (c,r). NNPM (MA 1302:8).

First line: This is my Carnac whose unmeasured dome

Collation: 1 leaf of white wove (type 22), 19.1 x 16.5 cm., pp. [1–2], paged "37–38"; bound.

Date: [1847–1848], dated "August 6 1845".

Contents: Early draft of 4 lines; text in *CP*, pp. 62, 296.

B161. Citation: "The Earth" A.ms., 1 side. Ink (c). NNPM (MA 1302:8).

Title: The Earth

First line: Which seems so barren once gave birth

Collation: 1 leaf of white wove (type 22), 19.1 x 16.5 cm., pp. [1–2]; bound.

Date: [1847–1848], dated "December 1845".

Contents: Fair copy of 3 lines; text in *CP*, p. 160.

B162.   Citation: ["This is the house that I built"] A.ms., 1 side. Ink (c). CSmH (HM 924: before A, 11).

First line: This is the house that I built

Collation: 1 leaf of white wove (type 1a), 31.8 x 19.3 cm., pp. [1–2].

Date: [1847–1848].

Contents: Early draft of 4 lines; text in W 2:170.

B163.   Citation: "At midnight's hour I raised my head" A.ms., 1 side. Ink (c). NNPM (MA 1302:7).

First line: At midnight's hour I raised my head

Collation: 1 leaf of white wove (type 22), 19.3 x 16.6 cm., pp. [1–2]; bound.

Date: [1847–1848].

Contents: Fair copy of 11 lines; text in CP, p. 164.

B164.   Citation: "The Friend" A.ms., 2 sides. Ink (c,r) Pencil (d). CSmH (HM 13188).

Title: The Friend.

First line: The great friend | Dwells at the land's end

Collation: 2 leaves of white wove (type 5), 25 x 20 cm., pp. [1–4]; mounted as 1 leaf.

Date: [1848].

Contents: Intermediate draft of 2 stanzas, 42 lines; text in CP, pp. 201–2, 325. For other contents see B95b, D7d.

B165.   Citation: "Manhood" A.ms., 1 side. Ink (c) Pencil (r,n*). RPB.

Title: Manhood

First line: I love to see the man, a long-lived child

Collation: 1 leaf of white wove (type 5), 25.1 x 19.8 cm., pp. [1–2].

Date: [1848].

Contents: Late draft of 26 lines; text in *CP*, pp. 225, 331.

B166a. Citation: "The moon moves up her smooth and sheeny path" A.ms., 1 side. Ink (c) Pencil (r). RPB.

First line: The moon moves up her smooth and sheeny path

Collation: 1 leaf of white wove (type 5), 25.1 x 19.8 cm., pp. [1–2].

Date: [1848].

Contents: Intermediate draft of 13 lines; text in *CP*, pp. 226, 331.

B166b. Citation: "The moon moves up her smooth and sheeny path" A.ms., 2 sides. Ink (c) Pencil (d). TxU.

First line: The moon moves up her smooth and sheeny path

Collation: 1 leaf of white wove (type 5), 25.2 x 19.9 cm., pp. [1–2].

Date: [1848].

Contents: Late draft of 13 lines; text varies from *CP*, pp. 226, 331. For other contents see B155b, B156b.

B167. Citation: "Farewell" A.ms., 3 sides. Ink (c,r,d) Pencil (r,d). NNPM (MA 920).

Title: Farewell.

First line: Sister mine, where'er thou art,

Collation: 2 leaves of blue wove (type 3), 24.9 x
19.6 cm., pp. [1–4]; mounted and bound.

Date: [After 14 June 1849].

Contents: Early draft of 87 lines; text in CP, pp.
215, 327–28.

Note: CP lists these as two drafts. Another copy, in
Emerson's hand, is at MH (RWEMA).

B168a. Citation: "For though the [eaves] were rabitted"
A.ms., 2 sides. Ink (c,r) Pencil (d). CSmH (HM
13182).

First line: For though the eaves were rabitted

Collation: 2 leaves of blue wove (type 3), 24.8 x
19.9 cm., pp. [1–4], paged ["190–91"].

Date: [September 1849].

Contents: Early draft of 8 lines; text varies from CP,
pp. 189, 323.

Note: CP reads the first line as "For though the
caves were rabitted", but only eaves suits the poem's
subject and imagery.

B168b. Citation: "For though the [eaves] were rabitted"
[see Section H]

B169. Citation: [Poem] A.ms., 2 sides. Ink (c). CSmH
(HM 13182).

First line: You Boston folks & Roxbury people | Will
want Tom Hyde to mend your kettle.

Collation: 1 leaf of blue wove (type 5), 24.8 x 19.4
cm., pp. [1–2], paged "383".

Date: 28 October 1849.

Contents: Fair copy of 2 lines; text unpublished. For other contents, see E13e.

Note: Following a prose passage he later used in *Walden*, Thoreau indented and wrote these lines as a couplet. The absence of quotation marks suggests originality, but he may have copied the lines from another source.

B170.   Citation: "I will obey the strictest law of love" A.ms., 2 sides. Ink (c,r) Pencil (r,d). NYPL (Ms. Division).

First line: I will obey the strictest law of love

Collation: 1 leaf of blue wove (type 5), 24.8 x 19.4 cm., pp. [1–2], paged "387"; in folder marked "Miscellaneous Papers".

Date: [November 1849].

Contents: Early draft of 9 stanzas, 43 lines; text in *CP*, pp. 387–88, 491–92. For other contents see E13f.

B171.   Citation: "Loves invalides are not those of common wars" A.ms., 1 side. Ink (c) Pencil (r,d). CSmH (HM 13182:II).

First Line: Loves invalides are not those of common wars,

Collation: I leaf of blue wove (type 5), 24.6 x 19.7 cm., pp. [1–2].

Date: [November 1849].

Contents: Early draft of 2 stanzas, 8 lines; text in *CP*, p. 168. For other contents see E13g.

Note: *CP* prints this as a separate poem, but it is actually part of its predecessor, "I will obey the strictest law of love", p. 387.

B172. Citation: *The Transmigration of the Seven Brahmans* A.ms., 19 sides. Ink (c) Pencil (r). MH (bMS Am 278.5[12.1]).

Title: The world is founded upon the *svaddha* | The Transmigrations | of the | Seven Brahmans

First line: The divine eye, which Sanatcoumara had given me; made me perceive the seven Brahmans,

Collation: 10 leaves of white wove (type 5), 25.1 x 19.9 cm., pp. [1–20].

Date: [1849–1850].

Contents: Late draft of a prose translation from a French translation by Langlois (1834); text and a facsimile are in *The Transmigration of the Seven Brahmans,* ed. Arthur Christy (New York: William Edwin Rudge, 1932).

B173a. Citation: "The Old Marlborough Road" A.ms., 4 sides. Ink (c,r) Pencil (r,d). NNPM (MA 1302:9).

First line: And once again

Collation: 2 leaves of blue wove, 24.5 x 19.7 cm., pp. [1–4], paged "139–42"; bound in [vol. 3] of the *Journal.*

Date: 16 July 1850.

Contents: Early draft of 10 stanzas, 86 lines; text in *CP,* pp. 17–19, 169, 284.

B173b. Citation: "The Old Marlborough Road" A.ms., 2 sides. Ink (c,r). MH (bMS Am 278.5 [21:B]).

Title: The Old Marlboro Boad

First line: Where they once dug for money

Collation: 1 leaf of white wove (type 18), 24.1 x 19.2 cm., pp. [1–2].

Date: [Before 23 April 1851].

Contents: Late draft of 68 lines; text in *CP*, pp. 17–19, 284–85.

B173c. Citation: "The Old Marlborough Road" A.ms., 4 sides. Ink (c*) Pencil (r). MCon.

Title: The Old Marlboro Road

First line: Where they once dug for money

Collation: 2 leaves of white laid (type 5), 24.5 x 19.1 cm., pp. [1–2], paged "25–27" in the late draft of "Walking".

Date: [1861–1862].

Contents: Late draft of 65 lines; text varies from *CP*, pp. 17–19. For other contents see C11l.

Note: Copied in Sophia's hand, revised by Henry.

B174. Citation: "Old meeting-house bell" A.ms., 2 sides. Ink (c). NNPM (MA 1302:9).

First line: Old meeting-house bell

Collation: 1 leaf of blue wove (type 5), 24.5 x 19.7 cm., pp. [1–2], paged "141–42"; bound in [vol. 3] of the *Journal*.

Date: 16 July 1850.

Contents: Fair copy of 6 lines; text in *CP*, p. 170.

B175. Citation: "Is consigned to the nine" A.ms., 1 side. Ink (c,r) Pencil (d). NNPM (MA 1302:9).

First line: Is consigned to the nine.

Collation: 1 fragment of blue wove (type 5), 9.5 x 19.8 cm., bound between pp. "142" and "151" of [vol. 3] of the *Journal*.

Date: [July 1850].

Contents: Late draft of 10 lines; text in *CP*, pp. 171, 319. For other contents see B178a.

Note: The pages between "142" and "151" are missing.

B176. Citation: "Tall Ambrosia" A.ms., 1 side. Ink (c,r). NNPM (MA 1302:9).

First line: Among the signs of autumn I perceive

Collation: 1 leaf of blue wove (type 5), 24.5 x 19.7 cm., pp. [1–2], paged "151–52"; bound in [vol. 3] of the *Journal*.

Date: 31 August [1850].

Contents: Early draft of 12 lines; text in *CP*, pp. 173, 320.

B177. Citation: "Th' ambrosia of the gods 's a weed on earth" A.ms., 1 side. Ink (c,r) Pencil (c,r). NNPM (MA 1302:9).

First line: Th' ambrosia of the gods 's a weed on earth

Collation: 1 leaf of blue wove (type 5), 24.5 x 19.7 cm., pp. [1–2], paged "151–52"; bound in [vol. 3] of the *Journal*.

Date: 31 August [1850].

Contents: Early draft of 8 lines; text in *CP*, pp. 174, 320.

B178a. Citation: "It is no dream of mine" A.ms., 1 side. Ink (c) Pencil (d). NNPM (MA 1302:9).

First line: I am its stony shore

Collation: 1 fragment of blue wove (type 5), 9.5 x 19.8 cm., pp. [1–2]; bound in [vol. 3] of the *Journal* between pages "142" and "151".

Date: [August 1850].

Contents: Early draft of 2 lines; text in *CP*, pp. 26, 288. For other contents see B175.

B178b. Citation: "It is no dream of mine" A.ms., 1 side. Ink (c) Pencil (r,d). CSmH (HM 924:D, 56).

First line: It is a real place,

Collation: 1 leaf of white wove (type 18), 23.9 x 19.1 cm., pp. [111–12] in draft D of *Walden*.

Date: [1852].

Contents: Late draft of 18 lines; text in *CP*, pp. 26, 288.

B179. Citation: "Among the worst of men that ever lived" A.ms., 1 side. Ink (c,r). NNPM (MA 1302:9).

First line: Among the worst of men that ever lived

Collation: 1 leaf of blue wove (type 5), 24.5 x 19.7 cm., pp. [1–2], paged "151–52"; bound in [vol. 3] of the *Journal*.

Date: [August 1850].

Contents: Intermediate draft of 9 lines; text in *CP*, pp. 172, 319.

B180a. Citation: "What's the railroad to me" A.ms., 1 side. Ink (c). NNPM (MA 1302:9).

First line: What's the rail-road to me?

Collation: 1 leaf of blue wove (type 5), 24.5 x 19.7 cm., pp. [1–2], paged "151–52"; bound in [vol. 3] of the *Journal*.

Date: [August 1850].

Contents: Fair copy of 7 lines; text in *CP*, pp. 25 287.

B180b. Citation: "What's the railroad to me" A.ms., 1 side.
Ink (c). CSmH (HM 924:F, 13).

First line: What's the railroad to me

Collation: 1 leaf of white wove (type 19), 23.7 x
19.2 cm., pp. [25–26] in draft F of *Walden*.

Date: [1853–1854].

Contents: Late draft of 7 lines; text in CP, pp. 25,
287.

B181. Citation: "I saw a delicate flower had grown up 2
feet high" A.ms., 1 side. Ink (c). NNPM (MA
1302:9).

First line: I saw a delicate flower had grown up 2
feet high

Collation: 1 leaf of blue wove (type 5), 24.5 x 19.7
cm., pp. [1–2], paged "161–62"; bound in [vol. 3]
of the *Journal*.

Date: 6 [September 1850].

Contents: Fair copy of 25 lines; text in CP, p. 175.

B182. Citation: "To day I climbed a handsome rounded
hill" A.ms., 1 side. Ink (c) Pencil (r). NNPM (MA
1302:9).

First line: To day I climbed a handsome rounded
hill

Collation: 1 leaf of blue wove (type 5), 24.5 x 19.7
cm., pp. [1–2], paged "163–64"; bound in [vol. 3]
of the *Journal*.

Date: 6 September 1850.

Contents: Fair copy of 7 lines; text in CP, p. 176.

B183a. Citation: "I am the little Irish boy" A.ms., 2 sides.
Ink (c) Pencil (d). NNPM (MA 1302:10).

First line: I am the little Irish boy

Collation: 1 leaf of white wove, 24.9 x 19.6 cm., pp. [1–2], paged "161–64" bound in [vol. 4] of the *Journal*.

Date: 28 November 1850.

Contents: Fair copy of 8 stanzas, 37 lines; text in *CP*, pp. 177–78, 320–21.

B183b. Citation: "I am the little Irish boy" A.ms., 1 side. Ink (c). NNPM (MA 1302:13).

First line: I am the little Irish boy,

Collation: 1 leaf of white wove (type 18), 24 x 18.7 cm., pp. [1–2]; laid in [vol. 7] of the *Journal*.

Date: [1851–1852].

Contents: Fair copy of 16 lines; text in *CP*, pp. 177, 320–21.

Note: Thoreau probably intended this copy for draft D of *Walden*.

B184. Citation: "In Adams fall" A.ms., 1 side. Ink (c). NNPM (MA 1302:11).

First line: In Adams fall

Collation: 1 leaf of blue wove (type 11), 24.1 x 17.7 cm., pp. [1–2], paged "6"; bound in [vol. 5] of the *Journal*.

Date: February 1851.

Contents: Fair copy of 4 lines; text in *CP*, p. 245.

B185. Citation: "I do not fear my thoughts will die" A.ms., 2 sides, Ink (c) Pencil (r). NNPM (MA 1302:14).

First line: I do not fear my thoughts will die

Collation: 1 leaf of blue wove (type 10), 24 x 18.7 cm., pp. [1–2], paged "83"; bound in [vol. 8] of the *Journal.*

Date: 13 November 1851.

Contents: Fair copy of 11 lines; text in *CP,* p. 179.

B186.   Citation: "The vessel of love, the vessel of state" A.ms., 1 side. Ink (c). CSmH (HM 13196).

First line: The vessel of love, the vessel of state

Collation: 1 leaf of white wove (type 18), 23.8 x 19.1 cm., pp. [1–2].

Date: September 1852.

Contents: Fair copy of 2 stanzas, 8 lines; in an intermediate draft of the essay "Love." Text in *CP,* pp. 182, 231. For other contents see C12a.

B187.   Citation: "I'm contented you should stay" A.ms., 1 side. Ink (c). CSmH (HM 924:D, 47).

First line: I'm contented you should stay

Collation: 1 leaf of white wove (type 18), 23.9 x 19.1 cm., pp. [93–94] in draft D of *Walden.*

Date: [1852].

Contents: Late draft of 4 lines; text in *CP,* pp. 207, 326.

B188.   Citation: "Man Man is the Devil" A.ms., 1 side. Ink (c) Blue pencil (d). NNPM (MA 1302:19).

First line: Man Man is the Devil

Collation: 1 leaf of blue wove (type 7), 24.5 x 19.3 cm., pp. [1–2], paged "147"; bound in [vol. 13] of the *Journal.*

Date: 3 January 1853.

Contents: Fair copy of 2 lines; text in *CP*, p. 186.

B189.   Citation: "Light-winged Smoke, Icarian bird" A.ms.,
2 sides. Ink (c) Pencil (r,d). CSmH (HM 924:E,
77–8).

First line: Light-winged Smoke, Icarian bird

Collation: 2 leaves of blue wove (type 8), 24.6 x
19.3 cm., pp. [153–56] in draft E of *Walden*.

Date: [1853].

Contents: Late draft of 13 lines; text in *CP*, pp. 27,
288.

B190.   Citation: "When the toads begin to ring" A.ms., 1
side. Ink (c). NNPM (MA 1302:23).

First line: When the toads begin to ring

Collation: 1 leaf of white wove (type 19), 23.7 x
19.2 cm., pp. [1–2], paged "129"; bound in [vol. 17]
of the *Journal*.

Date: 26 April 1854.

Contents: Fair copy of 3 lines; text in *CP*, p. 183.

B191.   Citation: "He knows no change who knows the
true" A.ms., 1 side. Ink (c). CSmH (HM 924:G,
46).

First line: He knows no change who knows the true

Collation: 1 leaf of white wove (type 17), 24.3 x
19.1 cm., pp. [91–92] in draft G of *Walden*.

Date: [1854].

Contents: Late draft of 2 stanzas, 8 lines; text in *CP*,
pp. 208, 326.

B192. Citation: "In two years' time 't had thus" A.ms., 1
       side. Ink (c). NNPM (MA 1302:30).

       First line: 'Twas 30 years ago

       Collation: 1 leaf of white laid (type 3), 24.9 x 18.8
       cm., pp. [1–2], paged "228"; bound in [vol. 24] of
       the *Journal*.

       Date: 28 October 1857.

       Contents: Fair copy of 2 stanzas, 16 lines; text in CP,
       pp. 20, 286.

B193. Citation: "Forever in my dream & in my morning
       thought" A.ms., 1 side. Ink (c,r). NNPM (MA
       1302:30).

       First line: Forever in my dream & in my morning
       thought

       Collation: 1 leaf of white laid (type 3), 24.9 x 18.8
       cm., pp. [1–2], "234"; bound in [vol. 24] of the
       Journal.

       Date: 29 October 1857.

       Contents: Late draft of 24 lines; text in CP, pp. 184,
       321.

B194. Citation: "The chicadee" A.ms., 1 side. Ink (c).
       NNPM (MA 1302:30).

       First line: The chicadee

       Collation: 1 leaf of white laid (type 3), 24.9 x 18.8
       cm., pp. [1–2], paged "270"; bound in [vol. 24] of
       the *Journal*.

       Date: 8 November 1857.

       Contents: Fair copy of 2 lines; text in CP, p. 187.

B195. Citation: "Die and be buried who will" A.ms., 2
       sides. Ink (c) Pencil (n*). RPB.

First line: Die and be buried who will

Collation: 1 leaf of white laid (type 2), 25.4 x 20.1 cm., pp. [1–2]; paged "147" in the essay draft of "Ktaadn."

Date: [1858–1859].

Contents: Fair copy of 4 lines; text in *CP*, p. 28. For other contents see D24d.

B196. Citation: "The Rosa Sanguinea" A.ms., 1 side. Ink (c) Pencil (r). NYPL (Berg).

Title: The Rosa Sanguinea

First line: As often as a martyr dies,

Collation: 1 leaf of white laid (type 5), 24.6 x 19.5 cm., pp. [1–2]; laid in the "Notes on Fruits" slipcase.

Date: [After 2 December 1859].

Contents: Late draft of 4 lines; text in *CP*, pp. 397, 404.

B197. Citation: "Any fool can make a rule" A.ms., 1 side. Ink (c) Blue pencil (d). NNPM (MA 1302:36).

First line: Any fool can make a rule

Collation: 1 leaf of white wove (type 6), 25.1 x 18.8 cm., pp. [1–2]; bound in [vol. 30] of the *Journal*.

Date: 3 February 1860.

Contents: Fair copy of 2 lines; text in *CP*, p. 187.

B198. Citation: "All things decay" A.ms., 1 side. Ink (c). NNPM (MA 1302:37).

First line: All things decay

Collation: 1 leaf of blue laid (type 3), 24.6 x 19.2 cm., pp. [1–2]; bound in [vol. 31] of the *Journal*.

Date: 25 March 1860.

Contents: Fair copy of 2 lines; text in CP, p. 187.

B199. Citation: "Voyagers Song" A.ms., 1 side. Ink (c*). CSmH (HM 13190).

Title: Voyagers Song.

First line: Gentle river, gentle river

Collation: 1 leaf of white wove (anom.), 23.7 x 19.7 cm., pp. [1–2].

Date: [1867], dated "June 1837".

Contents: Copy of an early draft of 20 lines; text in CP, pp. 86, 302.

Note: Sophia Thoreau made this copy for the 1868 edition of A Week.

B200. Citation: "I am a parcel of vain strivings tied" A.ms., 2 sides. Ink (c*). VtMiM.

Title: Sic Vita

First line: I am a parcel of vain strivings tied

Collation: 1 leaf of white wove, 23.7 x 19.5 cm., pp. [1–2].

Date: [1867], originally before July 1841.

Contents: Copy of an early draft of 7 stanzas, 42 lines; text in CP, pp. 81–82, 300.

Note: Sophia Thoreau made this copy for the 1868 edition of A Week. Other copies are at MConA (by Sophia) and MH (R. W. Emerson).

B201. Citation: "Woof of the sun, ethereal gauze" A.ms., 1 side. Ink (c*). CSmH (HM 13190).

Title: Haze.

First line: Woof of the sun, ethereal gauze

Collation: 1 leaf of white wove (anom.), 23.7 x 19.7 cm., pp. [1–2].

Date: [1867], originally before April 1843.

Contents: Fair copy of 13 lines; text in *CP*, pp. 59, 295.

Note: Copied by Sophia Thoreau for *A Week* (1868).

C.

LECTURES AND ESSAYS, 1837–1862

The manuscripts in this section represent the "bread and butter" of Thoreau's literary career. Although he never earned much total income from his writings, the largest fees by far came from periodicals and Lyceum committees, who employed him not as steadily as he wished. Most of the pieces he wrote for *The Dial* survive, whether actually published there or not. New York and Boston editors usually failed to return his drafts, however, leaving us no trace of several early pieces: "The Landlord" (1843), "Paradise (to be) Regained" (1843), "Herald of Freedom" (1844); and only stray fragments of his most famous essay, "Civil Disobedience" (1849). On the other hand, at least two unpublished works have survived, one of such magnitude that I have assigned it an entirely separate section (G).

Most of the lectures and essays Thoreau wrote after 1850 appear here, often in fragmentary sequences because they were broken and scattered via the Manuscript Edition. Even so, enough paper survives to depict the complexities of Thoreau's creative process, as he worked from notes to lecture and finally to essay drafts. His posthumous essays, "Walking", "Life Without Principle", "Autumnal Tints", and "Wild Apples", are difficult to classify and describe; when feasible, I have divided them according to dates and stages of composition. For any lectures or essays Thoreau later revised as book chapters, see section D.

C1a.   Citation: "Died Miss Anna Jones" A.ms., 2 sides. Pencil (c,r) Ink (traces pencil). MH (bMS Am 278.5 [3]).

Title: Died | In this town, on the 12th | inst, Miss Anna Jones, | aged 85

First line: When we hear of the departure of a fellow being

Collation: 1 fragment of white wove (anom.), pp. [1–2].

Date: [Before 25 November 1837].

Contents: Early draft of an obituary; text in K. W. Cameron, "Thoreau's Three Months Out of Harvard and His First Publication", ESQ, No. 5 (1956), pp. 9–10.

Note: Thoreau's original interview with Anna Jones appears in the "Index Rerum" (F2a).

C1b.   Citation: "Died Miss Anna Jones" A.ms., 2 sides. Pencil (c,r) Ink (traces pencil). MH (bMS Am 278.5 [3]).

Title: Died | In this town, on the 12th | inst, Miss Anna Jones, | aged [ ]

First line: When a fellow being departs for the land of spirits

Collation: 1 fragment of white wove (anom.), pp. [1–2].

Date: [Before 25 November 1837].

Contents: Late draft of an obituary; text in Cameron, ESQ, No. 5 (1956), pp. 9–10.

C2.   Citation: The Service A.ms., 23 sides. Ink (c) Pencil (n*). NNPM (MA 607).

Title: The Service. | Qualities of the Recruit. | Spes sibi quisque. Virgil | Each one his own hope.

First line: The brave man is the elder son of creation, who has stept boyantly into his inheritance,

Collation: 12 leaves of gray wove (type 3), 24.8 x 19.9 cm., pp. [1–24]; tied, with a.l.s. M. Fuller and a.n.s. G. Hellman.

Date: July 1840.

Contents: Fair copy; text varies from *TS*, pp. 9–20. A facsimile is in *TM* 2:935–70. For later versions see D5m–n. For other contents see B22a.

C3a. Citation: "Natural History of Massachusetts" A.ms., 4 sides. Ink (c,r) Pencil (r,d). MHarF.

First line: With the autumn begins in some manner a new spring. The plover is heard whistling high in the air over the dry pastures—

Collation: 3 leaves of white wove (type 7), 24.9 x 19.5 cm., pp. [1–6]; mounted, framed in hinged wall cases.

Date: [1840 (c); 1842 (r)].

Contents: Portion of essay draft; text varies from *W* 5:112–14. For other contents see B88.

C3b. Citation: "Natural History of Massachusetts" A.ms., 2 sides. Ink (c) Pencil (n). CSmH (HM 926: 2v).

First line: Pilgrims cup. [underscored]

Collation: 1 fragment of blue wove, 25 x 20.2 cm., pp. [1–2].

Date: [1840].

Contents: Note for draft; a list of flower and animal species. For other contents see B17a.

C4a.   Citation: "A Walk to Wachusett" A.ms., 28 sides.
Ink (c). NYPL (Berg).

Title: A Walk to Wachusett. | The needles of the
pine | All to the west incline.

First line: Like Rasselas and other inhabitants of
Happy Vallies, I had always felt a desire to scale the
blue wall that bounds the western prospect.

Collation: 14 leaves,
    13 of white wove (type 1), 32 x 19.9 cm.,
    1 of white wove (type 11), 24.6 x 19.3 cm.,
pp. [1–28], paged* "62–87"; part of notebook, 66
leaves bound π^1 [A–F$^{16/8}$ G^8] + 1, pp. [1–164],
paged* "1–132", with 16 leaves missing.

Date: [October 1842].

Contents: Portion of essay draft; text varies from
W 5:135–52. For a description see L. Lane, Jr.,
"Thoreau at Work: Four Versions of 'A Walk to
Wachusett'", BNYPL 69 (1965):3–16. For other
versions, early and late, see D5k–l, E9a. For other
contents see B40b, B41b, B9o.

Note: For a partial description of the July 1842
journey see the "composition book" of Richard Fuller
at MB (Mss Am. 550 [1]), transcribed in TSB 121
(Fall, 1972):1–4.

C4b.   Citation: "A Walk to Wachusett" A.ms., 2 sides.
Pencil (c). CSmH (HM 926:6v).

First line: But Peter, by the mountain rills,

Collation: 1 leaf of blue wove, 25 x 20.2 cm., pp.
[1–2].

Date: [1842].

Contents: Note for essay, an extract of Wordsworth's
"Peter Bell"; text resembles W 5:143–44. For other
contents see B17a.

C5a.   Citation: *Sir Walter Raleigh* A.ms., 101 sides. Ink
(c) Pencil (r,d,n). CSmH (HM 935).

First line: [7r] If an English Plutarch were to be
written——Raleigh would be the best Greek or
Roman among them.

Collation: 52 leaves,
    46 of blue wove (type 2), 25 x 19.9 cm.,
    3 fragments of white wove (type 11), 12.3 x 19.4
    cm.,
    2 of white laid, 25 x 20.2 cm.,
    1 of white wove (type 18), 24 x 18.6 cm.,
pp. [1–104], foliated* "1–52"; bound, with a.n.s.
A. Kern on order of leaves.

Date: [Before 8 February 1843].

Contents: Lecture draft, containing notes, revised
Journal entries, other insertions; text resembles *SWR*,
pp. 17–100.

C5b.   Citation: *Sir Walter Raleigh* A.ms., 2 sides. Ink (c).
MH (bMS Am 278.5 [4,A]).

First line: Though we are inclined to believe this
was sometimes not a real but an apparent meaness
and if he did not go contrary to the vulgar—

Collation: 1 fragment of blue wove (type 2), 10.7 x
19.7 cm., pp. [1–2].

Date: [Before 8 February 1843].

Contents: Portion of lecture draft; text varies from
SWR, p. 30.

C5c.   Citation: *Sir Walter Raleigh* A.ms., 83 sides. Ink (c)
Pencil (r,d). CSmH (HM 943).

Title: Sir Walter Raleigh.

First line: Perhaps no one in English history more distinctly represents the heroic character than Sir Walter Raleigh.

Collation: 45 leaves,
    42 of white wove (type 11), 24.5 x 19.5 cm.,
    3 of gray wove, 24.5 x 18.5 cm.,
    pp. [1–90], paged "1–83"; bound.

Date: [1843–1844].

Contents: Essay draft; text varies from SWR, pp. 17–90. For early versions see E9a.

C5d.   Citation: *Sir Walter Raleigh* A.ms., 2 sides. Ink (c,r) Pencil (r,d). MH (bMS Am 278.5 [19]).

First line: Raleigh's History of the World, which commences with a sermon on human life & was done like himself and with no small success.

Collation: 1 leaf of white wove (type 11), 24.7 x 19.1 cm., pp. [1–2].

Date: [1843–1844].

Contents: Portion of essay draft; text varies from SWR, pp. 50–51. For later version see W 1:106–8.

C6a.   Citation: "A Winter Walk" A.ms., 18 sides. Ink (c,r,d) Pencil (r,d,p). NNPf.

First line: caddice worms, the larvae of the Phicipennes. Their small cylindrical cases built around themselves,

Collation: 9 leaves of white wove (type 11), 24.7 x 19.2 cm., pp. [1–18], paged "17, 21–24, 29–40"; with ts. copy by F. B. Sanborn.

Date: [1843].

Contents: Portion of essay draft; text varies from W 5:170–75, 177–83.

Note: Sanborn attributes the penciled hand to R. W. Emerson.

C6b. Citation: "A Winter Walk" A.ms., 2 sides. Ink (c,r) Pencil (r,d). MH (MS Am 1280.214.1 [5]).

First line: to its brink, all paths seek it out, birds fly to it, quadrupeds flee to it, and the very ground inclines toward it.

Collation: 1 leaf of white wove (type 11), 24.6 x 19.7 cm., pp. [1–2], paged "25–26".

Date: [1843].

Contents: Portion of essay draft; text varies from W 5:175–76. For early versions see E9c, E10a–c.

C6c. Citation: "A Winter Walk" A.ms., 2 sides. Ink (c,r) Pencil (r). VtMiM.

First line: To me it has a strange sound of home and thrilling as the voice of one's distant and noble kindred.

Collation: 1 leaf of white wove (type 11), 24.7 x 19.7 cm., pp. [1–2], paged "27–28"; mounted, in folder marked "Fragments". Verso has a.n.s. R. W. Emerson.

Date: [1843].

Contents: Portion of essay draft; text varies from W 5:176–77. For other contents see B60b.

C6d. Citation: "A Winter Walk" A.ms., 2 sides. Ink (c,n*). NNPM (MA 1719).

First line: our warm sympathy to the Siberian traveller, on whose morning route the sun is rising,

Collation: 1 leaf of white wove (type 11), 24.7 x 19.7 cm., pp. [1–2], paged "41–42".

Date: [1843].

Contents: Rejected portion of essay draft; text varies from *W* 5:183 and *FLJ* 1:142–46. A facsimile is in *PT*, p. 32. For other contents see B104.

C7a.   Citation: "Wendell Phillips Before the Concord Lyceum" A.ms., 8 sides. Ink (c,r). NNPM (MA 1303).

First line: We have now for the third winter had our spirits refreshed and our faith in the destiny of the commonwealth strengthened by the presence & the eloquence of Wendell Phillips

Collation: 4 leaves of white wove (type 1a), 31.8 x 19.8 cm., pp. [1–8], paged "203–10".

Date: 12 March 1845.

Contents: Early draft of essay-letter; text varies from *W* 4:311–15.

C7b.   Citation: "Wendell Phillips Before the Concord Lyceum" A.ms., 2 sides. Ink (c) Pencil (r). MH (bMS Am 278.5 [2,2]).

First line: His motions were not his personal aggrandisement but the glory and honor of his country.

Collation: 1 fragment of white wove (anom.), pp. [1–2]. Verso is handbill announcement for the Concord Lyceum.

Date: [Before 12 March 1845].

Contents: Portion of early draft; text resembles *W* 4:312.

C8.   Citation: "Thomas Carlyle and his Works" A.ms., 7 sides. Ink (c,r) Pencil (r,d). NNPM (MA 1303).

First line: Carlyle's works are not to be studied—

Collation: 4 leaves of white wove (type 1a), 31.8 x
19.3 cm., pp. [1–8], paged "221–25".

Date: [Before 4 February 1846].

Contents: Portions of early draft; text resembles *W*
4:339–40. For other leaves containing draft portions
see D10a and D10f.

C9a. Citation: "Civil Disobedience" A.ms., 6 sides. Ink
(c). MH (bMS Am 278.5 [20,A]).

First line: The word Government is commonly
thought to stand for some great and positive virtue
and respectability;

Collation: 3 leaves of white wove (type 5), 25.1 x
20 cm., pp. [1–6].

Date: [After 26 January 1848].

Contents: Portion of essay draft; text resembles *W*
4:356–58.

C9b. Citation: "Civil Disobedience" A.ms., 14 sides. Ink
(c) Pencil (c,r,d). MH (bMS Am 278.5 [14:B,
C,F]).

First line: resistance to the previously existing Government—it has been the business of the new Government to preserve itself so to preserve order or the
new foundation then laid.

Collation: 7 leaves of blue wove (type 5), 24.7 x
19 cm., pp. [3–10, 17–18, 21–24].

Date: [Before 26 January 1848].

Contents: Portions of lecture draft; text resembles *W*
4:357–60, 370–72.

C9c. Citation: "Civil Disobedience" A.ms., 2 sides. Ink
(c). CSmH (HM 924: before A, 8v).

First line: Yet this quality is not wisdom, but prudence rather.

Collation: 1 leaf of blue wove (type 5), 24.2 x 19.1 cm., pp. [1–2], paged "381".

Date: [Before 26 January 1848].

Contents: Portion of lecture draft; text resembles W 4:367–68. For other contents see D16e.

C10a. Citation: [On Reform] A.ms., 128 sides. Ink (c,r) Pencil (c,r,d). MH (bMS Am 278.5 [18]).

First line: The reformers are no doubt the true ancestors of the next generation—

Collation: 66 leaves,
  (a) 46 of white wove (type 11), 24.7 x 19.5 cm., pp. [1–92], paged "1–78",
  (b) 5 of blue wove (type 1), 25.1 x 20 cm., pp. [93–98, 111–14],
    14 of white wove (type 14), 24.5 x 19 cm., pp. [99–110, 115–30],
    1 fragment of white wove (anom.), pp. [131–32];
in two folders, "18A" and "18B".

Date: (a) [1843–1844 (c), 1848 (r)]; (b) [1846–1847 (c), 1848 (r)].

Contents: Unpublished essay draft; possibly a sequel to "Civil Disobedience." For other contents see B24c.

Note: Thoreau worked on this essay before and after "Civil Disobedience", but he used only a small portion of it in A Week (see W 1:130–32), and later copied revised portions into the first and last chapters of Walden, draft D. An edited text appears in Reform Papers, ed. Wendell Glick, The Writings of Henry D. Thoreau (Princeton, N.J.: Princeton University Press, 1973).

C10b. Citation: [On Reform] A.ms., 3 sides. Ink (c,r) Pencil (r). Prof. E. Seybold, Jacksonville, Ill.

First line: But suppose his indigestion is sound, still we might ask,

Collation: 2 leaves of white wove (type 5), 25.1 x 20.1 cm., pp. [1–4]; mounted and bound.

Date: [1848–1849].

Contents: Portion of unpublished essay draft.

C11a. Citation: "Walking" A.ms., 47 sides. Ink (c,r,d) Pencil (c,r). MH (bMS Am 278.5 [21,B]).

Title: Walking or The Wild Read in April 1851

First line: Wordsworth on a pedestrian tour through Scotland, was one evening, just as the sun was setting with unusual splendor,

Collation: 26 leaves of white wove (type 18), 24.1 x 19.2 cm., pp. [11–14, 19–30, 33–44, 47–56, 65–74, 91–92], paged "2–263".

Date: [Before 23 April 1851].

Contents: Portions of lecture draft; text varies from W 5:205–48, passim.

C11b. Citation: "Walking" A.ms., 2 sides. Ink (c) Pencil (r). ICarbS.

First line: The traveller Parrot says of the Kalmucks that "so great is their attachment to a roving life,

Collation: 1 leaf of white wove (type 18), 24 x 18.5 cm., pp. [1–2]; mounted.

Date: [Before 23 April 1851].

Contents: Portion of lecture draft; text resembles W 5:205–7. See also J 3:27 and W. Harding, "Thoreau

and the Kalmucks: A Newly Discovered Manuscript",
NEQ 32 (1959):91–92.

C11c.   Citation: Walking" A.ms., 2 sides. Ink (c,r,d) Pencil
(r,d). ViU (6345–e:22).

First line: area and variety to the traveller these
various fields taken together appear more extensive
than a single prairie of the same size would.

Collation: 1 leaf of white wove (type 18), 23.8 x
19 cm., pp. [1–2], paged "68"; mounted.

Date: [Before 23 April 1851].

Contents: Portion of lecture draft; text of verso resembles *W* 5:212.

C11d.   Citation: "Walking" A.ms., 2 sides. Ink (c,r) Pencil
(d,n). NYPL (Berg).

First line: A constant intercourse with nature is necessary not only to the physical but the moral and
intellectual health.

Collation: 1 leaf of white wove (type 18), 23.9 x
19.3 cm., pp. [1–2], paged "80"; with ts. copy.

Date: [Before 23 April 1851].

Contents: Portion of lecture draft; text of third paragraph resembles *W* 5:218.

C11d¹.   Citation: "Walking" A.ms., 2 sides. Ink (c,r) Pencil
(r). MnM.

First line: I do not know of any poetry to quote
which adequately expresses this yearning for the wild.

Collation: 1 leaf of white wove (type 18), 24 x 19
cm., pp. [1–2], paged "124"; mounted, bound in Set
No. 206 of the Manuscript Edition.

Date: [Before 23 April 1851].

Contents: Portion of lecture draft; text varies from
W 5:232–33.

C11e.   Citation: "Walking" A.ms., 2 sides. Ink (c,r) Pencil
(r). ICarbS.

First line: we are already little men. Give me a culture which imports much muck from the meadows,

Collation: 1 leaf of white wove (type 18), 24 x
19.2 cm., pp. [1–2], paged "141".

Date: [Before 23 April 1851].

Contents: Portion of lecture draft; text varies from
W 5:237–38.

C11f.   Citation: "Walking" A.ms., 2 sides. Ink (c) Pencil
(r). W. A. Strutz, Bismarck, N.D.

First line: We have heard of a Society for the Dif-
fusion of Useful Knowledge.

Collation: 1 leaf of white wove (type 18), 23.8 x
19 cm., pp. [1–2], paged "144"; mounted, bound in
Set No. 282 of the Manuscript Edition.

Date: [Before 23 April 1851].

Contents: Portion of lecture draft; text varies from
W 5:239–40.

C11g.   Citation: "Walking" A.ms., 2 sides. Ink (c,r) Pencil
(d). IElP.

First line: A man's ignorance sometimes is not only
useful but beautiful,

Collation: 1 leaf of white wove (type 18), 23.8 x
19 cm., pp. [1–2]; mounted, bound in Set No. 259
of the Manuscript Edition.

Date: [Before 23 April 1851].

Contents: Portion of lecture draft; text varies from *W* 5:240. For an early version see *J* 2:150.

C11g¹. Citation: "Walking" A.ms., 2 sides. Ink (c,r) Pencil (c,r). CaAEU.

First line: perchance he is walking on the railroad, then indeed the cars go by without his hearing them,

Collation: 1 leaf of white wove (type 18), 24.1 x 18.9 cm., pp. [1–2], paged "145"; mounted, bound in Set No. 280 of the Manuscript Edition.

Date: [Before 23 April 1851].

Contents: Portion of lecture draft; text varies from *W* 5:241, 244.

C11g². Citation: "Walking" A.ms., 2 sides. Ink (c,r) Pencil (r,d). P. R. Bernier, Boston, Mass.

First line: with regard to Nature whose elysian fields never reach quite up to our doors,

Collation: 1 leaf of white wove (type 18), 24.4 x 20.1 cm., pp. [1–2], paged "82"; mounted, bound in Set No. 321 of the Manuscript Edition.

Date: [Before 23 April 1851].

Contents: Portion of lecture draft; text varies from *W* 5:242.

C11h. Citation: "Walking" A.ms., 2 sides. Ink (c) Pencil (r). MH-W.

First line: I took a walk on Spaulding's farm the other afternoon.

Collation: 1 leaf of white wove (type 18), 23.8 x 19 cm., pp. [1–2], paged "151"; mounted, bound in Set No. 238 of the Manuscript Edition.

Date: [Before 23 April 1851].

Contents: Portion of lecture draft; text varies from *W* 5:243.

C11i. Citation: "Walking" A.ms., 2 sides. Ink (c) Pencil (r). CtY (Za T391 B906 1).

First line: We are accustomed to say in New England that few and fewer pigeons visit us every year.

Collation: 1 leaf of white wove (type 18), 23.7 x 18.9 cm., pp. [1–2], paged "155"; mounted, bound in Set No. 234 of the Manuscript Edition.

Date: [Before 23 April 1851].

Contents: Portion of lecture draft; text varies from *W* 5:244.

C11j. Citation: "Walking" A.ms., 2 sides. Ink (c). R. Adams, Chapel Hill, N.C.

First line: We hug the earth, — how rarely we mount!

Collation: 1 leaf of white wove (type 18), 24 x 19 cm., pp. [1–2], paged "157"; mounted, bound in Set No. 337 of the Manuscript Edition.

Date: [Before 23 April 1851].

Contents: Portion of lecture draft; text varies from *W* 5:244–45.

C11k. Citation: "Walking" A.ms., 29 sides. Ink (c,r) Pencil (r,d). MH (bMS Am 278.5 [21:A,B,C]).

Title: This concerns Walking & the Wild— | Only the ones marked on the 1st 2½ ps—then all.

First line: Courage — 1 — 255

Collation: 17 leaves of white wove (type 12), 24.7 x 19.3 cm., pp. [1–10, 15–18, 31–32, 61–64, 77–90].

Date: [Before 6 February 1857].

Contents: Indexes and notes for essay draft.

C11l.   Citation: "Walking" A.ms., 102 sides. Ink (c,r,d) Pencil (r). MCon.

Title: Walking

First line: I wish to speak a word for Nature, for absolute Freedom and Wildness, as contrasted with a Freedom and Culture merely civil,

Collation: 86 leaves,
  (a) 68 of white wove (type 12), 24.5 x 19.1 cm., pp. [1–6, 23–24, 39–54, 57–140, 143–46, 149–72], paged "1–4, 17–18, 29–35, 37–87, 89–99",
  (b) 9 of white wove (type 18), 24 x 18.5 cm., pp. [7–16, 21–22, 27–30, 37–38], paged "5–12, 16, 21–22, 28",
  (c) 6 of white laid (type 5), 24.6 x 19 cm., pp. [17–20, 31–36, 55–56], paged "13–15, 23–27, 36",
  (d) 3 of white wove (anom.), pp. [25–26, 141–42, 147–48], paged "19–20, 85–88";
bound, with front board stamped MANUSCRIPT. | ——— | THOREAU.

Date: (a) [1857 (c), 1861–1862 (r)]; (b) [1851 (c) 1857–1862 (r)]; (c) [1861–1862 (c,r)]; (d) [1861–1862 (c,r)].

Contents: Essay draft, containing notes, revised portions of lecture drafts, and some passages transcribed by Sophia Thoreau; text varies from W 5:205–48. For other contents see B173c.

C11m.   Citation: "Walking" [see Section H].

C11n.   Citation: "Walking" A.ms., 2 sides. Ink (c) Pencil (r.d). R. H. Greer, Spencer, Mass.

First line: The island of Atlantis, and the islands and gardens of the Hesperides, a sort of terrestrial Paradise—

Collation: 1 leaf of white wove (type 5), 24.5 x 19 cm., pp. [1–2]; mounted, bound in Set. No. 250 of the Manuscript Edition.

Date: [1857 (c); 1861–1862 (r)].

Contents: Portion of essay draft; text varies from W 5:219–21.

C110.   Citation: "Walking" A.ms., 2 sides. Ink (c) Pencil (r). MWor.

First line: Little is to be expected of a nation when the vegetable mould is exhausted,

Collation: 1 leaf of white wove (type 12), 24.5 x 19.2 cm., pp. [1–2]; mounted, bound in Set No. 358 of the Manuscript Edition.

Date: [1857].

Contents: Portion of essay draft; text varies from W 5:229–31.

C12a.   Citation: "Love" A.ms., 15 sides. Ink (c,r) Pencil (r,d). CSmH (HM 13196).

Title: Love & Friendship

First line: I do not know but I incline to praise Friendship most, but I would not extol the one relation at the expense of the other.

Collation: 9 leaves of white wove (type 18), 23.8 x 19.1 cm., pp. [1–18], with a.n.s. F. B. Sanborn.

Date: [Before September 1852].

Contents: Worksheets and essay draft; text varies from W 6:199–208. For other contents see B148b, B149b, B185.

Note: This ms. represents the "disconnected fragments" Thoreau sent Blake as a wedding gift, promis-
ing a "completer essay" later. See *Corr.*, p. 288.

C12b.   Citation: "Love" A.ms., 2 sides. Ink (c,r). TxU.

First line: Where there is not discernment, the behavior even of the purest soul may in effect account
of coarseness.

Collation: 1 leaf of blue wove (type 8), 24.4 x 19.2
cm., pp. [1–2], paged "3"; mounted.

Date: [Before September 1852].

Contents: Portion of essay draft; text varies from *W*
6:200–201.

C13a.   Citation: "Chastity and Sensuality" A.ms., 10 sides.
Ink (c,r) Pencil (r,d). CSmH (HM 13196).

Title: Chastity & Sensuality.

First line: The subject of Sex is a remarkable one,
since, though its phenomena concern us so much
both directly and indirectly,

Collation: 5 leaves of blue wove (type 8), 24.4 x
19.2 cm., pp. [1–10], with a.n.s. F. B. Sanborn.

Date: [Before September 1852].

Contents: Early draft; text varies from *W* 6:204–9.

C13b.   Citation: "Chastity and Sensuality" A.ms., 11 sides.
Ink (c). TxU.

Title: Chasity and Sensuality.

First line: The subject of Sex is a remarkable one,
since, though its phenomena concern us so much
both directly and indirectly,

Collation: 6 leaves of blue wove (type 8), 24.4 x 19.2 c.m., pp. [1–12]; sewn.

Date: [Before September 1852].

Contents: Fair copy; text varies from W 6:204–9.

Note: In the first sentence of the second paragraph Thoreau's ms. reads "copulation", for which its editor, R. W. Emerson, substituted "marriage".

[Item C14 eliminated in press.]

C15a. Citation: "Life Without Principle" A.ms., 1 side. Ink (c) Pencil (c,r). VtMiM.

First line: of sound timber, & kept tuned always, it was he—so that when the bow of events is drawn across him

Collation: 1 leaf of white wove (type 12), 24.5 x 19.3 cm., pp. [1–2]; in folder marked "Fragments".

Date: [Before 26 December 1854].

Contents: Portion of early lecture draft, dropped from the essay text.

Note: Thoreau called this early version "Getting a Living" or "What Shall It Profit".

C15a[1]. Citation: "Life Without Principle" A.ms., 2 sides. Ink (c) Pencil (c). R. R. Miller, Bristol, R.I.

First line: My text this evening is "What shall it profit a man if he gain the whole world, and lose his own soul?"

Collation: 1 leaf of white wove (type 12), 24.8 x 19.2 cm., pp. [1–2]; mounted, formerly bound in Set No. 130 of the Manuscript Edition.

Date: [Before 26 December 1854].

Contents: Portion of early lecture draft; text varies from *W* 5:456–57. A partial transcription is in *Chapter and Verse*, No. 5 (Bristol, R.I.: The Current Company, 1972), p. 18.

C15b. Citation: "Life Without Principle" A.ms., 2 sides. Ink (c,r). H. S. Newton, Charleston, S.C.

First line: doubt, flowers are thus colored & painted to attract and guide the bee.

Collation: 1 leaf of white wove (type 12), 24.4 x 19.3 cm., pp. [1–2], paged "37"; mounted, bound in Set No. X (Publisher's Copy) of the Manuscript Edition.

Date: [Before 26 December 1854].

Contents: Portion of early lecture draft; text resembles *W* 4:458–59.

C15c. Citation: "Life Without Principle" A.ms., 1 side. Ink (c,r) Pencil (r,d). ICarbS.

First line: The great majority are strictly men of society—we live on solid surface and are interested chiefly in what is transitory.

Collation: 1 leaf of white wove (type 12), 24.7 x 19.2 cm., pp. [1–2].

Date: [Before 26 December 1854].

Contents: Portion of early lecture draft; text resembles *W* 4:469–70. For an early version see *J* 3:460–61. A transcribed text is in Stoller, p. 12.

C15d. Citation: "Life Without Principle" A.ms., 1 side. Ink (c) Pencil (r,d). MEd.

First line: But it is unsafe to defer thus to the opinions of your community—

Collation: 1 leaf of white wove (type 12), 24.5 x 19.3 cm., pp. [1–2]; mounted, bound in Set No. 569 of the Manuscript Edition.

Date: [Before 26 December 1854].

Contents: Portion of early lecture draft; text resembles W 4:469–70.

C15e. Citation: "Life Without Principle" A.ms., 2 sides. Ink (c,r). RPB.

First line: wealth & the approbation of man are to them success. The enterprises of society are something final & sufficing to them.

Collation: 1 fragment of white wove (type 19), 11.9 x 19.4 cm., pp. [1–2]; mounted, bound in Set No. 389 of the Manuscript Edition.

Date: [Before 26 December 1854].

Contents: Portion of early lecture draft; text resembles W 4:469–70. For an early version see J 3:460–61.

C15f. Citation: "Life Without Principle" A.ms., 2 sides. Ink (c,r) Pencil (c,r,d). MH (bMS Am 278.5 [1,A]).

First line: When our life ceases to be inward and private, who can tell us any news

Collation: 1 leaf of white wove (type 12), 24.7 x 19.3 cm., pp. [1–2].

Date: [Before 26 December 1854].

Contents: Portion of early lecture draft; text resembles W 4:471.

C15g. Citation: "Life Without Principle" A.ms., 2 sides. Ink (c) Pencil (r,d). ViU (6345–e:14).

First line: If anybody thinks a thought how sure we are to hear of it.

Collation: 1 leaf of white wove (type 12), 24.5 x 19.3 cm., pp. [1–2]; mounted, with ts. copy.

Date: [Before 26 December 1854].

Contents: Portion of early lecture draft; text resembles W 4:471–76. For early versions see J 3:328; 4:194, 483.

C15h.   Citation: "Life Without Principle" A.ms., 34 sides. Ink (c,r) Pencil (r,d). MH (bMS Am 278.5 [20:B,D,F,G]).

First line: Pickering, in his work on Races, says that "The missionaries [at the Hawaiian Islands] regarded as one main obstacle to improvement

Collation: 20 leaves,
   17 of white wove (type 12), 24.9 x 19.1 cm., pp. [7–8, 13–16, 19–32, 35–38, 43–50, 53–54],
   1 of white wove (type 19), 24 x 19.2 cm., pp. [39–40], paged "230".
   2 of white wove (anom.),
pp. [17–18, 33–34].

Date: [Before 26 December 1854].

Contents: Portions of early lecture draft; text resembles W 4:458, 462, 476–79. For an early version of pp. [7–8] see J 5:410.

C15i.   Citation: "Life Without Principle" A.ms., 18 sides. Ink (c) Pencil (r,d). MH (bMS Am 278.5 [6:A, C,D,E]).

First line: What are the mechanics about—whose hammers we hear on all sides—building some lofty rhyme—or only houses, barns, & woodsheds?

Collation: 9 leaves,
   8 of white wove (type 12), 24.7 x 19.4 cm., pp.
   [1–4, 9–10, 17–22, 25–28],
   1 of white wove (type 13), 24.5 x 19.1 cm., pp.
   [23–24].

Date: [Before 26 December 1854].

Contents: Portions of early lecture draft, all on the subject of workmen, dropped from the essay text. For early versions see D15b and J 2:490–93; 3:4–5, 9–11, 32, 327–28. For a late version see C15x.

C15j. Citation: "Life Without Principle" A.ms., 1 side. Ink (c). RPB.

First line: V Ap. 3d 59—the man who thought I was calculating my wages when making a minute in my notebook.

Collation: 1 fragment of white wove (anom.) 6.5 x 12.8 cm., pp. [1–2].

Date: [Before 9 October 1859].

Contents: Note for late lecture draft; text resembles W 4:458–61.

Note: Thoreau revised most of this version, called "Life Misspent", for his essay draft.

C15k. Citation: "Life Without Principle" A.ms., 8 sides. Ink (c,r) Pencil (c,r,d). MH (bMS Am 278.5 [20: C,E,F]).

First line: [F] A praetor or proconsul would suffice to settle the questions which absorb the attention of the English Parliament and the American Congress.

Collation: 4 leaves,
   2 of white wove (4), 25.1 x 20 cm., pp. [9–12],
   1 of white wove (anom.), pp. [41–42],

1 of blue laid (type 2), 24.7 x 19.7 cm., pp. [51–52].

Date: [Before 9 October 1859].

Contents: Notes and portions of late lecture draft; text resembles *W* 4:470, 478.

C15l.   Citation: "Life Without Principle" A.ms., 2 sides. Ink (c) Pencil (r). MH (bMS Am 278.5 [5]).

First line: Early for several mornings I have heard the sound of a flail.

Collation: 2 leaves of white wove (type 13), 24.8 x 19.5 cm., pp. [1–4].

Date: [Before 9 October 1859].

Contents: Portion of late lecture draft; text resembles *W* 4:469–70. For an early version see *J* 11:158.

C15m.   Citation: "Life Without Principle" A.ms., 2 sides. Ink (c) Pencil (r). T. L. Bailey, Shaker Heights, Ohio.

First line: After reading many books on various subjects for some months I take up a "Report on Farms" by a committee of Middlesex husbandmen.

Collation: 1 leaf of white wove (type 4), 25.1 x 20.1 cm., pp. [1–2]; mounted, bound in Set. No. 127 of the Manuscript Edition.

Date: [Before 9 October 1859].

Contents: Portion of late lecture draft; text resembles *W* 4:471–76. For an early version see *J* 3:327-28.

C15n.   Citation: "Life Without Principle" A.ms., 2 sides. Ink (c,r) Pencil (r,d). Mrs. R. W. Jackson, Waccabuc, N.Y.

First line: This world is a place of business. What an infinite bustle!

Collation: 1 leaf of white wove (type 13), 24.5 x 19.3 cm., pp. [1–2]; mounted, bound in Set No. 21 of the Manuscript Edition.

Date: [1858–1859 (c), 1861–1862 (r)].

Contents: Portion of essay draft; text varies from W 4:456.

Note: Thoreau's original title for this final version was "The Higher Law".

C15o. Citation: "Life Without Principle" A.ms., 6 sides. Ink (c,r) Pencil (c,r,d). MH (bMS Am 278.5 [1,B]).

First line: How shall a man continue his culture after manhood?

Collation: 3 leaves,
    1 fragment of blue laid (type 2), 12.3 x 19.6 cm.,
    1 of white wove (type 13), 24.3 x 19.3 cm.,
    1 fragment of blue wove (type 5), 11.2 x 19.8 cm.,
pp. [1–6], paged "33" and "XVI–64".

Date: [1859–1860 (c), 1861–1862 (r)].

Contents: Notes, portions of essay draft; text resembles W 4:468.

C15p. Citation: "Life Without Principle" A.ms., 2 sides. Ink (c,r,d) Pencil (c,r,d). VtMiM.

First line: In our science and philosophy even there is commonly no true and absolute account of things.

Collation: 1 leaf of white wove (type 13), 24.3 x 19.1 cm, pp. [1–2]; in folder marked "Fragments".

Date: [1859–1860 (c), 1861–1862 (r)].

Contents: Portion of essay draft; text varies from *W* 4:469.

C15q.   Citation: "Life Without Principle" A.ms., 2 sides. Ink (c) Pencil (r,d). CaNBFU.

First line: In some Lyceums they tell me that they have voted to exclude the subject of religion!

Collation: 1 fragment of white wove (type 13), 12.7 x 19.5 cm., pp. [1–2]; mounted, bound in Set No. 542 of the Manuscript Edition.

Date: [1859–1860 (c), 1861–1862 (r)].

Contents: Portion of essay draft; text varies from *W* 4:469–70.

C15r.   Citation: "Life Without Principle" A.ms., 2 sides. Ink (c) Pencil (r,d). NNPM (MA 2556).

First line: "What does he lecture for?" I confess that it made me quake in my shoes.

Collation: 1 leaf of blue laid (type 2), 24.6 x 19.2 cm., pp. [1–2]; mounted.

Date: [1860 (c), 1861–1862 (r)].

Contents: Portion of essay draft; text varies from *W* 4:470.

C15s.   Citation: "Life Without Principle" A.ms., 2 sides. Ink (c) Pencil (r). CtLkH.

First line: People are going to see Kossuth—but the same man does not attract me.

Collation: 1 fragment of white wove (type 13), 11.2 x 19.2 cm., pp. [1–2]; mounted, bound in Set No. 352 of the Manuscript Edition.

Date: [1859–1860 (c), 1861–1862 (r)].

Contents: Portion of essay draft; text varies from *W* 4:470-71.

C15t. Citation: "Life Without Principle" A.ms., 2 sides. Ink (c,d) Pencil (r). W. Harding, Geneseo, N.Y.

First line: I do not know but it is too much to read one newspaper a week.

Collation: 1 leaf of white wove (type 13), 24.6 x 19.3 cm., pp. [1–2]; mounted, bound in Set No. 449 of the Manuscript Edition.

Date: [1859–1860 (c), 1861–1862 (r)].

Contents: Portion of essay draft; text varies from *W* 4:471. For an early version see *J* 11:86–88.

C15u. Citation: "Life Without Principle" A.ms., 2 sides. Ink (c,r,d). T. Y. Davis, Sterling, Ill.

First line: news. Its facts appear to float in the atmosphere, insignificant as the sporules of fungi,

Collation: 1 fragment of white wove (type 13), 12.8 x 19.4 cm., pp. [1–2]; mounted, bound in Set No. 380 of the Manuscript Edition.

Date: [1859–1860 (c), 1861–1862 (r)].

Contents: Portion of essay draft; text varies from *W* 4:472.

C15v. Citation: "Life Without Principle" A.ms., 4 sides. Ink (c) Pencil (c,r,d). MH (bMS Am 278.5 [14:A, D]).

First line: From time to time I find the newspapers talking about the prospect of a war,

Collation: 2 leaves.

   1 of white wove (type 13), 24.5 x 19.2 cm.,

1 of white wove (type 4), 25.1 x 20.1 cm., pp. [1–2, 11–12].

Date: [1859–1860 (c), 1861–1862 (r)].

Contents: Portions of essay draft; text resembles *W* 4:472–76. For an early version of pp. [1–2] see *J* 8:189–90.

C15w.   Citation: "Life Without Principle" A.ms., 2 sides. Ink (c,r). MiDW.

First line: passing rolled stones—spruce blocks—& asphaltum—you have only to look into some of our minds which have been subjected to this treatment so long.

Collation: 1 fragment of white wove (type 13), 12 x 18 cm., pp. [1–2]; mounted, bound in Set No. 330 of the Manuscript Edition.

Date: [1859–1860 (c), 1861–1862 (r)].

Contents: Portion of essay draft; text varies from *W* 4:475–76. A transcribed text is in Stoller, pp. 12–13.

C15x.   Citation: "Life Without Principle" A.ms., 8 sides. Ink (c) Pencil (r,d). MH (bMS Am 278.5 [6:B,C, D]).

First line: His hammer, his chisels, his wedges, his shims [word underscored] (shamus?) or half-rounds, his iron spoon—are hoary with age, as with granite dust.

Collation: 5 leaves of blue laid (type 2), 24.7 x 19.8 cm., pp. [5–8, 11–16].

Date: [1859–1860 (c)].

Contents: Rejected portion of essay draft; text partly resembles *J* 11:348. See also C15i, D15b.

C15y.   Citation: "Life Without Principle" [see Section H].

C15z.   Citation: "Life Without Principle" [see Section H].

C16a.   Citation: "A Plea for Captain John Brown" A.ms.,
         18 sides. Ink (c) Pencil (r,d). CSmH (HM 13203).

         Title: A Plea for Captain John Brown.

         First line: I trust that you will pardon me for being
         here.

         Collation: 9 leaves,
             7 of white laid (type 5), 24.5 x 19.5 cm.,
             2 of white wove (type 13), 24.6 x 19.5 cm.,
         pp. [1–18], paged "1–60b".

         Date: [22–30 October 1850 (c), 1860 (r)].

         Contents: Portions of lecture/essay draft; text varies
         from W 4:409–10 passim. For other contents see
         F19b. For a textual study of the essay see R. L.
         Albrecht, "Thoreau and His Audience: 'A Plea for
         Captain John Brown' ", AL 32 (1961):393–402.

C16b.   Citation: "A Plea for Captain John Brown" A.ms.,
         18 sides. Ink (c) Pencil (r,d). CSmH (HM 13202).

         First line: [4v] When the troubles in Kansas began
         he sent several of his sons thither.

         Collation: 9 leaves,
             6 of white laid (type 5), 24.5 x 19.5 cm.,
             3 of white wove (type 13), 24.6 x 19.4 cm.,
         pp. [1–18], paged "3–50".

         Date: [22–30 October 1859 (c), 1860 (r)].

         Contents: Portions of lecture/essay draft; text varies
         from W 4:410–40, passim. For other contents see
         F18b.

C16c.   Citation: "A Plea for Captain John Brown" A.ms., 2 sides. Ink (c,n) Pencil (n,p). M. Ferguson, West Concord, Mass.

First line: The news papers seem to ignore, or perhaps are really ignorant of the fact,

Collation: 1 leaf of white laid (type 5), 24.5 x 19.2 cm., pp. [1–2], paged "17"; mounted, bound in Set No. 586 of the Manuscript Edition.

Date: [22–30 October 1859].

Contents: Portion of lecture draft; text varies from W 4:416. For other contents see F28d.

C16d.   Citation: "A Plea for Captain John Brown" A.ms., 1 side. Ink (c,r) Pencil (r,d). CSmH (HM 954).

First line: One would say that there was no such thing as a man in the community, for he is never referred to, but only this or that party or sect.

Collation: 1 leaf of white wove (type 13), 24.6 x 19.3 cm., pp. [1–2].

Date: [22–30 October 1859].

Contents: Portion of lecture draft; text resembles W 4:423. For an early version see J 12:423. For other contents see F29f.

C16e.   Citation: "A Plea for Captain John Brown" A.ms., 4 sides. Ink (c) Pencil (c,r,d). MH (bMS Am 278.5 [14,E]).

First line: One would say that there was not one man in the community, for he is rarely if ever referred to, but only this or that party or sect.

Collation: 2 leaves of white wove (type 13), 24.7 x 19.4 cm., pp. [13–16].

Date: [22–30 October 1859 (c), 1860 (r)].

Contents: Portion of lecture/essay draft; text resembles *W* 4:423. For an early version see *J* 12:423. For other contents see C9b.

C16f. Citation: "A Plea for Captain John Brown" A.ms., 2 sides. Ink (c). ViU (6345–e:7).

First line: was the greatest compliment which this country could pay them. They were ripe for her gallows.

Collation: 1 leaf of white laid (type 5), 24.4 x 19.4 cm., pp. [1–2], paged "47".

Date: [22–30 October 1859 (c), 1860(r)].

Contents: Portion of lecture/essay draft; text varies from *W* 4:432–33. For an early version see *J* 12:425–27.

C17. Citation: "After the Death of John Brown" A.ms., 7 sides. Ink (c,r,d). NNPM (V–2, 9B).

Title: Henry D. Thoreau said—

First line: So universal and widely related is any transcendent moral greatness—

Collation: 5 leaves of white laid (type 5), 24.5 x 19.4 cm., pp. [1–10]; mounted, bound with a.l.s. F. B. Sanborn.

Date: [Before 2 December 1859].

Contents: Lecture/essay draft; text varies from *W* 4:451–54.

C18. Citation: [Memorial service for John Brown] A.ms., 10 sides. Ink (c). NNPM (V–2, 9B).

Title: Wordsworth

First line: May not we with sorrow say,

Collation: 114 leaves, 104 from other sources and
10 from Thoreau,
    7 of white laid (type 5), 24.5 x 19.4 cm.,
    3 of blue laid (type 2), 24.9 x 19.7 cm.,
pp. [1–20], paged "73–74, 77, 81, 84, 90, 91, 93,
101–3"; mounted and bound.

Date: [After 2 December 1859].

Contents: Order of the Concord service, with editorial continuity and some transcription of readings
supplied by Thoreau.

C19a.   Citation: "The Succession of Forest Trees" A.Ms.,
2 sides. Ink (c). MH (bMS Am 278.5 [2,1]).

First line: Gurowski in his "America & Europe" p 49
says "Europe has received all the animals and useful
nutritious seeds & plants from Asia & transposed them
to America."

Collation: 1 fragment of blue laid (anom.), pp.
[1–2].

Date: [Before 20 September 1860].

Contents: Note for lecture; text resembles *W* 5:187,
201–3 and *J* 11:261–63.

C19b.   Citation: "The Succession of Forest Trees" A.ms., 1
side. Ink (c,r) Pencil (r,d). Mrs. E. Weigel, Mis-
soula, Mont.

First line: From my knowledge of the habits of
quadrupeds & birds I had affirmed this confidently
many years ago—

Collation: 1 leaf of white laid (type 5), 24.5 x 19.5
cm., pp. [1–2]; mounted, bound in Set No. 372 of
the Manuscript Edition.

Date: [Before 20 September 1860].

Contents: Portion of lecture draft; text varies from W 5:190–91.

Note: For Thoreau's later revision and expansion of the essay draft, see F30.

C20a.   Citation: "Autumnal Tints" A.ms., 2 sides. Ink (c) Pencil (r). CSmH (HM 13191:EX).

First line: Now too (Oct. 17, if not earlier) the 2 aspens are perhaps in their prime.

Collation: 1 leaf of green wove, 24.5 x 19.4 cm., pp. [1–2], paged "162".

Date: [1858–1859].

Contents: Worksheet for lecture; text resembles W 5:278. For an early version see J 7:498.

C20b.   Citation: "Autumnal Tints" A.ms., 3 sides. Ink (c) Pencil (r,d). NYPL (Berg).

First line: Many leaves of the small white oaks— within the trees, partially concealed by the green ones, have turned to a dull crimson.

Collation: 2 leaves of white wove (anom.), pp. [1–4]; with ts. copy.

Date: [1858–1859].

Contents: Worksheet for lecture; text resembles J 10:40,55. For other contents see Corr., p. 510.

C20c.   Citation: "Autumnal Tints" A.ms., 2 sides. Ink (c). L. F. Kleinfeld, Forest Hills, N.Y.

First line: There are 2 periods when the leaves are in their glory—their green and perfect youth in June, and their ripe old age.

Collation: 1 fragment of white wove (anom.), pp. [1–2]; mounted, bound in First Impression (1 of 200 copies) of the Walden Edition.

Date: [1858–1859].

Contents: Worksheet for lecture; text varies from
J 7:512; 11:230.

C20c[1].   Citation: "Autumnal Tints" A.ms., 2 sides. Ink (c,r)
Pencil (c,r). D. Siegel, Weston, Mass.

First line: I were to search closely I should find
horse chestnuts—& weeping willows not to mention
apple trees—

Collation: 1 leaf of white wove, 25.1 x 20 cm., pp.
[1–2]; mounted, bound in Set No. 381 of the Manuscript Edition.

Date: [Before 22 February 1859].

Contents: Worksheet for lecture; text resembles W
5:266. For an early version see J 5:440–44.

Note: For another ms. bound into this set, see D23b[1].

C20d.   Citation: "Autumnal Tints" A.ms., 2 sides. Ink (c).
J. M. Dorsey, Detroit, Mich.

First line: previous one. The large white—swamp
white and black oaks are now perhaps as ripe as
ever—as well as *small* red & scarlet oaks.

Collation: 1 leaf of white wove (anom.), pp. [1–2].

Date: [After 11 February 1859].

Contents: Worksheet for lecture; text varies from
J 11:211, 247–48. A transcribed text is in Stoller,
pp. 10–11. For other contents see *Corr.*, p. 545.

C20e.   Citation: "Autumnal Tints" A.ms., 1 side. Ink (c).
TxU.

First line: Our late fellow citizen who planted that
admirable row of elms some ¾ of a mile long at the
west end of the Street,

Collation: 1 leaf of white wove (anom.), pp. [1–2]; mounted, bound in First Impression (1 of 200 copies) of the Walden Edition.

Date: [After 16 February 1859].

Contents: Worksheet for lecture; text resembles *W* 5:263–64, 271. Text and facsimile are in J. J. Moldenhauer, "A New Manuscript Fragment by Thoreau", *ESQ*, No. 33 (1963), pp. 17–21.

C20f. Citation: "Autumnal Tints" A.ms., 2 sides. Ink (c,r) Pencil (r,d). VtMiM.

First line: It is remarkable that the autumnal change of our woods has left no deeper impression on our own literature yet.

Collation: 1 leaf of white wove (type 4), 25.2 x 20.2 cm., pp. [1–2], paged "2"; in folder marked "Fragments".

Date: [Before 22 February 1859].

Contents: Portion of lecture draft; text resembles *W* 5:249. For an early version see *J* 11:254–55.

C20g. Citation: "Autumnal Tints" A.ms., 2 sides. Ink (c,r) Pencil (r). Mrs. J. J. McDevitt III, Rydal, Pa.

First line: I think that the change to some higher color in a leaf is an evidence that it has arrived at a late and more perfect maturity,

Collation: 1 leaf of white wove (type 4), 25.1 x 19.8 cm., pp. [1–2]; mounted, bound in Set No. 357 of the Manuscript Edition.

Date: [Before 22 February 1859].

Contents: Portion of lecture draft; text resembles *W* 4:250–51.

C20h. Citation: "Autumal Tints" [see Section H].

C20i.   Citation: "Autumnal Tints" A.ms., 2 sides. Ink (c) Pencil (r,d). ViU (6345–e:19).

First line: I notice the scarlet leaves of the cultivated cherry.

Collation: 1 leaf of white wove (type 13), 24.5 x 19.3 cm., pp. [1–2], paged "42"; mounted.

Date: [Before 22 February 1859].

Contents: Portion of lecture draft; text resembles W 5:252. For an early version see J 11:310.

C20j.   Citation: "Autumnal Tints" A.ms., 2 sides. Ink (c,r) Pencil (r). M. H. Baker, Concord, Mass.

First line: the fern [word underscored] the aftermath appears in patches of bright yellowish green.

Collation: 1 leaf of white wove (type 4), 24.9 x 19.6 cm., pp. [1–2]; mounted, bound in Set No. 547 of the Manuscript Edition.

Date: [Before 22 February 1859].

Contents: Portion of lecture draft; text resembles W 5:253–54.

C20j^1.   Citation: "Autumnal Tints" A.ms., 2 sides. Ink (c,r) Pencil (r). CSdS.

First line: to long voyages. [paragraph] We can just go over the low Ammanannia Meadow & cut off a bend,

Collation: 1 leaf of white wove (type 13), 24.6 x 19.4 cm., pp. [1–2]; mounted, bound in Set No. 57 of the Manuscript Edition.

Date: [Before 22 February 1859].

Contents: Portion of lecture draft; text unpublished but intended for ca. W 4:258–60. For an early version see J 11:163–65.

C20k.   Citation: "Autumnal Tints" A.ms., 2 sides. Ink (c).
R. R. Borst, Auburn, N.Y.

First line: About the end of the month commonly,
after a warm soaking rain storm in the night perchance,

Collation: 1 leaf of white wove (type 13), 24.6 x
19.5 cm., pp. [1–2]; mounted, bound in Set No. 407
of the Manuscript Edition.

Date: [Before 22 February 1859].

Contents: Portion of lecture draft; text resembles *W*
5:263. For an early version see *J* 11:130.

C20l.   Citation: "Autumnal Tints" A.ms., 2 sides. Ink (c,r)
Pencil (r,d,n). WaSpW.

First line: When I turn round, half way up Fair
Haven Hill, by the orchard wall, & look NW,

Collation: 1 leaf of white wove (type 4), 25.1 x
20.2 cm., pp. [1–2], paged "96"; mounted, bound in
Set No. 436 of the Manuscript Edition.

Date: [Before 22 February 1859].

Contents: Portion of lecture draft; text resembles *W*
5:283. For early versions see *J* 2:311–12; 10:72–73.

C20m.   Citation: "Autumnal Tints" A.ms., 2 sides. Ink (c,r)
Pencil (r). R. W. Knight, Marblehead, Mass.

First line: it may be a rare & unobserved tint, as
many a plant is comparatively unobserved at all
seasons.

Collation: 1 leaf of white wove (type 13), 24.5 x
19.5 cm., pp. [1–2], paged "102"; mounted, bound
in Set No. 82 of the Manuscript Edition.

Date: [Before 22 February 1859].

Contents: Portion of lecture draft; text partly resembles *W* 5:289. For an early version see *J* 11:242–
46. For a late version see C20z.

C20n. Citation: "Autumnal Tints" A.ms., 2 sides. Ink (c)
Pencil (r,d). ViU (6345–e:20).

First line: on the hill side. The maples being in
their prime before the pines are conspicuously parti-
colored,

Collation: 1 leaf of white wove (type 13), 24.5 x
19.3 cm., pp. [1–2], paged "106"; mounted, with ts.
copy.

Date: [Before 22 February 1859].

Contents: Portion of lecture draft; text resembles *W*
5:261.

C20o. Citation: "Autumnal Tints" A.ms., 2 sides. Ink (c)
Pencil (r). MA (RBR T39 1906 v.1).

First line: Now, the red maple fires are gone out,
with very few exceptions,

Collation: 1 leaf of white laid (type 5), 24.5 x 19.4
cm., pp. [1–2], paged "124"; mounted, bound in Set
No. 65 of the Manuscript Edition.

Date: [Before 22 February 1859].

Contents: Portion of lecture draft; text resembles *J*
11:210–11.

C20p. Citation: "Autumnal Tints" A.ms., 4 sides. Ink (c,r)
Pencil (n). ICarbS.

Title: 2(Copied from Aut. Tints | 1(Fall of Leaf—

First line: Hellebore 20th of June some already half
turned yellow — v. July 4 59

Collation: 2 leaves of white laid (type 2), 25 x 20
cm., pp. [1–4].

Date: [July–October 1859].

Contents: Notes for essay, copied from lecture draft.

C20q. Citation: "Autumnal Tints" A.ms., 36 sides. Ink (c,r) Pencil (r,n). MH (bMS Am 278.5 [13:A,D,F]).

First line: White maple leaves toward Balls Hill reddish-looking reddish brown at a distance.

Collation: 24 leaves and fragments (anom.), pp. [1–2, 29–60, 73–78, 87–94]; with miscellaneous clippings and business a.l.s. laid in.

Date: [After 26 July 1859].

Contents: Notes for essay, copied from Journal (June–July 1859).

C20r. Citation: "Autumnal Tints" A.ms., 2 sides. Ink (c,d) Pencil (r). NNPM (MA 2255).

Title: Autumnal Tints. | In Two Parts | 1.

First line: Europeans coming to America are surprised by the brilliancy of our autumnal foliage.

Collation: 1 leaf of white laid (type 5), 24.5 x 19.4 cm., paged "1–2"; mounted.

Date: [1859–1860 (c), 1861–1862 (r)].

Contents: Portion of essay draft; text varies from W 5:249.

C20s. Citation: "Autumnal Tints" A.ms., 42 sides. Ink (c,r) Pencil (c,r,d). MH (bMS Am 278.5 [13:B, C,E]).

Title: [13:E] Autumnal Tints

First line: [13:E] I remember one who proposed to write an epic poem to be called The Leaf.

Collation: 23 leaves,
    12 of white laid (type 2), 25.2 x 20.1 cm.,
    11 of white laid (type 5), 24.5 x 19.4 cm.,
pp. [3–27, 61–68, 79–86], paged "12, 20–22, 25–27, 30, 35–39, 45, 74".

Date: [1859–1860 (c), 1861–1862 (r)].

Contents: Portions of essay draft; text varies from
W 5:251–52, 258–71, 287.

Note: Three leaves in group B are in the hand of
Sophia Thoreau.

C20t. Citation: "Autumnal Tints" A.ms., 2 sides. Ink (c,r,
d) Pencil (n,p). NNCoC.

First line: Close at hand it appeared but a dull
purple, & made little impression on the eye.

Collation: 1 leaf of white wove (type 13), 24.6 x
19.3 cm., pp. [1–2], paged "8–9"; mounted, bound in
Set No. 408 of the Manuscript Edition.

Date: [1859–1860 (c), 1861–1862 (r)].

Contents: Portion of essay draft; text varies from W
5:252–53.

C20u. Citation: "Autumnal Tints" [see Section H].

C20v. Citation: "Autumnal Tints" A.ms., 2 sides. Ink (c,r)
Pencil (r). NYPL (Berg).

First line: down plants as high as his head & cannot
be said to know that they exist though he may have
cut many tons of them—

Collation: 1 leaf of blue laid, 25.2 x 19.3 cm., pp.
[1–2], paged "36"; mounted, with ts. copy.

Date: [1859–1860 (c), 1861–1862 (r)].

Contents: Portion of essay draft; text varies from
W 5:257.

C20w. Citation: "Autumnal Tints" A.ms., 3 sides. Ink (c,r,
d) Pencil (p). NYPL (Berg).

First line: What do we know of sapphire, amethyst, emerald, ruby, amber, & the like,—most of us who take these names in vain?

Collation: 2 leaves,
  1 of white wove (type 13), 24.6 x 19.5 cm., pp. [1–2], paged "48–49",
  1 of white wove (anom.), pp. [3–4];
with ts. copy.

Date: [1859–1860 (c), 1861–1862 (r)].

Contents: Portion of lecture/essay draft; text varies from *W* 5:274–75.

C20x.   Citation: "Autumnal Tints" A.ms., 2 sides. Ink (c,r) Pencil (r,n). VtMiM.

First line: A village needs these innocent stimulants of bright & cheering prospects to keep off melancholy & superstition.

Collation: 1 leaf of white wove (type 13), 24.5 x 19.3 cm., pp. [1–2], paged "52–53".

Date: [1859–1860 (c), 1861–1862 (r)].

Contents: Portion of lecture/essay draft; text varies from *W* 5:276–77.

C20y.   Citation: "Autumnal Tints" A.ms., 2 sides. Ink (c). Pencil (r). NjP (Ex. 3960.6.1906)

First line: Stand under this tree & see how finely its leaves are cut against the sky,

Collation: 1 leaf of white wove (type 13), 24.6 x 19.7 cm., pp. [1–2], paged "55–56"; mounted, bound in Set No. 219 of the Manuscript Edition.

Date: [1859–1860 (c), 1861–1862 (r)].

Contents: Portion of lecture/essay draft; text varies from *W* 5:278.

C20z.   Citation: "Autumnal Tints" A.ms., 2 sides. Ink (c,r) Pencil (r). IaU.

First line: When I turn round half way up Fair Haven Hill, by the orchard wall, and look N.W.

Collation: 1 leaf of white wove (type 13), 24.6 x 19.5 cm., pp. [1–2]; mounted, bound in Set No. 68 of the Manuscript Edition.

Date: [1859–1860 (c), 1861–1862 (r)].

Contents: Portion of essay draft; text resembles *W* 5:283. For an early version see C20m.

C20aa.   Citation: "Autumnal Tints" A.ms., 2 sides. Ink (c) Pencil (r) ViU (6345–e:16).

First line: botanical rambles, I find that, first, the idea, or image, of a plant occupies my thoughts,

Collation: 1 leaf of white wove (type 13), 24.4 x 19.3 cm., pp. [1–2], paged "70–71".

Date: [1859–1860 (c), 1861–1862 (r)].

Contents: Portion of lecture/essay draft; text varies from *W* 5:286–87. For an early version see *J* 11:268. For similar phrasing in one of Thoreau's letters (19 May 1859) see *Corr.*, p. 551.

C21a.   Citation: "Wild Apples" A.ms., 2 sides. Ink (c) Pencil (r). CU-S.

First line: are so remarkably sour, that they are held in disesteem; ['have many a foul word and shrewd curse given them'] indeed their acidity is so extreme

Collation: 1 leaf of white wove (type 13), 24.6 x 19.4 cm., pp. [1–2], paged "31"; mounted, bound in Set No. 506 of the Manuscript Edition.

Date: [Before 8 February 1860].

Contents: Portion of lecture draft; text resembles *W* 5:295, 299–300. For early versions see *J* 2:396; 4:359; 10:137.

C21b. Citation: "Wild Apples" A.ms., 2 sides. Ink (c) Pencil (r,d). ViU (6345–e:12).

First line: the woods in the autumnal air or as they lie in the dewy grass, and not when they have wilted in the house.

Collation: 1 leaf of blue wove, .13.9 x 20.5 cm., pp. [1–2]; mounted.

Date: [Before 8 February 1860].

Contents: Portion of lecture draft; text varies from *W* 5:315–16. For an early version see *J* 9:378–79, 387–88. A facsimile text is in R. B. Shuman, "Thoreau's Passage on the 'Frozen-Thawed Apple' ", *ESQ*, No. 18 (1960), pp. 34–35.

C21c. Citation: "Wild Apples" A.ms., 4 sides. Ink (c,r,n*) Pencil (r,d). NjPentS.

First line: come to thaw them—for they are extremely sensible to its rays—are found to be filled with a rich sweet cider with which I am better acquainted than with wine.

Collation: 2 leaves of white wove (type 13), 24.5 x 19.4 cm., pp. [1–4], paged "52–55"; with a.n.s. J. T. Fields.

Date: [Before 8 February 1860].

Contents: Portion of lecture draft; text resembles *W* 5:319–21. A facsimile and text are in *ESQ*, No. 18 (1960), pp. 34–39.

Note: The first leaf is now in the private collection of Mr. Irving Wallace, Los Angeles, Calif.

C21d.   Citation: "Wild Apples" A.ms., 2 sides. Ink (c,r) Pencil (r,d). ICarbS.

First line: for walkers, sometimes red inside, perfumed with a beautiful blush—faery food, too beautiful to eat—apple of the Hesperides—apple of the evening sky.

Collation: 1 leaf of white wove (type 13), 24.6 x 19.4 cm., pp. [1–2].

Date: [Before 8 February 1860].

Contents: Portion of lecture draft; text varies from W 5:320–21.

C21e.   Citation: "Wild Apples" A.ms., 34 sides. Ink (c,r) Pencil (r,d,n). MH (bMS Am 278.5 [9,A–G]).

Title: [11r] Wild Apples. | The History of the Apple Tree.

First line: [11r] It is remarkable how closely the history of the Apple-tree is connected with that of man.

Collation: 22 leaves,
    12 of white wove (type 13), 24.5 x 19.4 cm., pp. [1–24],
    1 of white laid (type 5), 24.5 x 19.4 cm., pp. [27–28],
    9 of (anom.), pp. [25–26, 29–42].

Date: [1859–1860 (c), 1861–1862 (r)].

Contents: Portions of lecture/essay draft; text varies from W 5:290–94, 301–2, 307–8, 312–13, 318–20, 322.

C21e^1.   Citation: "Wild Apples" A.ms., 2 sides. Ink (c,r) Pencil (r). NRRI.

First line: grown more stout, he recognizes it for a fellow emigrant from the old country,

Collation: 1 leaf of white laid (type 5), 24.5 x 19.4 cm., pp. [1–2]; mounted, bound in Set No. 441 of the Manuscript Edition.

Date: [1861–1862].

Contents: Portion of essay draft; text varies from W 5:303–4.

C21f.   Citation: "Wild Apples" A.ms., 2 sides. Ink (c) Pencil (r). VtMiM.

First line: I have seen no account of these among the Fruits and Fruit-trees of America,

Collation: 1 leaf of white laid (type 5), 24.5 x 19.4 cm., pp. [1–2]; in folder marked "Fragments".

Date: [1862].

Contents: Portion of essay draft; text varies from W 5:309–10.

C21g.   Citation: "Wild Apples" A.ms., 2 sides. Ink (c,r). T. M. Fassett, Rochester, N.Y.

First line: and cider & it is not every winter that produces it in perfection.

Collation: 1 leaf of white wove (type 13), 24.5 x 19.4 cm., pp. [1–2]; mounted.

Date: [1862].

Contents: Portion of essay draft; text varies from W 5:320–21.

D.

MAJOR WRITINGS, 1845–1862

This section contains Thoreau's most famous literary manuscripts, the drafts of his two books, *A Week on the Concord
and Merrimack Rivers* (1849)[1] and *Walden* (1854); and of
three lecture series, published posthumously as *The Maine
Woods* (1864), *Cape Cod* (1865), and *A Yankee in Canada*
(1866). The last two manuscripts vary significantly from their
published forms, owing to the extensive editorial refinements
of Sophia Thoreau.

Because of some special problems, my arrangement of these
papers varies from work to work. The manuscript of *A Week*
is undoubtedly the most complex and confused in Thoreau's
canon. He composed the book over a ten-year span, "harvesting" materials from various early sources—*Journal*, notebooks,
lectures, essays—and conflating them into a huge mosaic. As
Linck C. Johnson notes in his recent study,[2] Thoreau wrote
two drafts of *A Week* between 1845 and 1847. In 1847–1848
he revised and expanded the second draft, culling his usual
sources, dropping some passages, and making fair copy of
heavily revised pages. He either submitted this draft to the
printer or prepared a final fair copy; the latter has not
survived.

Thoreau used many different types of paper in *A Week*, so
the various stages of his writing may be dated and identified.
But a chronological listing of the manuscripts would make
little sense to readers; my arrangement therefore follows the
final order of Thoreau's published text, by chapters. Often the
relation between manuscript and text is tenuous, even dubious,
but I have tried to place the various fragments wherever their
contents seemed to resemble *A Week* most closely.

The manuscript of *Walden*, by contrast, is a model of clarity
and order, thanks to the labors of J. Lyndon Shanley and
other scholars. Shanley first identified and arranged the manuscript at CSmH, sorting the paper types and textual contents
into eight major drafts, which he labeled and dated as follows:

---

1. Cited hereafter as *A Week*.
2. "The Manuscripts of Henry D. Thoreau's *A Week on the
Concord and Merrimack Rivers*" (Ph.D. diss., Princeton University,
1974).

Before A and *A* (1846–1847), *B* (1848), *C* (1849), *D* (1852), *E* (1853), *F* (1853–1854), and *G* (1854). The present listing follows this order, but moves all of the *Before A* fragments to later drafts and also lists several notebooks and loose leaves now in other respositories. Most of these scattered pieces have a discernible location in the respective drafts. F. B. Sanborn wrote marginal notes on many of the papers at CSmH, usually giving page references to the Riverside Aldine edition of *Walden* (2 vols.; Boston: Houghton Mifflin Co., 1897). A full transcription of the drafts at CSmH appears in Ronald Clapper, "The Development of *Walden*: A Genetic Text" (Ph.D. diss., UCLA, 1967).

The most important inference we can draw from the *Walden* manuscript is that it depicts Thoreau turning away from the digressive, "mosaic" methods he used in writing *A Week*. Instead of compiling a large and amorphous draft, for *Walden* he eventually wrote a series of drafts, each one overlapping, but not duplicating, its predecessors and extending the book's dimensions. As Shanley has noted, these successive recastings trace the growth of Thoreau's ideas and images; they also verify his structural plan for the entire narrative. The early drafts (1846–1849) coincide with his writing of *A Week*; thus, some of the notebooks and lecture fragments contain interchangeable portions of the two texts. Not until 1852 did *Walden* begin to acquire its distinctive character, becoming in the end a book that had ripened, season after season, with its author.

The manuscripts of *A Yankee in Canada, Cape Cod,* and *The Maine Woods* appear in their order of composition, not publication. Like the materials in section C, these works developed in a familiar pattern, as lectures and then essays; but Thoreau imparted to them a loose coherence by focusing on common subjects and locales. Not in the same class as *A Week* or *Walden*, these "excursions" are interesting yet distinctly minor narratives in the Thoreau canon. He was able to revise only *The Maine Woods* for collected publication, and even that text does not always represent his final intentions.

Many of the manuscripts in this section contain drafts of poems; for their descriptions see the cross references to section B.

D1a.   Citation: *A Week* [Notebook 1] A.ms., 208 sides. Ink (c) Pencil (r,d). NNPM (MA 1303).

First line: While we ascended the stream, plying the oars, or shoving our way along, with might and main,

Collation: 115 leaves of white wove (type 1a), 31.8 x 19.8 cm., pp. [1–230], paged "1–266"; bound π^2 [A–L^{12}] + 2, pp. [1–272], with 26 leaves missing, 5 tipped.

Date: [1844–1846].

Contents: Notes, transcribed *Journal* entries from [Vols. 1–9, 1], draft portions; text considerably longer than *J* 1:438–87. For other contents see B26b, B62b, B75b, B77d, B112b, B113b, B114b, B115b, B116b, B117b, B118b, B119b, B123, B124, B125, B126b, B127, B128a, B129a, B130a, B131, B132a, B133, B134, B135, C7a, C8, D2b, D10a, E12a.

Note: Thomas Blanding has recently identified several of the missing leaves at CSmH (HM 924, 956, 13188, 13194, 13195) and in the collection of W. S. Thomas. For descriptions see B44b, B97b, B107b, B108b, B109b, B162, D4a, D5h, D7a, D10a–b.

D1b.   Citation: *A Week* [Notebook 2] A.ms., 49 sides. Ink (c,r,d) Pencil (r,d). NNPM (MA 608).

First line: Any book of great authority and genius would seem to our imagination to permeate and pervade all space.

Collation: 25 leaves of white wove (type 21), 20.2 x 16.7 cm., paged "1–126"; bound π^2 [A–G^{12}] + 2, pp. [1–176], with 63 leaves missing. Covers signed* "Paragraphs &c mostly Original".

Date: [1842 (c); 1845 (r)].

Contents: Transcribed *Journal* entries (1842–1844) and draft portions; text resembles *W* 1:80–92, 92–

Show how it is that a writer's nationality and individual genius may be fully manifested in a Play or other Literary work upon a Foreign or Ancient subject — and yet full justice be done to the subject.

Man has been called a bundle of habits. This truth, I imagine, was the discovery of a philosopher — one who spoke as he thought, and thought before he spoke — to he realized it, and felt it to be, as it were, literally true. It has a deeper meaning and admits of a wider application than it generally allowed. The various bundles which we label, French, English, and Scotchmen, differ only in this, that while the first is made up of gay, showy, and fashionable habits — the second is crowded with those of a more sombre hue, bearing the stamp of utility and comfort — and the contents of these, it may be, are as rugged and unyielding as their very envelope. The color and texture of these contents vary with different bundles, but the material is uniformly the same.

Man is an abstract and general term, it denotes the genus; French, English, Scotch, &c. are but the differentiæ. It is with the genus alone that the philosopher and poet have to do. Where then shall they study it? As well here as there, surely, if it be everywhere the same;

1   College Theme No. 44, 16 December 1836 (Item A21).
An example of Thoreau's early handwriting.

2 "Farewell" A memorial (Item B167). A memorial poem to Helen Thoreau, who died on 14 June 1849.

3 "Autumnal Tints" (Item C20r). First page of the essay draft, composed in the winter of 1859–1860.

At the time the following pages were written, I lived alone in the woods, a mile from any neighbor, in a house which I had built myself, on the shore of Walden Pond, in Concord ... and earned my living by the labor of my hands. I lived there two years & two months. At present I am a sojourner in civilized life again.

5 *Journal* Pine box, allegedly built by Thoreau to hold the surviving volumes.

6 *Journal* (Item E12a). Entry for 5 July 1845, the second day of Thoreau's residence at Walden Pond.

7 "Indian Notebooks" (Item F10). Five of the eleven notebooks, kept by Thoreau between 1849 and 1861.

8 "Indian Notebook" (Item F10e). Page 119 of volume 4, containing extracts from works published between 1849 and 1851; copied by Thoreau in the winter of 1851–1852.

112, 150–65. A text, with facsimiles and notes, is in TC 3:901–69. For other contents see F3. For missing leaves see B16d, B17a, B18a, B31, B87, D5e, F9, F10b.

D2a.   Citation: *A Week*, "Concord River" A.ms., 14 sides. Ink (c) Pencil (r,d). NNPM (MA 1303).

First line: The Concord or Musketaquid or Grass-ground river (the original name, or some suppose, being "formed of the Indian words, *musket*, signifying 'grass',

Collation: 7 leaves of white wove (type 1a), 31.8 x 19.8 cm., pp. [1–14], paged "178–90".

Date: [Before 25 March 1845].

Contents: Notes for lecture draft; text varies from *W* 1:1–11.

D2b.   Citation: *A Week*, "Concord River" A.ms., 7 sides. Ink (c,r,d) Pencil (c,r,d). NYPL (Berg).

Title: Were it the will of Heaven yon osier bough | Were vessel safe enough the seas to plough.

First line: The village of Concord is situated on Concord river, about 15 miles from where it empties into the Merrimack.

Collation: 4 leaves of white wove (type 11), 24.7 x 19.5 cm., paged* "1–8".

Date: [Before 25 March 1845].

Contents: Portion of early lecture draft; text varies from *W* 1:1–11. For other contents see B116b.

Note: The couplet is adapted from Plutarch; see *W* 5:391.

D2c.   Citation: *A Week*, "Concord River" A.ms., 1 side. Ink (c) Pencil (r). MCon.

First line: "In a low level upon a fresh river a branch of Merrimack is seated Concord,

Collation: 1 fragment of white wove (anom.), pp. [1–2]; laid in with ms. of "Walking".

Date: [Before 25 March 1845].

Contents: Extract from Josselyn copied for lecture; text resembles *W* 1:8.

D3a.   Citation: *A Week*, "Saturday" A.ms., 33 sides. Ink (c,r,d) Pencil (c,r,d). NYPL (Berg).

Title: Sat. Aug. 31st 1839.
First line: The village of Concord is situated on Concord river, about 15 miles from where it empties into the Merrimack.

Collation: 16 leaves of white wove (type 11), 24.7 x 19.5 cm., pp. [1–32], paged* "8–40".

Date: [Before 25 March 1845].

Contents: Portion of early lecture draft; text varies from *W* 1:12–41. For other contents see B77c.

D3b.   Citation: *A Week*, "Saturday" A.ms., 4 sides. Ink (c,r) Pencil (r,d). MH (bMS Am. 278.5 [4,C]).

First line: The villager crossing the bridge stood awhile & gazed at us gliding swiftly from his sight— following our other fates

Collation: 2 leaves,
    1 of white wove (type 11), 24.9 x 18.3 cm., paged "7–8",
    1 of white wove (type 14), 24.6 x 19 cm.,
pp. [1–4].

Date: [1844 (c), 1846 (r)].

Contents: Draft portion; text resembles *W* 1:15–16. For later versions see *J* 1:450, 465–66, 476–77.

D4a.   Citation: *A Week*, "Sunday" A.ms., 30 sides. Ink
        (c,r,d) Pencil (c,r,d). CSmH (HM 13195).

        Title: Sept 1st 1839 | In each dew drop of the
        morning | Lies the promise of a day.

        First line: In the morning the whole river and
        adjacent country was covered with a dense fog—
        through which the smoke of our fire curled up like
        a subtler mist.

        Collation: 16 leaves,
            15 of white wove (type 11), 24.5 x 19.4 cm., pp.
            [1–30],
            1 of white wove (type 1a), 31.9 x 19.3 cm., pp.
            [31–32],
        paged "70–131".

        Date: [1843–1844 (c), 1847–1848 (r)].

        Contents: Draft portion; text varies from *W* 1:42–
        102, 115–18. For other contents see B19c, B95c.

        Note: See D1a, Note.

D4b.   Citation: *A Week*, "Sunday" A.ms., 12 sides. Ink
        (c,r) Pencil (r,d). MH (bMS AM 278.5 [15,B]).

        First line: a young maiden once sailed in my boat
        thus solitary and unattended, but by invisible spirits.

        Collation: 6 leaves,
            1 of white wove (type 11), 24.5 x 19.3 cm., pp.
            [7–8],
            4 of white wove (type 14), 24.4 x 19 cm., pp.
            [25–32],
            1 of blue wove (type 9), 24.2 x 19 cm., pp. [129–
            30].

        Date: [1844–1846].

        Contents: Draft portions, text resembles *W* 1:38,
        43, 45, 70, 77. In pp. [25–32] some paragraphs re-
        semble *W* 1:322, 327, 360–61. For other contents see
        B53b, B120, B126a.

D4c.   Citation: *A Week*, "Sunday" A.ms., 2 sides. Ink (c,r) Pencil (r,d). MH (bMS Am 278.5 [2,4]).

First line: If you regard what others think of you, no country is enlightened,

Collation: 1 leaf of white wove (type 14), 24.6 x 19.4 cm., pp. [1–2].

Date: [1846].

Contents: Draft portion; text resembles *W* 1:63–67.

D4d.   Citation: *A Week*, "Sunday" A.ms., 2 sides. Ink (c) Pencil (r,d). MH (bMS Am 278.5 [14,D]).

First line: there are those living today in the midst of the scenery of life, themselves actors in it,

Collation: 1 leaf of white wove (type 5), 25.1 x 20.1 cm., pp. [1–2].

Date: [1848].

Contents: Draft portion; text resembles *W* 1:72–73.

D4e.   Citation: *A Week*, "Sunday" A.ms., 2 sides. Ink (c) Pencil (r,d). MH (bMS Am 278.5 [2,5]).

First line: There is papyrus by the river-side, and rushes for light, and the goose only flies overhead,

Collation: 1 leaf of white wove (type 14), 24.5 x 18.9 cm., pp. [1–2].

Date: [1846].

Contents: Draft portion; text resembles *W* 1:108–11. For other contents see B22c.

D5a.   Citation: *A Week*, "Monday" A.ms., 28 sides. Ink (c,r) Pencil (c,r,d,n). CSmH (HM 956, 1–15r).

Title: Sept 2nd

First line: Early this morning we were again on our way—steering through a fog as before—

Collation: 15 leaves,
    14 of white wove (type 11), 24.4 x 19.5 cm.,
    1 of white wove, 40.7 x 19.2 cm.,
pp. [1–30], foliated* "1–10a, 11–15"; bound, cover stamped "Maine Woods" [sic].

Date: [1843 (c), 1844 (r)].

Contents: Draft portion; text briefer than *W* 1:122–87 and also varies from *FLJ* 1:7–29. For other contents see B114a, D6a.

D5b.   Citation: *A Week*, "Monday" A.ms., 2 sides. Pencil (c,r) Ink (r). MCon.

First line: But they did not all safe arrive in Dunstable the 13th or the 15th or the 30th day of May.

Collation: 1 leaf of white wove (type 5), 25.2 x 20.1 cm., pp. [1–2].

Date: [1848].

Contents: Draft portion; text varies from *W* 1:124–26. Verso contains surveying notes and calculations, ca. [1849].

D5c.   Citation: *A Week*, "Monday" A.ms., 12 sides. Ink (c,r,d) Pencil (c,r,d). CSmH (HM 13195).

First line: It is related in the history of Dunstable Just before his last march Lovewell was warned

Collation: 6 leaves,
    4 of blue wove (type 5), 24.6 x 19.8 cm.,
    1 of gray wove (type 6), 24.2 x 19 cm.,
    1 of white wove (type 11), 24.6 x 19.3 cm.,
pp. [1–12].

Date: [1847–1848].

Contents: Draft portions; text varies from W 1:126, 132–33, 173–75, 177–78, 182–84. For other contents see B16e.

D5d. Citation: *A Week,* "Monday" A.ms., 2 sides. Ink (c) Pencil (r). CSmH (HM 13182:III, 12).

First line: Because I stand aloof from politics, and devote myself to the search after truth,

Collation: 1 leaf of blue wove (type 9), 24.4 x 19 cm., pp. [1–2].

Date: [1845].

Contents: Draft portion; text resembles W 1:133–36. A facsimile is in *FLJ* 1:136. For other contents see B137.

D5e. Citation: *A Week,* "Monday" A.ms., 2 sides. Ink (c). CSmH (HM 926:3v).

First line: These sublime passages as they proceeded from so do they address what is most abiding and deepest in human nature.

Collation: 1 leaf of white wove (type 21), 20.2 x 15.9 cm., pp. [1–2], paged "101".

Date: [1842].

Contents: Draft portion; text resembles W 1:154–55. For other contents see B17a.

D5f. Citation: *A Week,* "Monday" A.ms., 2 sides. Ink (c,r) Pencil (d). MHarF.

First line: Any book of great authority and genius would seem to our imagination to pervade all space.

Collation: 1 leaf of white wove (type 11), 24.6 x 19.5 cm., pp. [1–2]; mounted for display in hinged wall case.

Date: [1843–1844].

Contents: Draft portion; text resembles *W* 1:155–57. For an early version see *J* 1:260–61, 265; for a late version see D5g.

D5g.   Citation: *A Week*, "Monday" A.ms., 1 side. Ink (c,r,d). VtMiM.

First line: I love the gradual & vague transitions of mature expressions which cannot be analyzed—

Collation: 1 leaf of blue wove (type 1), 24.7 x 20.1 cm., pp. [1–2]; in folder marked "Fragments".

Date: [1847].

Contents: Draft portion; text resembles *W* 1:155–57.

D5h.   Citation: *A Week*, "Monday" A.ms., 1 side. Ink (c). W. S. Thomas, Rochester, N.Y.

First line: Here rose the spirit of Capt. Jonathan Foster—the 19th day of May, in the 50th year of our independence.

Collation: 1 fragment of white wove (type 1a), 27.8 x 19.4 cm., pp. [1–2].

Date: [1845].

Contents: Draft portion; text resembles *W* 1:177–78. For a later version see D5i. For other contents see B107b, B108b, B109b.

D5i.   Citation: *A Week*, "Monday" A.ms., 1 side. Ink (c) Pencil (c). NNPM (MA 1823,2).

Title: Intelligence is but the shadow | of that light that hangs over me | perpetually.

First line: Here rose the spirit of Capt. Jonathan Toole the 19th day of May and the 50th year of our independence—

Collation: 1 leaf of white wove, 25 x 18.9 cm.; pasted to inside back cover of the *Journal*, [vol. *9*].

Date: [1843–1844].

Contents: Draft portion; text and facsimile in K. W. Cameron, "An Epitaph on the Cover of a Thoreau Journal", *ESQ*, No. 13 (1958), pp. 93–95.

D5j.   Citation: *A Week*, "Monday" A.ms., 20 sides. Ink (c,r) Pencil (r,d). MH (bMS Am 278.5 [15:A, J,N]).

First line: It is now easy to apply to this ancient scripture such a catholic criticism as it will become the part of some future age to apply to Christianity,

Collation: 10 leaves,
   3 of gray wove (type 1), 25 x 20.1 cm., pp. [1–6],
   2 of blue wove (type 5), 24.5 x 19.7 cm., pp. [57–58, 63–64],
   1 of gray wove (type 3), 24.8 x 20.1 cm., pp. [59–60],
   2 of blue wove (type 9), 24.4 x 18.8 cm., pp. [61–62, 65–66],
   1 of white wove (type 5), 25.1 x 20 cm., pp. [67–68],
   1 of white wove (anom), pp. [87–88].

Date: [1845–1848].

Contents: Draft portions; text resembles *W* 1:154–61, 177–79, 181. For other contents see B109c.

D5k.   Citation: *A Week*, "Monday" A.ms., 14 sides. Ink (c) Pencil (r,d). MH (bMS Am 278.5 [10]).

First line: One pleasant summer morning, (July 19th, 1842) we started to walk to Wachusett,

Collation: 7 leaves,

1 of gray wove (type 1), 25 x 20.1 cm., pp. [1–2].
6 of blue wove (type 1), 25.1 x 19.9 cm., pp. [3–14].

Date: [1847].

Contents: Draft portion; text varies from *W* 1:169–74. For an early version see C4a. For other contents see E9a.

Note: The paper and text of this ms. indicate that it is later than *W* 5:136–50 but earlier and longer than *W* 1:169–74. For a contrary opinion see L. Lane, Jr., "Thoreau at Work: Four Versions of 'A Walk to Wachusett' ", *BNYPL* 69 (1965): 3–16.

D5l. Citation: *A Week*, "Monday" A.ms., 2 sides. Ink (c,r,d) Pencil (d,n*). RPB.

First line: [v] And now when we look again westward from these hills of Concord

Collation: 1 leaf of white wove (type 11), 24.4 x 19.9 cm., pp. [1–2].

Date: [1843 (c), 1844 (r)].

Contents: Draft portion; text varies from *W* 1:173–74. For an early version see C4.

D5m. Citation: *A Week*, "Monday" A.ms., 4 sides. Ink (c,r) Pencil (r,d). MH (bMS Am 278.5 [4,D]).

First line: A bugle heard in the stillness of the night sends forth its voice to the pastures of land

Collation: 2 leaves of white wove (type 11), 24.5 x 19.3 cm., pp. [1–2].

Date: [1843–1844].

Contents: Draft portion; text resembles *W* 1:182–84. For early versions see *TS*, p. 14, and *J* 1:159.

D5n.   Citation: *A Week,* "Monday" A.ms., 6 sides. Ink
(c,r) Pencil (r,d). MH (bMS Am 278.5 [2,8–9]).

First line: That training which exacts nothing between the hero's moods and the universe—

Collation: 2 leaves of white wove (type 14), 24.5 x
18.9 cm., pp. [15–18].

Date: [1846].

Contents: Draft portion; text resembles *W* 1:183.
For an early version see *TS,* p. 12.

D5o.   Citation: *A Week,* "Monday" A.ms., 2 sides. Ink
(c,r) Pencil (r,n). TxU.

First line: (Whoever) is harmoniously composed delights in harmony,

Collation: 1 leaf of blue wove (type 1), 25 x 19.9
cm., pp. [1–2], paged "214–15"; mounted.

Date: [1847].

Contents: Draft portion; text varies from *W* 1:183–
86. For other contents see B144.

D6a.   Citation: *A Week,* "Tuesday" A.ms., 28 sides. Ink
(c,r) Pencil (c,r,d,n). CSmH (HM 956, 15v–30).

First line: By three o'clock we had completed our
preparations and were again on the weigh.

Collation: 15 leaves,
    7 of white wove (type 11), 24.4 x 19.5 cm.,
    5 of white wove, 40.7 x 19.2 cm.,
    3 of blue wove (type 6), 24.5 x 20 cm.,
pp. [31–60], foliated* "16–30"; bound, cover stamped
"Maine Woods" [*sic*].

Date: [1843–1844].

Contents: Draft portion; text briefer than *W* 1:188–248 but longer than *FLJ* 1:30–32. For other contents see B112a, B113a, B114a.

Note: See D1a, Note.

D6b. Citation: *A Week*, "Tuesday" A.ms., 4 sides. Ink (c,r) Pencil (r,d). CSmH (HM 13195).

Title: [1v] Tuesday.

First line: [1r] By three o'clock we had completed our preparations and were ready to pursue our voyage as usual.

Collation: 2 leaves of blue wove (type 5), 24.6 x 19.9 cm., pp. [1–4].

Date: [1847 (c), 1848 (r)].

Contents: Draft portion; text varies from *W* 1:188–89, 244–45, and *FLJ* 1:30–32. For other contents see B19c.

D6c. Citation: *A Week*, "Tuesday" A.ms., 4 sides. Ink (c) Pencil (r,d). CSmH (HM 13182:I, 5–6).

First line: I had thought of returning to this house the next day—which was well kept and so nobly placed

Collation: 2 leaves of white wove (type 14), 24.5 x 19.1 cm., pp. [1–4], paged "5, 83".

Date: [1846].

Contents: Draft portion; text resembles *W* 1:191–92.

D6d. Citation: *A Week*, "Tuesday" A.ms., 10 sides. Ink (c,r) Pencil (r,d). MH (bMS Am 278.5 [15,L]).

First line: When we meet a person unlike ourselves, we are apt to find ourselves wholly in the unlikeness.

Collation: 5 leaves,
    1 of white wove (anom.), pp. [71–72],
    3 of blue wove (type 1), 25.2 x 20 cm., pp. [73–76, 81–82], paged "97–98",
    1 of gray wove, 24.7 x 19 cm., pp. [77–78].

Date: [1847].

Contents: Draft portion; text resembles W 1:199–202, 230. Other paragraphs resemble W 1:65–67, 111–12, 155–59, 166, 412–13.

D6e.   Citation: A Week, "Tuesday" A.ms., 2 sides. Ink (c) Pencil (r,d). CSmH (HM 926:4r).

First line: established by the note of the flicker heard from among the oaks on the hill side,

Collation: 1 leaf of white wove, 25.4 x 20.1 cm., pp. [1–2].

Date: [After 27 March 1842].

Contents: Draft portion; text resembles W 1:205–6. For early versions see J 1:351; W 5:110. For other contents see B17a.

D6f.   Citation: A Week, "Tuesday" A.ms., 7 sides. Ink (c,r) Pencil (r,d). MH (bMS Am 278.5 [16]).

First line: Some affirmed that it carried sail, and that such winds blew here as filled the sails of vessels on the ocean,

Collation: 4 leaves,
    3 of blue wove (type 1), 25.1 x 20 cm., pp. [1–6], paged "252–53 273–74",
    1 of white wove (type 5), 25.1 x 20 cm., pp. [7–8].

Date: [1847 (c), 1848 (r)].

Contents: Draft portion; text varies from *W* 1:223–26. For a late version of some paragraphs on clothing, see *W* 2:28–29.

D6g.   Citation: *A Week*, "Tuesday" A.ms., 2 sides. Ink (c) Pencil (r,d). ViU (6345-e).

Title: The Devil.

First line: In our holiest moment the devil with a leer stands close at hand.

Collation: 1 leaf of gray wove (type 1), 25 x 20.1 cm., pp. [1–2].

Date: [1841 (c), 1843 (r)].

Contents: Draft portion; text resembles *W* 1:236. For a late version see *J* 1:207–8.

D7a.   Citation: *A Week*, "Wednesday" A.ms., 6 sides. Ink (c) Pencil (r,d). CSmH (HM 13194).

First line: We made our way slowly up the river, through the fog—

Collation: 3 leaves,
    2 of white wove (type 11), 24.6 x 19.4 cm.,
    1 of white wove (type 1a), 31.9 x 19.3 cm.,
pp. [1–6], one side paged "129".

Date: [1844–1845 (c), 1847 (r)].

Contents: Draft portion; text varies from *W* 1:249, 261–62, 273, and also from *FLJ* 1:33–34, 42–44.

Note: See D1a, Note.

D7b.   Citation: *A Week*, "Wednesday" A.ms., 24 sides. Ink (c,r) Pencil (r,d). CSmH (HM 13195).

Title: Wednesday. | "Man is man's foe, and destiny."

First line: Here was another young day let loose to roam the earth.

Collation: 12 leaves,
  5 of blue wove (type 5), 24.5 x 19.8 cm.,
  4 of white wove (type 11), 24.5 x 19.5 cm.,
  2 of gray wove (type 6), 24.2 x 19 cm.,
  1 of blue wove (type 1), 25.2 x 20 cm.,
pp. [1–24].

Date: [1844 (c), 1847–1848 (r)].

Contents: Draft portion; text varies from *W* 1:249–51, 253, 260–61, 268, 271, and also from *FLJ* 1:46–61. For other contents see B97b.

D7c. Citation: *A Week*, "Wednesday" A.ms., 68 sides. Ink (c,r) Pencil (c,r,d). MH (bMS Am 278.5 [15: D,G,I,O,T]).

First line: not to be jostled against my neighbor without danger of being broken by the collision,

Collation: 34 leaves,
  14 of blue wove (type 1), 25.1 x 20 cm., pp. [11–14, 33–40, 91–100] paged "158–428,"
  6 of gray wove (type 3), 24.8 x 20.1 cm., pp. [45–56],
  1 of white wove (type 14), 24.6 x 19 cm., pp. [89–90],
  1 of white wove (type 5), 25.1 x 19.9 cm., pp. [101–2], paged "341,"
  1 of blue wove (type 9), 24.2 x 19.1 cm., pp. [133–34],
  1 of white wove (type 8), 23.8 x 19.1 cm., pp. [135–36],
  10 of white wove (type 11), 24.5 x 19.4 cm., pp. [137–46].

Date: [1844–1848].

Contents: Draft portions; text resembles *W* 1:252–53, 267–72, 289, 304–5, 310. Other paragraphs resemble *W* 1:132–33, 177, 182–84, 220, 376–77. For other contents see B132c.

D7d. Citation: *A Week*, "Wednesday" A.ms., 2 sides. Ink (c,r) Pencil (d). CSmH (HM 13188v)

First line: [v] As in the treaties of states there are secret articles inserted of vital importance

Collation: 1 leaf of white wove (type 5), 25 x 20.1 cm., pp. [1–2].

Date: [1848].

Contents: Draft portion; text resembles *W* 1:279. For other contents see B95b, B164.

D7e. Citation: *A Week*, "Wednesday" A.ms., 4 sides. Ink (c) Pencil (r). VtMiM.

Title: Conversation.

First line: Talking is very singular. Men and women get together and they talk.

Collation: 2 leaves of white wove (type 11), 24.7 x 19.8 cm., pp. [1–4]; in folder marked "Fragments."

Date: [1844 (c), 1847 (r)].

Contents: Draft portion copied from the *Journal*; text resembles *W* 1:295 and varies from *FLJ* 1:113–17. For a late version see *J* 1:460.

D7e[1]. Citation: *A Week*, "Wednesday" A.ms., 4 sides. Ink (c) Pencil (r). K. W. Rendell, Somerville, Mass.

First line: I trust that my obligations of this kind will be my lightest load,

Collation: 2 leaves of white wove, 25 x 18.1 cm., pp. [1–4].

Date: [1847].

Contents: Draft portion; text resembles *W* 1:295–96. For a late version see *J* 1:460.

Note: This item is an interesting anomaly. It bears no physical resemblance to Thoreau's other papers, and it is the only ms. known to appear from a European source. Yet the handwriting is unmistakably genuine, and the contents seem to match those of D7e.

D7f.   Citation: *A Week,* "Wednesday" A.ms., 4 sides. Ink (c,r) Pencil (r,d). TxU.

First line: Imagination is my capital, for I am poor in worldly goods, but I would fain keep that clothed and fed.

Collation: 2 leaves of blue wove (type 9), 24.3 x 19.2 cm., pp. [1–4]; mounted.

Date: [1845].

Contents: Draft portion; text resembles *W* 1:310–11.

D8a.   Citation: *A Week,* "Thursday" A.ms., 11 sides. Ink (c,r) Pencil (r,d). CSmH (HM 13195).

Title: Thursday Sept. 5th.

First line: When we awoke this morning we heard the ominous still, deliberate sound of rain drops on our cotton roof.

Collation: 6 leaves,
    5 of white wove (type 11), 24.6 x 19.3 cm.,
    1 of blue wove (type 1), 25.1 x 19.9 cm.,
pp. [1–12], paged "1–8 11."

Date: [1844 (c), 1847 (r)].

Contents: Draft portion; text varies from *W* 1:317–18, 335, 341, 354; and *FLJ* 1:46 ff. For other contents see B121a.

D8b. Citation: *A Week*, "Thursday" A.ms., 2 sides. Ink (c) CSmH (HM 1225).

First line: [v] There is no where any apology for despondency. There is always life, which rightly lived implies a divine satisfaction.

Collation: 1 leaf of blue wove (type 1), 25 x 17.9 cm., pp. [1–2]; bound.

Date: [1847].

Contents: Draft portion; text varies from *W* 1:320. For other contents see B145.

D8c. Citation: *A Week*, "Thursday" A.ms., 2 sides. Ink (c). CSmH (HM 924:Before A, 6v).

First line: be reflected many times, telling us precisely how he remembered it, and this seemed to him a good excuse for continuing the conversation,

Collation: 1 leaf of white wove (type 5), 25 x 20.1 cm., pp. [1–2].

Date: [1847].

Contents: Draft portion; one paragraph resembles *W* 1:322.

D8d. Citation: *A Week*, "Thursday" A.ms., 2 sides. Ink (c) Pencil (r,d). CSmH (HM 13182:I,8).

First line: [v] We were hospitably entertained in Concord, New Hampshire, which to the confusion of the inhabitants we persisted in calling New [underscored] Concord,

Collation: 1 leaf of blue wove (type 1), 25.1 x 20 cm., pp. [1–2].

Date: [1847].

Contents: Draft portion; text varies from *W* 1:322. Recto has paragraphs on reformers, resembling *W* 1:130 ff.

D8e.   Citation: *A Week*, "Thursday" A.ms., 6 sides. Ink (c,r) Pencil (r,d). MH (bMS Am 278.5 [11]).

First line: It was here that the Herald of Freedom was printed at the time our voyage was made.

Collation: 3 leaves of blue wove, 24.7 x 19 cm., pp. [1–6].

Date: [1847].

Contents: Draft portion; text resembles *W* 1:322–23. For an early version see *W* 4:306–8.

Note: This ms. contains notes on Nathaniel Rogers, the subject of Thoreau's early essay "Herald of Freedom". But the paper, hand, and contents all indicate that it was composed for *A Week*, then later all but dropped from the text.

D8f.   Citation: *A Week*, "Thursday" A.ms., 2 sides. Ink (c,r) Pencil (r,d). CtY (Za 7).

Title: Travelling

First line: No Tale pleased my youthful imagination more than the Journey of a Day or the Picture of Human Life,

Collation: 1 leaf of white wove (type 11), 24.7 x 19.7 cm., pp. [1–2].

Date: [1844].

Contents: Draft portion; text resembles *W* 1:325. For other contents see B118a.

D8g.   Citation: *A Week*, "Thursday" A.ms., 2 sides. Ink (c,r,d). NYPL (Berg).

First line: such travel is apt to take all the youth and nerve out of one man & make his after life pathetic.

Collation: 1 leaf of blue wove (type 1), 25.2 x 19.9 cm., pp. [1–2], paged "139"; in folder marked "Miscellaneous Holograph Notes."

Date: [1847].

Contents: Draft portion; text resembles *W* 1:326.

D8h.   Citation: *A Week*, "Thursday" A.ms., 6 sides. Ink (c) Pencil (r,d). CSmH (HM 13182:III,1–3).

First line: When the soldier is hit by a cannonball rags are as becoming as purple.

Collation: 3 leaves of blue wove (type 1), 25.2 x 20 cm., pp. [1–6], paged "310–11."

Date: [1847].

Contents: Draft portion; text resembles *W* 1:325–26. For other contents see B25c, B118d, B132c, B141, B142.

D8i.   Citation: *A Week*, "Thursday" A.ms., 2 sides. Ink (c) Pencil (r,d). CSmH (HM 924:C,1).

First line: They'll keep their nightly watch over my grave, while my spirit is admitted to new degrees of acquaintance with their spheres.

Collation: 1 leaf of white wove (type 11), 24.4 x 19.3 cm., pp. [1–2].

Date: [1843–1844].

Contents: Draft portion; text resembles *W* 1:345–47. For other contents see D14a.

D8j.   Citation: *A Week*, "Thursday" A.ms., 10 sides. Ink (c,r) Pencil (r,d). MH (bMS Am 278.5 [15,E]).

First line: Yet the universe is a sphere whose center is wherever there is intelligence.

Collation: 5 leaves,
   3 of blue wove (type 1), 25.1 x 20 cm., pp. [15–20], paged "415–29,"
   2 of white wove (type 14), 24.1 x 19 cm., pp. [21–24].

Date: [1846–1847].

Contents: Draft portion; text resembles *W* 1:353.

D9a.   Citation: *A Week*, "Friday" A.ms., 4 sides. Ink (c,r) Pencil (r). VtMiM.

Title: Friday Sept. 13th

First line: As we lay awake long before daylight listening to the sound of the current and of the wind—

Collation: 2 leaves of white wove (type 11), 24.6 x 19.5 cm., pp. [1–4]; in folder marked "Fragments."

Date: [1843–1844].

Contents: Draft portion; text varies from *W* 1:356–58.

D9b.   Citation: *A Week*, "Friday" A.ms., 4 sides. Ink (c) Pencil (r,d). CSmH (HM 13182:III,4–5).

First line: These changes we already beheld with prophetic vision, for summer passes into autumn in some unimaginable epoch and point of time, like the turning of a leaf

Collation: 2 leaves of blue wove (type 1), 25.2 x 20 cm., pp. [1–4], paged "369–72".

Date: [1847].

Contents: Draft portion; text resembles *W* 1:356–58, 374–76. For other contents see B10g, B13i, B114c, B136a.

D9c.   Citation: *A Week*, "Friday" A.ms., 10 sides. Ink (c,r) Pencil (r,d). MH (bMS Am 278.5 [15:C,H, K,Q]).

First line: It is a consoling fact that it is as hard for a melancholy man to speak from the depth of his sadness, as for a poet to give utterance to his inspirations.

Collation: 5 leaves,
    3 of blue wove (type 1), 25 x 20 cm., pp. [41–44, 127–28], paged "375–78, 417–18,"
    2 of white wove (type 14), 24.6 x 19 cm., pp. [9–10, 69–70].

Date: [1846–1847].

Contents: Draft portion; text resembles *W* 1:364, 374, 377, 388.

D9d.   Citation: *A Week*, "Friday" A.ms., 2 sides. Ink (c) Pencil (r). CSmH (HM 13182:III,11).

First line: plumb line—a level—a surgeons compass or thermometer or barometer.

Collation: 1 fragment of white wove (type 5), 13.1 x 20.2 cm.; pp. [1–2].

Date: [1848].

Contents: Draft portion; text resembles *W* 1:388. For other contents see B87.

D9e.   Citation: *A Week*, "Friday" A.ms., 2 sides. Ink (c,r) Pencil (r,d). CSmH (HM 13195).

First line: Our works of science, as they improve in accuracy, are liable to lose

Collation: 1 fragment of white wove (type 11), 13.9 x 19.3 cm., pp. [1–2].

Date: [1844 (c), 1847–1848 (r)].

Contents: Draft portion; text varies from *W* 1:388–90.

D9f.   Citation: *A Week*, "Friday" A.ms., 4 sides. Ink (c,r) Pencil (c,r). VtMiM.

First line: [1v] Men no where, east or west, live as yet a natural life, round which the vine clings, and which the elm willingly shadows.

Collation: 2 leaves of white wove (type 11), 24.6 x 19.5 cm., pp. [1–4]; in folder marked "Fragments."

Date: [1844].

Contents: Draft portion; text resembles *W* 1:404–5, 415, 417–18. For an early version see *J* 1:200. For other contents see B115a, B117a, B119a.

D9g.   Citation: *A Week*, "Friday" A.ms., 2 sides. Ink (c,r) Pencil (r,d). W. S. Thomas, Rochester, N.Y.

First line: I love to hear some men speak though I hear not what they say.

Collation: 1 leaf of blue wove (type 5) 24.6 x 19.5 cm., pp. [1–2], paged "103".

Date: [1848].

Contents: Draft portion; text varies from *W* 1:406–7.

D9h.   Citation: *A Week*, "Friday" A.ms., 2 sides. Ink (c,r) Pencil (r,d). MH (bMS Am 278.5 [2,3]).

First line: In what respect, we may ask, does sight differ *in kind* from touch—the eye from the finger—

Collation: 1 leaf of white wove (type 5), 25.1 x 19.9 cm., pp. [1–2].

Date: [1847–1848].

Contents: Draft portion; text resembles *W* 1:408.

D9i.   Citation: *A Week* [page proofs]. A.ms., 406 sides. Ink (r,n) Pencil (r). CSmH (PB 110229).

Collation: 210 leaves of white wove, 21.3 x 12.3 cm., folded in gatherings, [1] 2–35⁶, leaf 3 signed $*, pp. [1–7], 8–413, [414–20].

Date: [1848–1849].

Contents: Page proofs, heavily revised and corrected in Thoreau's hand; text varies from *W* 1:1–420. A facsimile of p. 61 is in *TM* 2:405.

D9j.   Citation: *A Week* [Thoreau's copy]. RPB.

Contents: On a few pages, notes and corrections of the printed text.

D10a.   Citation: *Walden* [Notebook 1] A.ms., 18 sides. Ink (c) Pencil (r,d). NNPM (MA 1303).

First line: There the sun lights me to holy beans pacing slowly backward and forward over the yellow gravelly on plain between the long green rows——

Collation: 9 leaves of white wove (type 1a), 31.8 x 19.8 cm., pp. [1–18], paged "222–43"; bound.

Date: [1845–1846], dated "March 13 1846."

Contents: Notes and early draft portions; text longer than *J* 1:438–87. For other contents see C8, D1a.

D10b.   Citation: *Walden* [from Notebook 1] A.ms., 10 sides. Ink (c,r) Pencil (r,d). CSmH (HM 924:Before A, 9–13, 21).

First line: Like all children he lived alone, not in society—nor where rumor & fame reach.

Collation: 6 leaves of white wove (type 1a), 31.8 x 19.3 cm., pp. [1–12], paged "229–31."

Date: [1845–1846].

Contents: Notes and draft portions; text resembles
W 2:30–31, 47, 148, 163–65, 170. For other contents
see B162.

D10c.   Citation: *Walden* [Notebook 2] A.ms., 82 sides. Ink
(c) Pencil (r,d). NNPM (MA 1302:8).

Title: Henry D. Thoreau | March 26th 1846

First line: The change from foul weather to fair from
blank sluggish hours to serene elastic ones

Collation: 43 leaves of white wove (type 22), 19.1 x
16.5 cm., paged "1–101"; bound, π^2[A–F^{12}] + 2,
pp. [1–152], with 33 leaves missing.

Date: 4 July 1845 to 26 March 1846.

Contents: Notes, original *Journal* entries, early draft
portions; order of text varies from J 1:361–402. For
other contents see B159, B160, B161, E12c.

D10d.   Citation: *Walden* [from Notebook 2] A.ms., 10
sides. Ink (c) Pencil (r,d,n*) Blue pencil (d). CSmH
(HM 924:Before A,1–5).

Title: Sunday Aug. 24, 1845

First line: Bread may not always nourish us, but it
always does us good—

Collation: 5 leaves of white wove (type 22), 19.1 x
16.2 cm., pp. [1–10], paged "7–10, 61–64, 85."

Date: [1845 (c), 1847–1848 (r)].

Contents: Notes, original *Journal* entries, early draft
portions; text resembles W 2:102, 171, 229–30.

D10e.   Citation: *Walden* [Notebook 3] A.ms., 70 sides. Ink
(c) Pencil (r,d). NNPM (MA 1302:7).

First line: distant capes. Perhaps, we think, there
may be neighbors still—as there used to be

Collation: 35 leaves of white wove (type 22), 19.3 x
16.6 cm., paged "7–140"; bound, π^2[A–F^{12}] + 2,
pp. [1–152], with 41 leaves missing. Cover marked
"Miscellany . . . | The Walden Period?"

Date: [1845–1846].

Contents: Notes, original *Journal* entries, early draft
portions; order of text varies from J 1:402–37. For
other contents see B146b, B147b, B163, E12b.

Note: An index to the volume appears on its front
and back fly-leaves.

D10f.   Citation: *Walden* [Notebook 4] A.ms., 65 sides.
          Ink (c,r,d) Pencil (p). NYPL (Berg).

          Title: Walden April 17 1846

          First line: Even nations are ennobled by affording
          protection to the weaker races of animals.

          Collation: 35 leaves of green wove (type 2), 24.2 x
          19.7 cm., pp. [1–70], paged "1–79". For binding see
          D24b.

          Date: [1846].

          Contents: Notes, original *Journal* entries, portions of
          early draft. For other contents see D24b, E12d.

D10g.   Citation: *Walden* [from Notebook 4] A.ms., 14
          sides. Ink (c,r,d) Pencil (r,d). CSmH (HM 924:
          Before A, 14–20).

          First line: I have seen some impudent Connecticut
          / or Down east man in his crack coaster / with a tort
          sail,

          Collation: 7 leaves of green wove (type 2), 24.3 x
          19.3 cm., pp. [1–14], paged "8^1–9^1, 105, 141–43, 160".

          Date: [1846].

Contents: Notes, original *Journal* entries, portions of early draft; text resembles *W* 2:7, 42–43, 45, 48, 64, 102, 104, 108, 117, 175–76, 248–49, 336.

Note: Thomas Blanding emends the first line to read " . . . in his crack coaster with a *taut* sail."

D10h.   Citation: *Walden* [from Notebook 4] A.ms., 2 sides. Ink (c) Pencil (r,d). CSmH (HM 13182:I,7).

First line: And the vast majority of men who at one period of their lives have been compelled to study Latin & Greek

Collation: 1 leaf of green wove (type 2), 24.2 x 19.4 cm., pp. [1–2], paged "39".

Date: [1846].

Contents: Portion of early draft; text resembles *W* 2:112–15, 346.

D10i.   Citation: *Walden* [from Notebook 4] A.ms., 4 sides. Ink (c) Pencil (r,d). CSmH (HM 924:F,1–2).

First line: Thus lie the sand and clay all winter under the living surface an inert mass

Collation: 2 leaves of green wove (type 2), 24.2 x 19.1 cm., pp. [1–4].

Date: [1846].

Contents: Portion of early draft; text resembles *W* 2:336–38.

D11.   Citation: *Walden* [early fragments] A.ms., 6 sides. Ink (c) Pencil (r,d). CSmH (HM 924:Before A, 22–24).

Title: In Carew's Coelum Britannicum | Mercury makes this reply | to the Pretensions of Poverty

First line: Thou dost presume too much, poor needy wretch,

Collation: 3 fragments,
  1 of white wove, 20 x 10.7 cm.,
  1 of green wove, 4.6 x 19.9 cm.,
  1 of green wove, 12.5 x 19.6 cm., pp. [1–6].

Date: [After 8 April 1847].

Contents: Notes, portions of early draft; text resembles *W* 2:69, 72–73, 89–90, 100, 237.

D12a. Citation: *Walden* [draft A] A.ms., 242 sides. Ink (c,r) Pencil (r,d). CSmH (HM 924:A).

Title: Walden or Life in | the Woods by Henry Thoreau | Addressed to my Townsmen

First line: I should not presume to talk so much about myself and my affairs as I shall in this lecture

Collation: 121 leaves of blue wove (type 1), 25.1 x 19.9 cm., pp. [1–242], paged "1–137, 1–235", with about 41 leaves missing.

Date: [Before 10 February 1847].

Contents: Portion of first draft; text considerably briefer than *W* 2:3–336. For description and edited text see Shanley, pp. 93–208. A brief account is W. H. Menger, "Thoreau's Walden Manuscript", *Trace* 44 (Autumn, 1961):209–15. For other contents see B18c, B138a, B140, B146a, B147a, B157.

D12b. Citation: *Walden* [from draft A] A.ms., 2 sides. Ink (c,r) Pencil (r,d). TxU.

First line: present moment—and will never be more divine in the lapse of all the ages.

Collation: 1 leaf of blue wove (type 1), 25.2 x 19.9 cm., pp. [1–2], paged "47"; mounted. In draft A, follows leaf 46.

Date: [Before 10 February 1847].

Contents: Portion of first draft; text resembles *W* 2:107–8.

D12c.   Citation: *Walden* [from draft A] A.ms., 2 sides. Ink (c,r) Pencil (r,d). MB (Ms Am. 631).

First line: notes of other birds—Think of it! It would put nations on the alert.

Collation: 1 fragment of blue wove (type 1), 12.2 x 19.6 cm., pp. [1–2]; mounted. In draft A, follows leaf 63.

Date: [Before 10 February 1847].

Contents: Portion of first draft; text resembles *W* 2:141–42.

D12d.   Citation: *Walden* [from draft A] A.ms., 2 sides. Ink (c,r) Pencil (r,d). MH (bMS Am 278.5 [15,V]).

First line: Most have not delved 6 feet below the surface of the earth or climbed a hundred feet above it.

Collation: 1 leaf of blue wove (type 1), 25.1 x 20 cm., pp. [149–50]. In draft A, follows leaf 121.

Date: [Before 10 February 1847].

Contents: Portion of first draft; text resembles *W* 2:365.

D12e.   Citation: *Walden* [index of draft A] A.ms., 1 side. Ink (c) Pencil (c). NNPM (MA 1823,1).

First line: Through verses on 19 then most all of rest. How spent morn & house work 39 to 43 Reality 46-8-9

Collation: 1 leaf of white wove, 25 x 18.9 cm.; pasted to inside front cover of the *Journal* [vol. 9], with ts. copy by J. L. Shanley.

Date: [1847–1848].

Contents: Index of first draft; text in Shanley, p. 101.

D13a.   Citation: *Walden* [from draft B] A.ms., 2 sides. Ink (c,r,d) Pencil (r,d). NNPM (MA 2505).

First line: At the time the following pages were written I lived alone in the woods, a mile from my neighbors,

Collation: 1 fragment of white wove (type 5), 12 x 19.6 cm., pp. [1–2]; mounted, formerly bound in the Manuscript Edition. In draft B, precedes leaf 4.

Date: [Before 22 November 1848].

Contents: Portion of second draft; text varies from W 2:3.

D13b. Citation: *Walden* [draft B] A.ms., 164 sides. Ink (c,r,d) Pencil (r,d). CSmH (HM 924:B).

First line: [4r] parted company long ago. I require of a writer that he give me a simple and sincere account of his own life,

Collation: 85 leaves of white wove (type 5), 25.1 x 20.1 cm., pp. [1–170], paged "9–122, 7–137", with about 93 leaves missing.

Date: [1848–1849].

Contents: Portion of second draft; text briefer than W 2:4–349.

D13c. Citation: *Walden* [from draft B] A.ms., 2 sides. Ink (c,r,d) Pencil (r,d). NNPM (MA 2109).

First Line: they are printed as rare and curious as ever. It is even worth the expense of youthful days and costly hours if you learn only some words of ancient language

Collation: 1 leaf of white wove (type 5), 24.9 x 19.5 cm., pp. [1–2], paged "39". In draft B, follows leaf 55.

Date: [1848–1849].

Contents: Portion of second draft; text varies from W 2:111–12.

D13c¹.   Citation: *Walden* [from draft B] A.ms., 2 sides. Ink (c) Pencil (r). R. R. Miller, Bristol, R.I.

First line: that now reviews the vision. No dust has settled on that robe; no time has elapsed since that divinity was revealed.

Collation: 1 fragment of white wove (type 5), 12.1 x 18.8 cm., pp. [1–2]; mounted, bound in Set No. 295 of the Manuscript Edition. In draft B, follows leaf 55.

Date: [1848–1849].

Contents: Portion of second draft; text varies from *W* 2:110–11. A facsimile of the recto is in *Chapter and Verse*, No. 5 (Bristol, R.I.: The Current Company, 1972), p. 55.

D13d.   Citation: *Walden* [from draft B] A.ms., 2 sides. Ink (c). ViU (6345-e:18).

First line: If your branches wither send out your fibres into every kingdom of nature for its contributions,

Collation: 1 fragment of white wove (type 5), 8.3 x 20.1 cm., pp. [1–2], paged "95". In draft B, follows leaf 68.

Date: [1848–1849].

Contents: Portion of second draft; text resembles *W* 2:148. For an early version see C10a.

D13e.   Citation: *Walden* [from draft B] A.ms., 1 side. Ink (c). VtMiM.

First line: Consider to what height & depth man's life has reached from the Patriarchs to the Presidents,

Collation: 1 leaf of white wove (type 5), 25.2 x 20 cm., pp. [1–2]; in folder marked "Fragments." In draft B, follows leaf 85.

Date: [1848–1849].

Contents: Portion of second draft; text resembles *W*
2:365.

D14a. Citation: *Walden* [draft C] A.ms., 61 sides. Ink
(c,r,d) Pencil (r,d). CSmH (HM 924:C).

Title: [3r] Walden, | or | Life in the Woods. |
Addressed to my Townsmen. | By | Henry D.
Thoreau.

First line: [3r] At the time the following pages were
written I lived alone in the woods, a mile from any
neighbor,

Collation: 31 leaves of white wove (type 5), 25 x
20.1 cm., pp. [3–64], paged "1–124," with about 46
leaves missing.

Date: [Before 28 February 1849].

Contents: Portion of third draft; text resembles *W*
2:4–82, 159–69, 191. For other contents see D8i.

D14a¹. Citation: *Walden* [from draft C] A.ms., 2 sides. Ink
(c) Pencil (r). D. Siegel, Weston, Mass.

First line: Not satisfied with defiling one another in
this world, we would all go to heaven together.

Collation: 1 leaf of white wove (type 5), 25.1 x
20.1 cm., pp. [1–2]. In draft C, precedes leaf 10.

Date: [1849].

Contents: Portion of third draft; text resembles *W*
2:16. For a late version, see *W* 5:480. A facsimile of
the recto appears in the catalogue for Charles Hamilton Autographs, Inc., Sale No. 26, Item 274, 18 April
1968.

D14b. Citation: *Walden* [from draft C] A.ms., 2 sides. Ink
(c) Pencil (c). CSmH (HM 924:Before A,6).

First line: Comparatively speaking tattooing is not necessarily the hideous custom it is described to be.

Collation: 1 leaf of white wove (type 5), 25 x 20.1 cm., pp. [1–2]. In draft C, follows leaf 10.

Date: [1849].

Contents: Portion of third draft; text resembles *W* 2:29. See also Shanley, pp. 22–23.

D14c.   Citation: *Walden* [from draft C] A.ms., 1 side. Ink (c). A. B. Adams, Rowayton, Conn.

First line: Or you may walk into the foreign land of Bedford on the banks of the ancient Shaushine

Collation: 1 leaf of white wove (type 5), 25.1 x 19.9 cm., pp. [1–2]; mounted, framed. In draft C, follows leaf 36.

Date: [1849].

Contents: Portion of third draft; text resembles *W* 2:185. For an early version see *J* 2:6.

D14d.   Citation: *Walden* [from draft C] A.ms., 2 sides. Ink (c) Pencil (r). Dr. L. E. Hames, Boston, Mass.

First line: When Quoil came down the hill, wearing his muff-colored coat as winter—

Collation: 1 leaf of white wove (type 5), 25.2 x 20.1 cm., pp. [1–2]; mounted. In draft C, follows leaf 61.

Date: [1849].

Contents: Portion of third draft; text resembles *W* 2:288–89. For an early version see *J* 1:414–17.

D15a.   Citation: *Walden* [draft D] A.ms., 150 sides. Ink (c,r,d) Pencil (r,d). CSmH (HM 924:D).

First line: We were astonished to meet away up here in New Hampshire an Italian with his hand organ,

Collation: 77 leaves,

    2 of white laid, 24.6 x 19.1 cm., pp. [1–4],

    65 of white wove (type 18), 23.9 x 19.1 cm., pp. [5–14, 21–82, 85–130, 133–44], paged (5 leaves only) "15–82",

    7 of white wove (type 16), 24.4 x 19.3 cm., pp. [15–20, 83–84, 145–46, 149–52],

    2 of white wove (type 19), 23.7 x 19.2 cm., pp. [131–32, 147–48],

    1 of gray wove (type 5), 24.5 x 19.1 cm., pp. [153–54].

Date: [April 1852].

Contents: Portion of fourth draft; text resembles *W* 2:8–364, but with many gaps. For other contents see B140b, B178b, B187.

D15b.   Citation: *Walden* [from draft D] A.ms., 2 sides. Ink (c,r) Pencil (r). MCon (818.3T 48Wri).

First line: are the result of a long experience. There sits a stone mason splitting granite for fence-posts before my window—

Collation: 1 fragment of white wove (type 18), 12.3 x 19.3 cm., pp. [1–2], paged "25"; mounted, bound in Set No. 416 of the Manuscript Edition. In draft D, follows leaf 4.

Date: [1852].

Contents: Portion of fourth draft; text intended for section ending on *W* 2:18. For an early version see *J* 2:491. For late versions see C15i, C15x.

D15c.   Citation: *Walden* [from draft D] A.ms., 2 sides. Ink (c) Pencil (r,d). MCon.

First line: Ah!! this process by which we get our coats is not what it should be.

Collation: 1 fragment of white wove (type 18), 12 x 19.2 cm., pp. [1–2]; in folder marked "Coat Manuscript". In draft D, follows leaf 18.

Date: [1852].

Contents: Portion of fourth daft; text resembles *W* 2:25. Verso contains surveying notes and calculations.

D15d.   Citation: *Walden* [from draft D] A.ms., 1 side. Ink (c) Pencil (r,p). NNPM (MA 1302:22).

First line: Simplicity is the law of nature for men as well as for flowers.

Collation: 1 leaf of white wove (type 16), 24 x 19.3 cm., pp. [1–2], paged "131"; laid in the *Journal*, [vol. 16]. In draft D, follows leaf 10.

Date: [After 29 February 1852].

Contents: Portion of fourth draft; text resembles *W* 2:87–88. For an early version see *J* 3:324.

D15e.   Citation: *Walden* [from draft D] A.ms., 1 side. Ink (c) Pencil (r,d). CSmH (HM 13182:III,10).

First line: What have I to do with plows. I cut another furrow than you see

Collation: 1 leaf of white wove (type 16), 24.4 x 19.3 cm., pp. [1–2]. In draft D, follows leaf 10.

Date: [1852].

Contents: Portion of fourth draft; text resembles *W* 2:91–92. For other contents see B36b, B37b.

D15e¹.   Citation: *Walden* [from draft D] A.ms., 2 sides. Ink (c) Pencil (p). Mrs. G. W. Pierce, Sanbornton, N.H.

First line: I have felt my spirits rise the moment I got into the road

Collation: 1 leaf of white wove (type 18), 24.1 x 19.3 cm., pp. [1–2], paged "59"; mounted, bound in Set No. X (Editorial Copy) of the Manuscript Edition. In draft D, follows leaf 10.

Date: [1852].

Contents: Portion of fourth draft; text resembles *W* 2:95–96. For a late version see *The Moon*, p. 24.

Note: This set belonged to E. Harlowe Russell, former owner of the Thoreau manuscripts (see Introduction).

D15f.   Citation: *Walden* [from draft D] A.ms., 2 sides. Ink (c) Pencil (r,d). MH.

First line: But some there are who find pleasure in the melody of birds and chirpings of crickets—aye—even the peeping of frogs.

Collation: 1 leaf of gray wove (type 5), 25 x 19.2 cm., pp. [1–2]. In draft D, follows leaf 41.

Date: [1852].

Contents: Portion of fourth draft; text resembles *W* 2:138–40.

D15g.   Citation: *Walden* [from draft D] A.ms., 2 sides. Ink (c) Pencil (r). T. Y. Davis, Sterling, Ill.

First line: grove of sizeable trees left in the township, supposed to have been planted by the pigeons that were once baited with beech-nuts near by;

Collation: 1 fragment of white wove (type 18), 11.8 x 19.3 cm., pp. [1–2]; mounted, bound in Set No. 476 of the Manuscript Edition. In draft D, follows leaf 57.

Date: [1852].

Contents: Portion of fourth draft; text varies from *W* 2:223-24.

D15h.   Citation: *Walden* [from draft D] A.ms., 4 sides. Ink (c,r) Pencil (c,r). MH (bMS Am 278.5 [21:C,D]).

First line: Sometimes with a companion who celebrated our adventures in some rhymes

Collation: 2 leaves of white wove (type 18), 24 x 19.1 cm., pp. [75-76, 91-92]. In draft D, follow leaf 61.

Date: [1852].

Contents: Portion of fourth draft; text resembles *W* 2:247.

D15h¹.   Citation: *Walden* [from draft D] A.ms., 2 sides. Pencil (c). C. B. Hansen, Westfield, N.J.

First line: The nearest flakes drive straight to the ground weaving their thick warp in the air—

Collation: 1 fragment of white wove (type 18), 12.2 x 19.3 cm., pp. [1-2]; mounted, bound in Set No. 453 of the Manuscript Edition.

Date: [1852].

Contents: Portion of fourth draft; text resembles *W* 2:299-305, passim.

D15i.   Citation: *Walden* [from draft D] A.ms., 2 sides. Ink (c,r) Pencil (r,d). CtY (Za 5).

First line: discoverer of America and researcher in central Africa are but faint types of the adventures of the faithful explorer of his own interior.

Collation: 1 leaf of white wove (type 16), 24.4 x 19.3 cm., pp. [1-2]. In draft D, follows leaf 74.

Date: [1852].

Contents: Portion of fourth draft; text resembles *W* 2:353–54.

D15j.   Citation: *Walden* [from draft D] A.ms., 2 sides. Ink (c) Pencil (r,d). MH (bMS Am 278.5 [2,7]).

First line: There is an independent humanity in nature which is not identical with man's,

Collation: 1 leaf of gray wove (type 5), 24.3 x 19.1 cm., pp. [13–14]. In draft D, follows leaf 77.

Date: [1852].

Contents: Portion of fourth draft; text resembles *W* 2:310–11. For an early version see *TS*, p. 9.

D15k.   Citation: *Walden* [from draft D] A.ms., 1 side. Ink (c,r). J. H. Jenkins III, Austin, Tex.

First line: is a mile off. Where rabbits & partridges multiply & muskrats are more numerous than ever—

Collation: 1 leaf of white wove, 24.8 x 20.1 cm., pp. [1–2]; mounted.

Date: [After 27 January 1852].

Contents: Portion of fourth draft; text unpublished. For early version see *J* 3:237–38.

D16a.   Citation: *Walden* [draft E] A.ms., 220 sides. Ink (c,r,d) Pencil (r,d). CSmH (HM 924:E).

First line: Men have an indistinct notion that if they keep up this activity of joint stocks and spades

Collation: 114 leaves,
   111 of blue wove (type 8), 24.6 x 19.3 cm., pp. [1–80, 83–122, 125–86, 189–228],
   1 fragment of white wove (type 18), 9 x 19.1 cm., pp. [81–82],
   1 of white wove (type 19), 23.7 x 19.2 cm., pp. [123–24],

1 of blue wove, 22.7 x 19.4 cm., pp. [187–88].

Date: [1853].

Contents: Portion of fifth draft; text resembles *W* 2:59–367, but with many gaps. For other contents see B18d, B138.

D16b. Citation: *Walden* [from draft E] A.ms., 6 sides. Ink (c) Pencil (r,d). ViU (6345).

First line: pretend to know. It is commonly higher in the winter and lower in the summer,

Collation: 3 leaves of blue wove (type 8), 24.4 x 29.2 cm., pp. [1–6]. In draft E, follow leaf 29.

Date: [1853].

Contents: Portion of fifth draft; text varies from *W* 2:200–203.

D16c. Citation: *Walden* [from draft E] A.ms., 2 sides. Ink (c,r) Pencil (r). NhExA.

First line: I set out one afternoon to go a fishing to Fair Haven, through the woods, to eke out my scanty fare of vegetables.

Collation: 1 fragment of blue wove (type 8), 12.3 x 18.8 cm., pp. [1–2]; mounted, bound in Set No. 318 of the Manuscript Edition. In draft E, follows leaf 41.

Date: [1853].

Contents: Portion of fifth draft; text varies from *W* 2:225–26.

D16c¹. Citation: *Walden* [from draft E] A.ms., 2 sides. Ink (c) Pencil (r). MH-Z.

First line: There have been caught in Walden, pickeril, one weighing seven pounds,

Collation: 1 leaf of blue wove (type 8), 24.6 x 19.4 cm., pp. [1–2]; mounted. In draft E, follows leaf 29.

Date: [1853].

Contents: Portion of fifth draft; text varies from *W* 2:204–5.

D16d. Citation: *Walden* [from draft E] A.ms., 2 sides. Ink (c,r) Pencil (r,d). NhU.

First Line: round greasy face, and bare breast—still thinking to improve her condition one day.

Collation: 1 leaf of blue wove (type 8), 24.6 x 19.3 cm., pp. [1–2]; mounted, bound in Set No. 135 of the Manuscript Edition. In draft E, follows leaf 41.

Date: [1853].

Contents: Portion of fifth draft; text varies from *W* 2:227–28.

D16e. Citation: *Walden* [from draft E] A.ms., 2 sides. Ink (c) Pencil (c). CSmH (HM 924:Before A,8).

First line: The building of the chimney was the most interesting part of my work.

Collation: 1 leaf of blue wove (type 8), 24.2 x 19.1 cm., pp. [1–2]. In draft E, follows leaf 73.

Date: [1853].

Contents: Portion of fifth draft; text varies from *W* 2:271–72.

D16f. Citation: *Walden* [from draft E] A.ms., 2 sides. Ink (c,r) Pencil (c,r,d). TxU.

First line: [v] the Walden ice. I was told that southern customers objected to its blue color

Collation: 1 leaf of blue wove (type 8), 24.4 x 19.2 cm., pp. [1–2]. In draft E, follows leaf 103.

Date: [1853].

Contents: Portion of fifth draft; text resembles *W* 2:327–28.

D16g. Citation: *Walden* [from draft E] A.ms., 2 sides. Ink (c,r) Pencil (r,d). MH (bMS Am 278.5 [15.S]).

First line: The sweltering and parched inhabitants of Madras, Bombay—Calcutta—Havana—Charleston & New Orleans drink at my well—

Collation: 1 leaf of blue wove (type 8), 24.2 x 19.1 cm., pp. [131–32], paged "97." In draft E, follows leaf 105.

Date: [1853].

Contents: Portion of fifth draft; text resembles *W* 2:328.

D16h. Citation: *Walden* [from draft E] A.ms., 2 sides. Ink (c). CtY (Za 8).

First line: Every one has heard the story, which has gone the rounds of New England, of a strong & beautiful bug

Collation: 1 leaf of blue wove (type 8), 24.4 x 19.1 cm., pp. [1–2]. In draft E, follows leaf 113.

Date: [1853].

Contents: Portion of fifth draft; text varies from *W* 2:366–67.

D17a. Citation: *Walden* [draft F] A.ms., 236 sides. Ink (c) Pencil (r,d) Blue pencil (d). CSmH (HM 924:F).

First line: [4r] with constructing his own coffin—
the architecture of the grave; and "carpenter" is but
another name for "undertaker."

Collation: 122 leaves,
119 of white wove (type 19), 23.7 x 19.2 cm., pp.
  [7–54, 57–188, 191–234, 237–250],
  1 fragment of blue wove, 8.6 x 19.5 cm., pp. [55–
    56],
  1 fragment of blue wove (type 8), 9 x 19.1 cm.,
    pp. [189–90],
  1 fragment of white wove, 3.3 x 18.5 cm., pp.
    [235–36].

Date: [1853–1854].

Contents: Portion of sixth draft; text varies from W
2:50–367, but with many gaps. For pp. [1–6] see
D24b. For other contents see B18e, B18ob, D1oi.

D17b.   Citation: *Walden* [from draft F] A.ms., 3 sides.
         Pencil (c). NYPL (Berg).

         First line: Another time as I was returning from the
         village in the dark of the evening I met Mrs. Ebby
         Hubbard

         Collation: 2 leaves of white wove (type 19), 23.8 x
         19.3 cm., pp. [1–4]; in folder marked "Miscellaneous
         Holograph Notes." In draft F, follow leaf 20.

         Date: [1853–1854].

         Contents: Portion of sixth draft; text resembles *W*
         2:188.

D17c.   Citation: *Walden* [from draft F] A.ms., 2 sides.
         Ink (c) CSmH (HM 924:Before A,7).

         First line: A lake is the landscape's most beautiful
         & expressive feature.

Collation: 1 fragment of white wove (type 19), 7 x
19.1 cm., pp. [1-2]. In draft F, follows leaf 36.

Date: [1853-1854].

Contents: Portion of sixth draft; text varies from W
2:206-7.

D18.   Citation: *Walden* [draft G] A.ms., 104 sides. Ink
(c) Pencil (r,d). CSmH (HM 924:G).

Title: Walden, | or | Life in the Woods. | By |
Henry D. Thoreau, | Author of "A Week on the
Concord & Merrimack Rivers"

First line: [3r] I do not propose to [drawing] write
an ode to dejection but to brag as lustily as Chaunti-
[drawing] cleer

Collation: 58 leaves,
    57 of white wove (type 17), 24.3 x 19.1 cm., pp.
    [1-2, 5-56],
    1 of white wove (type 5), 25.1 x 20 cm., pp.
    [3-4].

Date: [Before March 1854].

Contents: Portion of seventh draft; text varies from
W 2:1, 27-93, 147, 235-356, and with many gaps. For
another draft portion see G16a. For other contents
see B191.

Note: The title-page drawing is of a crowing rooster;
Thoreau's epigraph is followed by a quotation from
Sadi, not in the final text.

D19a.   Citation: *Walden* [page proofs] A.ms., 197 sides.
Pencil (r,n). CSmH (HM 925).

Collation: 197 leaves of white wove, 25.5 x 30.6
cm.; 3 printed pages per leaf.

Date: [March to May 1854].

Contents: Final corrections of entire printed text; *W* 2:2–367. For a description see *Walden*, ed. J. Lyndon Shanley, *The Writings of Henry D. Thoreau* (Princeton, N.J.: Princeton University Press, 1971), pp. 384–85.

D19b. Citation: *Walden* [Thoreau's copy] A.ms., 17 sides. Pencil (r,n). VtMiM.

Date: [After 9 August 1854].

Contents: On 17 pages, notes and corrections of the printed text. See R. L. Cook, "Thoreau's Annotations and Corrections in the First Edition of *Walden*", *TSB* 42 (1953):1.

D20. Citation: *A Yankee in Canada* A.ms., 194 sides. Ink (c,r,d) Pencil (r,d). CSmH (HM 949).

First line: I find that some of my townsmen expected last winter that I would give some account of Canada,

Collation: 102 leaves,
   101 of white wove (type 18), 23.8 x 19.3 cm., pp. [1–178, 181–202],
   1 fragment of blue wove (type 5), 9.3 x 19.7 cm., pp. [179–80].

Date: [Before 7 January 1852].

Contents: Early lecture draft; text briefer than *W* 5:3–101. For fragments of the *Journal* account see E13. For notes and notebook on Canada see F9.

D21a. Citation: *A Yankee in Canada* A.ms., 68 sides. Ink (c,r,d) Pencil (r,d). CSmH (HM 950).

Title: N. E. is by some affirmed to be an island bounded on the | north with the river Canada (so called from Monsieur Cane)." | Josselyn's Rareties.

First line: I find that some of my townsmen expected last winter that I would give them some account of Canada,

Collation: 57 leaves of white wove (type 18), 23.7 x 19.3 cm., pp. [1–114], foliated* "1–57"; bound.

Date: [Before 17 March 1852].

Contents: Portion of late lecture draft; text varies from *W* 5:3–34.

D21b. Citation: *A Yankee in Canada* A.ms., 4 sides. Ink (c) Pencil (r,d). MH (bMS Am 278.5 [12]).

Title: no. 4. | The Character of the Canadians, & The Fortifications of Quebec.

First line: Montmorenci County, not including the Isle of Orleans, which has recently been added to it,

Collation: 3 leaves,
    2 of white wove (type 18), 23.8 x 19.2 cm., pp. [1–4],
    1 fragment of white wove, 26 x 13.7 cm., pp. [5–6].

Date: [Before 17 March 1852].

Contents: Portion of late lecture draft; text varies from *W* 5:62.

D21c. Citation: *A Yankee in Canada* A.ms., 3 sides. Ink (c,r) Pencil (r,d). NYPL (Berg).

First line: them in the Indian way; they wrap square pieces of cloth round their feet instead of stockings,

Collation: 3 leaves of white wove (type 18), 24 x 19.3 cm., pp. [1–6], paged "133–35"; with ts. copy.

Date: [Before 17 March 1852].

Contents: Portion of late lecture draft; text varies from *W* 5:66–68.

D21d.   Citation: *A Yankee in Canada* A.ms., 1 side. Ink (c) Pencil (r,d). MiU.

First line: unengaged berths in the Lord Sydenham steamer, which was to leave Quebec before sundown,

Collation: 1 leaf of white wove (type 18), 23.8 x 18.9 cm., pp. [1–2]; mounted, bound in Set No. 370 of the Manuscript Edition.

Date: [Before 17 March 1852].

Contents: Portion of late lecture draft; text varies from *W* 5:72–73. A facsimile is in Stoller, p. 8.

D21e.   Citation: *A Yankee in Canada* A.ms., 1 side. Ink (c) Pencil (r,d). ViU (6345).

First Line: Yankee that got in there,—I thought the prospect nearly as good as from within the citadel itself,

Collation: 1 leaf of white wove (type 18), 23.8 x 19.3 cm., pp. [1–2], paged "152"; bound.

Date: [Before 17 March 1852].

Contents: Portion of late lecture draft; text varies from *W* 5:73. For an early version see *J* 2:74. A facsimile is in K. W. Cameron, "A Manuscript Fragment of Thoreau's Quebec Journey of 1850", *ESQ* No. 8 (1957), p. 19.

D21f.   Citation: *A Yankee in Canada* A.ms., 2 sides. Ink (c,r) Pencil (r,d). NYPL (Berg).

First line: The Government Garden has few nosegays, amid kitchen vegetables—

Collation: 2 leaves of white wove (type 18), 24 x 19.3 cm., pp. [1–2]; with a ts. copy.

Date: [Before 17 March 1852].

Contents: Portion of late lecture draft; text varies from *W* 5:64.

D21g. Citation: *A Yankee in Canada* A.ms., 1 side. Ink (c) Pencil (r). P. Brown, Lexington, Mass.

First line: I saw that the Canadians had a good excuse for not taking us over to the Isle of Orleans in a pirogue,

Collation: 1 leaf of white wove (type 18), 23.9 x 19.2 cm., pp. [1–2]; mounted, bound in Set No. 284 of the Manuscript Edition.

Date: [Before 17 March 1852].

Contents: Portion of late lecture draft; text varies from *W* 5:70–71.

D21h. Citation: *A Yankee in Canada* A.ms., 1 side. Ink (c) Pencil (r,d). ViU (6345–g).

First line: travelling once in Canada, & being in Quebec, thought it would be a good opportunity to obtain seeds of the real Canada crook neck squash;

Collation: 1 leaf of white wove (type 18), 23.8 x 19.2 cm., pp. [1–2].

Date: [Before 17 March 1852].

Contents: Portion of late lecture draft; text varies from *W* 5:87, 95.

D21i. Citation: *A Yankee in Canada* A.ms., 2 sides. Ink (c). ViU (6345–g).

Title: "The Canadian Naturalist" | by Philip Henry Gosse | London, 1840 (in Har. Col. Lib.)

First line: He lived "in the immediate neighborhood" of "the village of Compton"

Collation: 1 fragment of blue laid, 17.9 x 18.6 cm., pp. [1–2].

Date: [1851].

Contents: Note for lecture; text resembles *W* 5:91.

D22.   Citation: *A Yankee in Canada* A.ms., 216 sides. Ink
         (c,r,d) Pencil (r,d). CSmH (HM 953).

         Title: An Excursion To Canada. [underscored twice]
         | I. | Concord to Montreal. [underscored twice]

         First line: I fear that I have not got much to say
         about Canada, not having seen much; what I got by
         going to Canada was a cold.

         Collation: 169 leaves,
             164 of white wove (type 18), 23.9 x 19.1 cm.,
             5 of white wove, 19.6 x 15.3 cm.,
             pp. [1–338].

         Date: [Before May 1852].

         Contents: Essay draft; text longer than *W* 5:3–94.

D23a.   Citation: *Cape Cod* A.ms., 111 sides. Ink (c,r,d)
         Pencil (r,d) Blue pencil (n,p). CSmH (HM 13206).

         Title: A Course of Lectures on | Cape Cod.

         First Line: I do not see why there should not be a
         course of lectures on Cape Cod as well as on any-
         thing else; it is only another name for Human Cul-
         ture.

         Collation: 128 leaves,
         (a)   21 of white wove (type 5), 25.1 x 20.2 cm., pp.
                [1–2, 17–24, 33–34, 37–44, 55–56, 91–94,
                111–14, 117–18, 129–32, 135–36, 141–44,
                151–52],
         (b)   101 of white wove (type 16), 24.6 x 19.5 cm.,
                pp. [3–16, 25–32, 45–48, 51–54, 57–90,
                95–108, 121–22, 127–28, 133–34, 137–40,
                145–218, 225–50, 255–56],
                3 of white wove (type 17), 24.3 x 19 cm., pp.
                [49–50, 119–20, 123–24],
                2 of blue laid (type 1), 24.9 x 19.9 cm., pp.
                [109–10, 125–26],
         (c)   1 of white laid (type 5), 24.3 x 18.9 cm., pp.
                [153–54].

Date: (a) [1849]; (b) [1853–1855]; (c) [1859].

Contents: Portions of early draft, containing notes, revised lectures, and revised essays; text resembles *W* 4:3–273, but with many gaps.

Note: All surviving manuscripts belong to this draft.

D23b.   Citation: *Cape Cod* A.ms., 2 sides. Ink (c) Pencil (r,d). ViU (6345-e:11).

First line: far away, who as yet knew not of the wreck. I saw too how the beauty of the shore itself was wrecked for many a lonely walker there,

Collation: 1 leaf of white wove (type 16), 24.5 x 19.2 cm., pp. [1–2]; mounted.

Date: [1853].

Contents: Portion of early draft; text varies from *W* 4:12–14.

D23b¹.   Citation: *Cape Cod* A.ms., 2 sides. Ink (c) Pencil (r). D. Siegel, Weston, Mass.

First line: and formed this sand bank which we call Cape Cod. That is Hitchcocks account of it.

Collation: 1 leaf of white wove (type 5), 25.3 x 19.8 cm., pp. [1–2], paged "23"; mounted, formerly bound in Set. No. 481 of the Manuscript Edition, now tipped into Set No. 381.

Date: [1849].

Contents: Portion of early draft; text varies from *W* 4:20–21.

D23c.   Citation: *Cape Cod* A.ms., 1 side. Ink (c) Pencil (d). VtMiM.

First line: the stage on account of rain, we at length stopped for the night at Higgins' tavern in Orleans,

Collation: 1 leaf of white wove (type 16), 24.4 x 19.3 cm., pp. [1–2]; in folder marked "Fragments".

Date: [1853].

Contents: Portion of early draft; text varies from *W* 4:29–32.

D23c¹. Citation: "Cape Cod" [see section H].

D23d. Citation: *Cape Cod* A.ms., 2 sides. Ink (c) Pencil (r,d). NSchU.

First line: The next morning, (Thursday Oct 11th), it rained as hard as ever, but we were determined to proceed on foot nevertheless.

Collation: 1 leaf of white wove (type 5), 25.1 x 20 cm., pp. [1–2]; mounted, bound in Set No. 411 of the Manuscript Edition.

Date: [1849].

Contents: Portion of early draft; text varies from *W* 4:31–32.

D23d¹. Citation: *Cape Cod* A.ms., 2 sides. Ink (c). K. Harber, Rochester, N.Y.

First line: dashing against the land

Collation: 1 leaf of white wove (type 5), 25 x 20 cm., pp. [1–2]; mounted.

Date: [1849].

Contents: Portion of early draft; text varies from *W* 4:45–47.

D23e. Citation: *Cape Cod* A.ms., 2 sides. Ink (c) Pencil (r,d). ViU (6345-f).

First line: these were seen here and there on the waters of the Bay. Here in Wellfleet this pure sand plateau,

Collation: 1 leaf of white wove (type 5), 25 x 20 cm., pp. [1–2]; mounted.

Date: [1849].

Contents: Portion of early draft; text varies from *W* 4:62.

D23f.   Citation: *Cape Cod* A.ms., 2 sides. Ink (c) Pencil (r,d) ViU (6345-e:21).

First line: forest, in which not a house is to be discovered. Seamen therefore, though the distance between these two vallies is great, must not attempt to enter the wood,

Collation: 1 leaf of white wove (type 16), 24.5 x 19.3 cm., pp. [1–2]; mounted.

Date: [1853].

Contents: Portion of early draft; text varies from *W* 4:64.

D23g.   Citation: *Cape Cod* A.ms., 1 side. Ink (c) Pencil (r,d). NYPL (Ms. Division).

First line: While my companion talked with the women, I talked with the old man.

Collation: 1 leaf of white wove (type 5), 25.1 x 19.8 cm., pp [1–2], paged "119"; mounted, formerly bound in the Manuscript Edition.

Date: [1849].

Contents: Portion of early draft; text varies from *W* 4:81–82.

D23h.   Citation: *Cape Cod* A.ms., 5 sides. Ink (c) Pencil (r). MH (bMS Am 278.5 [8]).

Title: Indians of the Pemetegoit

First line: In the year 1604 the Sieur de Mont dispatched Champlain from the island of Sainte Croix to explore the coast of Noveau Belgii

Collation: 3 leaves,
2 of white wove (type 18), 23.9 x 19.1 cm., pp. [1–4],
1 fragment of white wove (type 8), 12.5 x 19 cm., pp. [5–6].

Date: [1849].

Contents: Note for early draft; text resembles *W* 4:85.

D23i.   Citation: *Cape Cod* A.ms., 2 sides. Ink (c,r). MWelHS.

First line: brought from the south and planted in the harbor of Wellfleet, till they obtained "the proper relish of Billingsgate,"

Collation: 1 leaf of white wove (type 18), 24.3 x 19.2 cm., pp. [1–2]; mounted, framed, in hinged display case.

Date: [1850].

Contents: Portion of early draft; text varies from *W* 4:82-86. A facsimile of the recto is in K. W. Cameron, "Two Pages of Thoreau's Notes for Cape Cod", *ESQ*, No. 19 (1960), pp. 38–39.

D23i¹.   Citation: *Cape Cod* A.ms., 2 sides. Ink (c) Pencil (r). [Private Collector] Needham, Mass.

First line: The ocean here is often but a tantalizing prospect

Collation: 1 leaf of white wove (type 18), 24.3 x 19.1 cm., pp. [1–21], paged "145"; mounted, bound in Set No. X (Publisher's Copy) of the Manuscript Edition.

Date: [1850].

Contents: Portion of early draft; text varies from W
4:110–12.

D23j.   Citation: *Cape Cod* A.ms., 2 sides. Ink (c) Pencil
(r). P. C. Richards, Brookline, Mass.

First line: The few scattered houses which we
passed on our way to the bay,

Collation: 1 leaf of white wove (type 16), 24.5 x
19.3 cm., pp., [1–2]; mounted, bound in the Manuscript Edition.

Date: [1853].

Contents: Portion of early draft; text varies from W
4:133–37.

D23k.   Citation: *Cape Cod* A.ms., 4 sides. Ink (c) Pencil
(r,d). ViU (6345-e:9,10).

First line: immediately sets back again into the sea
which carries with it the sand and whatever else is
in the way

Collation: 2 leaves of white wove (type 16), 24.5 x
19.3 cm., pp. [1–4]; mounted.

Date: [1853].

Contents: Portion of early draft; text varies from W
4:155–56, 171–72. See also W 4:190–92, 205–6.

D23l.   Citation: *Cape Cod* A.ms., 2 sides. Ink (c,r) Pencil
(c,r,d). Mrs. E. Nickerson, Manchester, Conn.

First line: nothing stood still but the shore. The
little beach birds trotted past along the beach,

Collation: 1 leaf of white wove (type 16), 24.3 x
19.1 cm., pp. [1–2]; mounted, bound in Set No. X
(Publisher's Copy) of the Manuscript Edition.

Date: [1853].

Contents: Portion of early draft; text varies from *W* 4:184–88.

D23m. Citation: *Cape Cod* A.ms., 2 sides. Ink (c,r) Pencil (r,d). MCon.

First line: the Cohasset Rock, again at Minot's Ledge, where is the new light-house

Collation: 1 leaf of white wove (type 16), 24.5 x 19.2 cm., pp. [1–2], paged "274"; mounted, bound in Set No. 562 of the Manuscript Edition.

Date: [1853].

Contents: Portion of early draft; text varies from *W* 4:262–64.

D24a. Citation: *The Maine Woods* ["Ktaadn" Notes] A.ms., 16 sides. Ink (c,r,d) Pencil (p). NYPL (Berg).

Title: Aug. 31st 1846

First line: Concord to Boston—Railroad station—tall man—sailors short of money—cars & Portland passenger to Ambagog.

Collation: 8 leaves of green wove (type 2), 24.4 x 19.2 cm., pp. [69–76], pages "79–87"; bound.

Date: [ca. 1847].

Contents: Transcribed field notes; the basis for *Journal* entries and lecture draft. Text resembles *W* 3:3–92, passim.; for descriptions see R. Cosbey, "Thoreau at Work: The Writing of 'Ktaadn'", *BNYPL* 65 (1961):21–30, and K. W. Cameron, "The Recent Sale of Thoreau Manuscripts", *ESQ*, No. 13 (1958), pp. 100–103. For other contents see D24b.

Note: A detailed history and description of items D24a–D26b appears in *The Maine Woods*, ed. Joseph J. Moldenhauer, *The Writings of Henry D. Thoreau* (Princeton, N.J.: Princeton University Press, 1972), pp. 355–85.

D24b.   Citation: *The Maine Woods*, "Ktaadn" A.ms., 150 sides. Ink (c,r,d) Pencil (p). NYPL (Berg).

First line: It was with strange but pleasant associations that we rowed over the North Twin Lake by moonlight—

Collation: 75 leaves of green wove (type 2), 24.4 x 19.2 cm., pp. [1–150], paged "89–241"; part of a notebook, 125 leaves bound [A–M¹²], pp. [1–288], paged "1–275", with 19 leaves missing.

Date: [Before January 1848].

Contents: Portion of lecture draft; text resembles *W* 3:39–87. For other contents see D10f, E12d.

Note: Thoreau's annotated copy of "Ktaadn and the Maine Woods", *Sartain's Union Magazine of Literature and Art* (July–November, 1848) is also at NYPL (Berg).

D24c.   Citation: *The Maine Woods*, "Ktaadn" A.ms., 4 sides. Ink (c,r) Pencil (r,d). W. S. Thomas, Rochester, N.Y.

First Line: There are singular reminescences in the life of a man of seasons

Collation: 2 leaves of white wove (type 5), 25.1 x 10.1 cm., pp. [1–4].

Date: [Before 31 March 1848].

Contents: Portion of essay draft; text resembles *W* 3:3–5. For a description see W. H. Baatz, "Henry David Thoreau", *URLB* 5 (1950):35.

D24d.   Citation: *The Maine Woods*, "Ktaadn" A.ms., 4 sides. Ink (c,r) Pencil (n*). RPB.

First line: a place to die & be buried! Here certainly men would live forever—and laugh at death and the grave.

Collation: 2 leaves of white laid (type 2), 25.4 x 20.1 cm., pp. [1–4], paged "147".

Date: [1858–1859].

Contents: Portion of book draft; text varies from W 3:90–92. For other contents see B195.

D25a.   Citation: *The Maine Woods*, "Chesuncook" A.ms., 77 sides. Ink (c,r) Pencil (p). MH (MS Lowell 9).

Title: Chesuncook.

First line: At 5 p.m. September 13th 185—, I left Boston in the steamer for Bangor by the outside course.

Collation: 71 leaves,
(a)   36 of white wove (type 12); 24.5 x 19.5 cm.,
(b)   35 of blue laid (type 2), 24.7 x 18.7 cm., pp. [1–142], paged "1–51, 61–87"; bound.

Date: (a) [Before 14 December 1853 (c), 1858 (r); (b) [1860].

Contents: Portion of book draft, containing revised lecture essay sheets; text varies from W 3:93–118, 123–36.

D25b.   Citation: *The Maine Woods*, "Chesuncook" A.ms., 1 side. Ink (c) Pencil (r). VtMiM.

First line: while they are narrower below. Not only the spruce and fir, but even the arbor-vitae and white pine,

Collation: 1 leaf of white wove (type 12), 24.5 x 19.2 cm., pp. [1–2], paged "58"; mounted, in folder marked "Fragments".

Date: [Before 14 December 1853 (c), 1858 (r)].

Contents: Portion of lecture draft, revised as essay; text varies from W 3:121.

D25c. Citation: *The Maine Woods*, "Chesuncook" A.ms.,
1 side. Ink (c,n*). RPB.

First line: a slight crackling of twigs deep in the
alders, and turned Joe's attention to it.

Collation: 1 fragment of white wove (type 12), 8.5 x
19 cm., pp. [1–2], paged "60".

Date: [Before 14 December 1853].

Contents: Portion of lecture draft; text varies from *W*
3:122.

D25d. Citation: *The Maine Woods*, "Chesuncook" A.ms.,
1 side. Ink (c) Pencil (p). MB (Ch B.6.17).

First line: After supper, the moon having risen, we
proceeded to hunt a mile up this stream, first carry-
ing about the falls.

Collation: 1 leaf of white wove (type 12), 24.4 x
19.2 cm., pp. [1–2], paged "76"; tipped in folder, with
ts. copy.

Date: [Before 14 December 1853].

Contents: Portion of lecture draft; text varies from *W*
3:130–31.

D25e. Citation: *The Maine Woods*, "Chesuncook" A.ms.,
6 sides. Ink (c,r) Pencil (c,r,d). MH (bMS Am 278.5
[17,C]).

First line: She is my body's god, my soul's goddess.
If God is my Father, and man is my Brother, she is
my Sister and my Mother.

Collation: 3 leaves,
1 of white wove (type 12), 24.5 x 19.5 cm.,
2 of white wove (type 5), 25.1 x 19.9 cm.,
pp. [37–42].

Date: [1853–1854].

Contents: Notes, portions of lecture draft; text resembles *W* 3:133–35.

D25f.   Citation: *The Maine Woods*, "Chesuncook" A.ms., 1 side. Ink (c) Pencil (p). ViU (6345–e:8).

First line: will rather preserve its life than destroy it. Is it the lumberman then who is the friend and lover of the pine—

Collation: 1 leaf of white wove (type 12), 24.4 x 19 cm., pp. [1–2], paged "85".

Date: [Before 14 December 1853].

Contents: Portion of lecture draft; text varies from *W* 3:135.

Note: James Russell Lowell deleted the final sentence of this ms. from the essay text, thus provoking Thoreau's famous letter of denunciation (see *Corr.*, pp. 515–16).

D26a.   Citation: *The Maine Woods*, "The Allegash and East Branch" A.ms., 10 sides. Ink (c) Pencil (r,d). CSmH (HM 13199).

Title: The Allegash and | East Branch | Maine Woods | 214

First line: I started on my 3d excursion to the Maine Woods Monday July 20th 1857,

Collation: 5 leaves of white laid (type 2), 25.2 x 20.2 cm., pp. [1–10].

Date: [Before 25 January 1858 (c), 1862 (r)].

Contents: Portion of essay draft, containing revised lecture sheets; text varies from *W* 3:174–77.

D26b.   Citation: *The Maine Woods*, "The Allegash and East Branch" A.ms., 30 sides. Ink (c,r) Pencil (c,r,d). MH (bMS Am 278.5 [17:A,B,D,E,F]).

Title: The mt. article might be called | Ktaadn—the 2d Chesuncook | the 3d The Allegash & | East Branch | The Whole "The Maine Woods" | H. D. T.

First line: The moose & Elk (not to mention the Beaver) will perchance one day become extinct—

Collation: 20 leaves,
   17 of blue laid (type 2), 24.7 x 19.7 cm., pp. [1–2, 5–30, 33–36, 47–48],
   3 of white wove (anom.), pp. [43–46, 49–50].

Date: [April–May 1862].

Contents: Notes, portions of essay and book draft; text resembles *W* 3:249–54, 290–98, 311–17, 326–27, 350–51.

E.

THE *JOURNAL,* 1837–1861

Thoreau's early *Journal* volumes (1837–1850) are today in a scattered and fragmentary condition, owing to his peculiar habits of composition during those years. Between October 1837 and January 1841 he wrote two large volumes, the first a "Red Journal of 546 pages" and the second a "Journal of 396 pages" (*J* 8:66). These first two volumes contained dated entries and early drafts of poems, lectures, or essays. He customarily removed the drafts for copying or insertion into later versions, and thus by 1841 the two volumes had become too mutilated for convenient use. In October and November of 1841 he transcribed their surviving contents into four smaller volumes, wryly entitled "Gleanings, Or What Time Has Not Reaped of My Journal". These new volumes he also "reaped" in time, for some of their leaves are missing as well.

From 1841 to 1850 Thoreau wrote and plundered eight successive volumes of his *Journal*, leaving behind a pile of remnants that his later editors either overlooked or thought too fragmentary to print. In their 1906 text Bradford Torrey and Francis H. Allen left several gaps in the *Journal*'s early years, notably from June 1840 to January 1841, July 1842 to March 1844, April to September 1846, and July 1848 to April 1850. About 460 manuscript pages for this period are now available, two-thirds of them still unpublished.

The following section contains a hypothetical reconstruction of the early *Journal* volumes, based on the evidence of paper types, pagination, indexes, and texts. I am heavily indebted to Thomas Blanding for his generous assistance in establishing the dates, order of pagination, and textual contents of the unpublished fragments, 1842–1850. At the risk of confusing readers, I have followed the two numbering sequences Thoreau used: *1–9* (1839–1844) and 1–33 (1845–1861). The early sequence always appears in italics, and the two original volumes appear as [First vol.; Second vol.].

Besides Thoreau's manuscripts, transcriptions by W. E. Channing of selected *Journal* entries are available at NNPM (MA 609) and ViU (6345-e:26). Channing made two sets of copies, the first in 1853 and the second in 1860, for "Concord Walks", an intended book of extracts from the journals of

Emerson, Thoreau, and Channing. Emerson borrowed the
second set to write his eulogy of Thoreau, and Channing later
used some of the material in *Thoreau, the Poet-Naturalist*;
but "Concord Walks" itself never appeared.

E1a.   Citation: *Journal* [First vol.] A.ms., 2 sides. Ink
        (c). Prof. R. Adams, Chapel Hill, N.C.

        Title: Henry D. Thoreau — 1837 [underscored]

        First line: "By all means use sometimes to be alone

        Collation: 1 leaf of white wove (type 9), 25 x 20 cm.,
        pp. [1–2].

        Date: [22 October 1837].

        Contents: Title page and motto; text varies from
        J 1:1–2. For other contents see B8, B23a.

        Note: This volume, which Thoreau called "the big
        Red Journal", originally contained 546 pages (see *J*
        1:138; 8:66), beginning with this leaf and ending on
        11 June 1840. A partial index to the volume appears
        in the "Index Rerum" at CSmH (HM 945); an edited
        version of the index is in *TM* 3:883–86. For other
        surviving leaves see B4, B10a, B12, B13a–b, B14a–b,
        B16b, B17a, B19a, B24a, B26a, B28a, B29a, B44a, C3.

E1b.   Citation: *Journal* [First vol.] A.ms., 2 sides. Ink (c).
        CSmH (HM 13201:4).

        Title: Gratitude ——

        First line: As in his strength, so in his weakness, does
        man's divinity appear.

        Collation: 1 leaf of white wove (type 9), 24.8 x 19.9
        cm., pp. [1–2].

        Date: 24 February 1838.

        Contents: Original entry; text and facsimile in *TM*
        1:268–10. For other contents see B10a.

E1c.   Citation: *Journal* [First vol.] A.ms., 2 sides. Ink (c)
        Pencil (c). CSmH (HM 13201: 10v).

        Title: The Cliffs.

First line: which sparingly we've shared, perchance but caught, the incence all the while it flitted past.

Collation: 1 leaf of white wove (type 9), 24.7 x 19.8 cm., pp. [1–2].

Date: 8 July 1838.

Contents: Original entry; text varies from *J* 1:51–52. A facsimile is in *TM* 1:271–72. For other contents see B10a, B13b, B16b.

E1d.   Citation: *Journal* [First vol.] A.ms., 2 sides. Ink (c) Pencil (d). CSmH (HM 926:8v).

First line: Fat sorts of p [torn]

Collation: 1 leaf of white wove (type 9), 24.9 x 20 cm., pp. [1–2].

Date: [1839].

Contents: Original entry, intended for *A Week* but dropped from the text. A later version appears in the "Moonlight" transcripts (see G12).

Note: Writing in 1854, Thoreau was to recall this spear-fishing episode of "some 15 years ago", of which this ms. is apparently the original version.

E2.   Citation: *Journal* [Second vol.] A.ms., 4 sides. Ink (c) Pencil (r,d). InU (Am. Lit. Mss., V.1).

Title: The Best Criticism

First line: Perhaps the best criticism of any book will be like his, who being asked how he liked a volume of very moderate size, answered that he had not yet finished it.

Collation: 2 leaves of white wove (type 8), 25 x 19.5 cm., pp. [1–4]; bound, with ts. copy.

Date: 13 December 1840.

Contents: Original entry; text unpublished. For late versions see *J* 1:447, and *W* 1:401.

Note: According to Thoreau, this volume, dated 14 June 1840 to 31 January 1841, originally contained 396 pages (*J* 1:188; 8:66). A partial index to the volume appears in the "Index Rerum" at CSmH (HM 945); an edited version is in *TM* 3:883–86. For other surviving leaves see D7c, D23h.

E3.   Citation: *Journal* [vol. 1] A.ms., 152 sides. Ink (c) Brown Ink (r) Pencil (r,d) Blue Pencil (d). NNPM (MA 1302:1).

Title: Henry D. Thoreau. | Gleanings — | Or What Time | Has Not Reaped | Of My | Journal

First line: "By all means use sometimes to be alone

Collation: 79 leaves of white wove (type 25), 11.2 x 9.3 cm., paged "1–154"; bound, π^2 [A–G^{12}] + 2, pp. [1–158], with 9 leaves missing.

Date: [November 1841], dated "October 22 1837–December 2 1839."

Contents: Transcribed entries; text in *J* 1:1–96. A facsimile of leaf 3 is in *MR* 4 (1962):97. For other contents see B11b, B14c, B18b, B19b, B51–B52, B53a, B54–B59, B60a, B61a–c, B62a, B63–B72, B73a.

E4.   Citation: *Journal* [vol. 2] A.ms., 135 sides. Ink (c) Brown ink (r) Pencil (r,d) Blue pencil (d). NNPM (MA 1302:2).

Title: From a Chapter on Bravery — Script. Dec. 1839.

First line: Bravery does not exhibit itself in ideas but in life it does not consist so

Collation: 80 leaves of white wove (type 25), 11.2 x 9.3 cm., paged "1–130"; bound, π^2 [A–G^{12}] + 2, pp. [1–176], with 10 leaves missing, 2 tipped.

Date: [November 1841], dated "December 1839–July 27 1840".

Contents: Transcribed entries; text in *J* 1:96–171. For other contents see B20b, B22b, B74a, B75a, B76.

E5. Citation: *Journal* [vol. 3] A.ms., 135 sides. Ink (c) Pencil (r,d). NNPM (MA 1718).

Title: Next to having lived a day well is a clear calm | overlooking all of our days.

First line: No pearlier tints than this mornings witnessed the valor of Hector and Idomenus,

Collation: 69 leaves of white wove, 10.4 x 8.5 cm., paged "1–136"; bound, π^2 [A–F^{12} G^8] + 2, pp. [1–144], with 3 leaves missing.

Date: [November 1841], dated "July 30 1840–January 22 1841".

Contents: Transcribed entries; text in *CC*, pp. 133–219. A facsimile of p. "64" is in *CC*, p. 132. For other contents see B77a, B78–B80, B81a, B82–B84, B87b.

E6a. Citation: *Journal* [vol. 4] A.ms., 143 sides. Ink (c) Pencil (r,d) Blue pencil (d). NNPM (MA 1302:4).

Title: Jan 23d 1841.

First line: A day is lapsing. I hear cockrils crowing in the yard, and see them stalking among the chips in the sun.

Collation: 74 leaves of white wove (type 23), 18.4 x 15.2 cm., paged "1–146"; bound, π^2 [A–F^{12}] + 2, pp. [1–152], with 2 leaves missing.

Date: [November 1841], dated "January 23–March 27 1841".

Contents: Transcribed and original entries; text in *J* 1:173–242. For other contents see B27b.

Note: Thoreau's transcription of the [Second vol.] ends on p. "33" of this volume. The entries after that point are presumably original, although he may have "gleaned" them from an unidentified source.

E6b. Citation: *Journal* [from vol. 4] A.ms., 13 sides. Ink (c). MH (MS Am 1280.214 [1]).

First line: The Sphinx is the pure intellect, seeking to render account of itself of the world——

Collation: 7 leaves,
  6 of white wove (type 11), 24.5 x 19.6 cm., pp. [1–12],
  1 of blue wove (type 2), 25.2 x 19.7 cm., pp. [13–14].

Date: [1843].

Contents: Fair copy of the entry for 10 March 1841; text varies from *J* 1:229–37.

Note: Thoreau possibly copied this analysis of Emerson's poem for publication, but the manuscript does not appear to belong with those in sections C or D.

E7. Citation: *Journal* [vol. 5] A.ms., 87 sides. Ink (c) Pencil (r,d). NNPM (MA 1302:5).

Title: Tuesday March 30th 1841

First line: I find my life growing slovenly when it does not exercise a constant suppression over itself.

Collation: 83 leaves of white wove, 21.6 x 16.5 cm., paged "1–144"; bound, π^2 [A–F^{12},G^8,H^{12}] + 2, pp. [1–192], with 13 leaves missing.

Date: 30 March–30 September 1841.

Contents: Original (or possibly transcribed) entries; text in *J* 1:242–87. For other contents see B33–B35, B36a, B37a, B38a, B39, B40a, B41a, B42, B43a, B45, B47a, B48a.

E8. Citation: *Journal* [vol. 6] A.ms., 139 sides. Ink (c) Pencil (r,d) Blue pencil (d). NNPM (MA 1302:6).

Title: Cambridge Nov. 29th 1841

First line: One must fight his way, after a fashion, even in the most civil and polite society;

Collation: 69 leaves of white wove, 20.7 x 17.5 cm., paged "4–141"; bound, π^2 [A–F^{12}] + 2, pp. [1–152], with 7 leaves missing.

Date: 12 November 1841 to 3 April 1842.

Contents: Original entries; text in J 1:287–360. For other contents see B50, B85–B86.

E9a.   Citation: *Journal* [vol. 7] A.ms., 8 sides. Ink (c) Pencil (r,d). MH (bMS Am 278.5 [4:E,F]).

First line: pulse out at that northeastern angle of the town. In the southeast part on either side of the stream

Collation: 4 leaves of white wove (type 17a), 24 x 19.5 cm., pp. [1–8], paged "91–92, 103–6, 119–20".

Date: 18 July, 8–9 August, 23 [August] 1842.

Contents: Original entries; text later used in "A Walk to Wachusett", *A Week*, and *Sir Walter Raleigh* (see W 5:136–37, 143; 1:365; *SWR*, pp. 91–92). For other contents see B89a. For a later copy of 19 July 1842 see D5k; for 28 July 1842 see E12a.

Note: These are the earliest entries to survive; [vol. 7] originally contained ca. 400 pages, covering 1842–1843.

E9b.   Citation: *Journal* [vol. 7] A.ms., 4 sides. Ink (c,r) Pencil (r,d). MH (bMS Am. 278.5 [4,G]).

First line: Gower writes like a man of common sense and good parts

Collation: 2 leaves of white wove (type 17a), 24 x 19.5 cm., pp. [151–52, 161–62].

Date: [September 1842].

Contents: Original entries; text later used in *A Week* (see J 1:450). For other contents see B21b.

E9c.   Citation: *Journal* [vol. 7] A.ms., 6 sides. Ink (c)
         Pencil (r,d). CSmH (HM 13182:III, 6–8).

         First line: Silently we unlatch the door—letting the
         drift fall in—

         Collation: 3 leaves of white wove (type 17a), 24 x
         19.2 cm., pp. [1–6], paged "193–98".

         Date: 14–15 October 1842.

         Contents: Original entries; text later used in "A
         Winter Walk" (see *W* 5:164–66). For late copies of
         29 September, 7 and 21 October 1842, see E12a. For
         other contents see B93a.

E9d.   Citation: *Journal* [vol. 7] A.ms., 6 sides. Ink (c)
         Pencil (r,d). MH (bMS Am 278.5 [4,E]).

         First line: I am charmed when in midsummer trav-
         ersing some remote fields set round with birchen leafy
         woods—

         Collation: 3 leaves of white wove (type 17a), 24 x
         19.5 cm., pp. [1–6], paged "239–40, 257–60".

         Date: 11 and 16 November 1842, 3 and 16 January
         1843.

         Contents: Original entries; text later used in *A Week*
         and *Walden* (see *W* 1:136, 201; 2:175).

E9e.   Citation: *Journal* [vol. 7] A.ms., 4 sides. Ink (c)
         Pencil (r,d). CSmH (HM 13182:I, 1–2).

         First line: my particular genius, I do embrace it: for
         even that vulgar and tavern-music, which makes one
         man merry, another mad,

         Collation: 2 leaves of white wove (type 17a), 24.2 x
         19.6 cm., pp. [1–4], paged "259".

         Date: [3 January 1843].

Contents: Original entries; extracted passage from the *Religio Medici* of Sir Thomas Browne.

E9f.   Citation: *Journal* [vol. 7] A.ms., 2 sides. Ink (c) Pencil (r,d). CSmH (HM 13182:III, 9).

Title: Wednesday

First line: Poetry is a purer draft of life.

Collation: 1 leaf of white wove (type 17a), 24 x 19.2 cm., pp. [1–2], paged "355–56."

Date: 11–[13] April 1843.

Contents: Original entries; text later used in *A Week* (see *W* 1:201). For other contents see B100.

E10a. Citation: *Journal* [vol. 8] A.ms., 2 sides. Ink (c) Pencil (r,d). MH (bMS Am 278.5 [4:F,G]).

First line: find any thought more warm and cheery than when I remember the summer—

Collation: 1 leaf of white wove (type 17a), 24 x 19.5 cm., pp. [1–2], paged "143–44".

Date: [14–18 April 1843].

Contents: Original entries or draft portions; text later used in "A Winter Walk" (see *W* 5:163). For other contents see B21b.

Note: This volume, its paper identical to that of [vol 7], contained about five hundred pages, covering April–August 1843. Thoreau exhausted this large notebook quickly, writing and then removing several long essay drafts.

E10b. Citation: *Journal* [vol. 8] A.ms., 1 side. Ink (c) Pencil (r,d). ICarbS.

First line: tent valor, such as they never witnessed— which never knew defeat nor fear.

Collation: 1 fragment of white wove (type 17a), 14 x 19.5 cm., pp. [1–2], paged "177".

Date: [14–18 April 1843].

Contents: Original entry or draft portion; text later used in "A Winter Walk" (see *W* 5:171–72). A facsimile is in Stoller, pp. 2–3. For other contents see B93b.

E10c.   Citation: *Journal* [vol. 8] A.ms., 5 sides. Ink (c) Pencil (r,d). MH (bMS Am 278.5 [4,F]).

First line: All the water on the globe insulates as in a kettle—and is either hastening to become ice or snow or ocean and vapor.

Collation: 3 leaves of white wove (type 17a), 24 x 19.2 cm., pp. [1–6], paged "179–80, 191–94, 197–98".

Date: 19 and 27 April, 19 May, 19 June 1843.

Contents: Original entries; text later used in "A Winter Walk" and *A Week* (see *W* 5:168, 178–80; 1:69, 405).

E10d.   Citation: *Journal* [vol. 8] A.ms., 6 sides. Ink (c) Pencil (r,d). MH (bMS Am 278.5 [4,F]).

First line: Tonight while I am arranging these sprigs of white cedar in my scrap-book

Collation: 3 leaves of white wove (type 17a), 24 x 19.5 cm., pp. [1–6], paged ["451–52, 463–64"].

Date: 14 and 25 [August]1843.

Contents: Original entries; text later used in *A Week* (see *W* 1:405).

E11a.   Citation: *Journal* [vol. 9] A.ms., 3 sides. Ink (c,r). TxU.

Title: Sat Aug 26 1843 —

First line: The future will no doubt be a more natural life than this.

Collation: 2 leaves of white laid (type 4), 24.8 x 19.4 cm., paged ["1–4"].

Date: 26 and 28 August, 1 September 1843.

Contents: Original entries; text later used in *A Week* (see *W* 1:280–81). An edited version is in R. W. Adams, *An Unpublished Bit of Thoreau's Journal* (Chapel Hill, N.C. [n.p., 1926]).

Note: A partial index of this volume appears on the inside front cover of [vol. 5] (E7). The original notebook contained about two hundred pages, covering August 1843–March 1844. Its covers survive at NNPM (MA 1823).

E11b.   Citation: *Journal* [vol. 9] A.ms., 2 sides. Ink (c,r). CSmH (HM 13182:I, 9).

Title: Sunday 24th Staten Is

First line: The poet is he that hath fat enough like bears and marmots to suck his claws o'winter.

Collation: 1 leaf of white laid (type 4), 24.8 x 19.2 cm., pp. [1–2], paged "5–6".

Date: 24 September 1843.

Contents: Original entries; text used in *A Week* (see *W* 1:101–2) and varies from *FLJ* 1:64–65.

E11c.   Citation: *Journal* [vol. 9] A.ms., 2 sides. Ink (c,r). MH (bMS Am 278.5 [4,C]).

First line: The villager crossing the bridge stood awhile to gaze at us gliding swiftly from his sight— following our other fates.

Collation: 1 leaf of white laid (type 4), 24.9 x 18.3 cm., pp. [1–2], paged "7–8".

Date: 25–26 [September] 1843.

Contents: Original entries; text used in *A Week* (see *W* 1:15–16). For a later copy see *J* 1:465–66.

E11d.   Citation: *Journal* [vol. 9] A.ms., 18 sides. Ink (c,r). CSmH (HM 13182:I, 10–18).

Title: Thursday 28th

First line: We have never conceived how many natural phenomena would be revealed to a simpler and more natural life.

Collation: 9 leaves of white laid (type 4), 24.9 x 18.3 cm., pp. [1–18], paged "9–16, 19–24, 27–30".

Date: 28 and 29 [September], 2–24 October, 1 November 1843.

Contents: Original entries; text used in *A Week* and *Walden* (see *W* 1:178, 358–59; 2:85–86, 342–43) and varies from *FLJ* 1:64–83. For other contents see B105–B106, B107a, B108a, B109a.

E11e.   Citation: *Journal* [vol. 9] A.ms., 2 sides. Ink (c) Blue pencil (n). ViU (6345–e:24).

First line: Meantime every one remembers by different principles, each of us seeking his proper food.

Collation: 1 leaf of white laid (type 4), 24.7 x 19.7 cm., pp. [1–2], paged "31".

Date: [1 November 1843].

Contents: Original entry; text unpublished.

Note: The handwriting on this ms. resembles Emerson's, but paper, text, and pagination correspond to those of [vol. 9].

E11f.   Citation: *Journal* [vol. 9] A.ms., 24 sides. Ink (c,r) Pencil (r,d). CSmH (HM 13182:I, 9–28, 3–4).

First line: You must store up none of the life in your gift—it is as fatal as to husband your breath.

Collation: 12 leaves of white laid (type 4), 24.9 x 19.2 cm., pp. [1–24], paged "33–52, 73–76".

Date: 1–21 November 1843, 7 January 1844, February [1844].

Contents: Original entries; text used in *A Week* (see W 1:91–92, 367–71, 391–92) and varies from *FLJ* 1:84–104. For a later version of pp. "73–76" see *J* 1:469–70. For other contents see B108a, B109a.

E11g.   Citation: *Journal* [vol. 9] A.ms., 2 sides. Ink (c,r). CSmH (HM 13182:II, 54).

First line: of the race the generation itself may be divine may be an inspired one. And the race of imperfect mortals die out.

Collation: 1 leaf of white laid (type 4), 25 x 19.2 cm., pp. "160–61".

Date: [February–March 1844].

Contents: Original entries; text unpublished.

E12a.   Citation: *Journal* [from vol. 1] A.ms., 26 sides. Ink (c) Pencil (r,d). NNPM (MA 1303).

First line: Yesterday I skated after a fox over the ice.

Collation: 13 leaves of white wove (type 1a), 31.8 x 19.8 cm., pp. [1–26], paged "137–75, 195–96"; bound.

Date: [1846–1847], dated "March 11 1845" to "March 13 1846".

Contents: Transcribed entries from [vols. 8, 9, 1]; text partly in *J* 1:438–87. For other contents see D1a.

Note: Thoreau's new numbering sequence for the *Journal* coincides with his Walden experiment, but his designations for specific volumes are uncertain until after May 1850. Between 1845 and 1850 several notebooks survive, which for convenience I have described as parts of two hypothetical volumes, [1–2], leading to the volume he numbered "3" in his second series. Thomas Blanding believes that possibly only E12b and E12c were numbered "1–2", and that leaves of an 1847 volume are at CSmH (HM 924, 956, 13182, 13194). For their descriptions see Section D.

E12b.   Citation: *Journal* [from vol. 1] A.ms., 134 sides. Ink (c) Pencil (r,d). NNPM (MA 1302:7).

First line: distant capes. Perhaps, we think, there may be neighbors still—as there used to be.

Collation: 35 leaves of white wove (type 22), 19.3 x 16.6 cm., paged "7–140"; bound, π^2 [A–F^{12}] + 2, pp. [1–152], with 41 leaves missing.

Date: [1845] to 22 February [1846].

Contents: Original entries; text in *J* 1:402–37. A facsimile of one leaf is in *MR* 4 (1962):153. For other contents see B146b, B147b, B163, D10e. For missing leaves see D10d.

Note: See D1a, Note.

E12c.   Citation: *Journal* [from vol. 1] A.ms., 82 sides. Ink (c) Pencil (r,d). NNPM (MA 1302:8).

Title: Henry D. Thoreau | March 26th 1846

First line: The change from foul weather to fair from blank sluggish hours to serene elastic ones

Collation: 43 leaves of white wove (type 22), 19.1 x 16.5 cm., paged "1–101"; bound, π^2 [A–F^{12}] + 2, pp.[1–152], with 33 leaves missing.

Date: 5 July [1845] to 26 March [1846].

Contents: Original entries; order of text varies from J 1:361–402. For other contents see B159–B161, D10c.

Note: See D1a, Note.

E12d. Citation: *Journal* [from vol. 1] A.ms., 90 sides. Ink (c,r) Pencil (r,d). NYPL (Berg).

Title: Walden April 17 1846

First line: Even nations are ennobled by affording protection to the weaker races of animals.

Collation: 45 leaves of green wove (type 2), 24.2 x 19.7 cm., pp. [1–90], paged "1–87, 243–75"; part of notebook, 125 leaves bound [A–M¹²], pp. [1–288], paged "1–275" with 19 leaves missing.

Date: 17 April to 2 December 1846.

Contents: Original entries, with field notes; text described in R. Gosbey, "Thoreau at Work: The Writing of 'Ktaadn'", *BNYPL* 65 (1961):21–30. See also D24a, Note. For other contents see D10f, D24a–b. For missing leaves see D10g–i.

E13a. Citation: *Journal* [vol. 2] A.ms., 61 sides. Ink (c,r) Pencil (r,n). CSmH (HM 13182:II, 1–33).

First line: 1 Swedenborg 58 verses transcend all thought 63 Left RWE

Collation: 34 leaves of blue wove (type 5), 24.6 x 19.7 cm., pp. [1–68], paged ["63–70, 75–80, 103–6, 139–48, 157–66, 173–76, 179–80, 189–92, 199–200, 215–16, 331–34, 337–40"].

Date: 30 July 1848 to October 1848.

Contents: Original entries; text later used in *A Week* (see W 1:4, 60, 66, 70–80, 131–33, 141, 148–50, 216, 275, 307); *Walden* (see W 2:48, 90, 110–13, 219–21, 356–58, 361); *The Maine Woods* (see W 3:82); *Cape Cod* (see W 4:64–65, 72, 90, 99–100, 225); "Walking" (see *W* 5:228–29); "Love" and "Chastity and Sensuality" (see *W* 6:199–204, 207). For other contents see B170. For other leaves see B19d, B109c, C9b–c, C150, D5c, D5j, D6b, D7b, D9g.

Note: This volume contained about five hundred pages, covering July 1848 to October 1850. Pagination sequence and textual references supplied by Thomas Blanding.

E13b.   Citation: *Journal* [vol. 2] A.ms., 2 sides. Ink (c,r) Pencil (r,d). MH (bMS Am 278.5 [2,6]).

First line: to discover that the earth is round, nor am I sure that a tortoise does not maintain it;

Collation: 1 leaf of blue wove (type 5) 24.5 x 19.7 cm., pp. [1–2], paged "60".

Date: [Before 30 July 1848].

Contents: Original entry; text later used in *Walden* (see *W* 2:353–54).

E13c.   Citation: *Journal* [vol. 2] A.ms., 2 sides. Ink (c) Pencil (r). TxU.

First line: Who doubts the influence of the character on the bodily features,

Collation: 1 leaf of blue wove (type 5) 24.7 x 19.5 cm., pp [1–2]; mounted.

Date: [August 1848], dated* "1843".

Contents: Original entry; text unpublished.

E13d.   Citation: *Journal* [vol. 2] A.ms., 8 sides. Ink (c,r) Pencil (r,d). CSmH (HM 13206).

First line: for it was many times freezing cold weather. (We noticed that the vessels were anchored at a distance from the shore

Collation: 4 leaves of blue wove (type 5), 24.7 x
19.5 cm., pp. [1–8], paged "351–58"; laid in with
Cape Cod mss.

Date: [October 1849].

Contents: Original entries; text unpublished but intended for *Cape Cod*.

E13e.   Citation: *Journal* [vol. 2] A.ms., 2 sides. Ink (c,r)
Pencil (r,d). CSmH (HM 13182:II, 34).

First line: Tom Hydes dying speech. When Tom
standing in the gallows was asked if he had anything
to say

Collation: 1 leaf of blue wove (type 5), 24.6 x 19.7
cm., pp. [1–2], paged "383".

Date: 28 October 1849.

Contents: Original entry; text later used in *Walden*
and *Cape Cod* (see W 2:360–31; 4:97). For other
contents see B169.

E13f.   Citation: *Journal* [vol. 2] A.ms., 2 sides. Ink (c,r)
Pencil (r,d). NYPL (Ms. Division).

First line: cause it to swell—small drops of resin(?)
stand out on every side of the twigs,

Collation: 1 leaf of blue wove (type 5), 24.8 x 19.4
cm., pp. [1–2], paged "387".

Date: [30 October 1848].

Contents: Original entry; text unpublished. For other
contents see B170.

E13g.   Citation: *Journal* [vol. 2] A.ms., 2 sides. Ink (c,r)
Pencil (r,d). CSmH (HM 13182:II, 35–9).

First line: How happens it that one we love can
ever do us wrong?—For thinking wrong & doing
wrong are one.

Collation: 4 leaves of blue wove (type 5), 24.6 x
19.7 cm., pp. [1–8], paged ["389–92, 397–402"].

Date: 9–10 December 1849 to 5 January 1850.

Contents: Original entries; text later used in *A Week*
(see *W* 1:386–91); *Cape Cod* (see *W* 4:255); and
"Love" (see *W* 6:201–3). For other contents see B171.

E13h. Citation: *Journal* [vol. 2] A.ms., 4 sides. Ink (c)
Pencil (r,d). VtMiM.

First line: I cannot imagine a woman no older than
I. The feminine is the mother of the masculine.

Collation: 2 leaves of blue wove (type 5), 24.8 x
19.7 cm., pp. [1–4], paged "417–20"; in folder marked
"Fragments".

Date: [January–February 1850].

Contents: Original entry; text later used in *A Week*
(see *W* 1:287). For a later version see E15c.

E13i. Citation: *Journal* [vol. 2] A.ms., 2 sides. Ink (c,r,d)
Pencil (n,p). TxU.

First line: We never tire of the beauty of certain
epithets which have been gradually bestowed by mankind, on the Harvest and Hunter's moons.

Collation: 1 leaf of blue wove (type 5), 24.8 x 19.8
cm., pp. [1–2], paged "423–24".

Date: [February 1850].

Contents: Original entry; text later used in "Night
and Moonlight" (see *W* 5:331–32).

E13j. Citation: *Journal* [vol. 2] A.ms., 24 sides. Ink (c,r)
Pencil (r,d). CSmH (HM 13182:II, 40–51).

First line: is confidence and successful love—but
when one rises above and laps over the other——

Collation: 15 leaves of blue wove (type 5), 24.6 x 19.7 cm., pp. [1–30], paged ["433–48, 453–54, 457–62"].

Date: 24 February to 19 April 1850.

Contents: Original entries; text later used in *Walden* (see *W* 2:243, 336, 364), "Walking" (see *W* 5:227–28), and "Love" (see *W* 6:198–201). An edited version of pp. ["440–45"] is in Kern, pp. [9–14].

E14.   Citation: *Journal* [vol. 3] A.ms., 163 sides. Ink (c,n) Pencil (r). NNPM (MA 1302:9).

First line: The Hindoos are more serenely and thoughtfully religious than the Hebrews—

Collation: 52 leaves of blue wove (type 5), 24.5 x 19.7 cm., paged "1–165"; bound π^2 [A–H^{10}] + 2, pp. [1–168], with 32 leaves missing.

Date: 12 May to 19 September 1850.

Contents: Original entries; text in *J* 2:3–69. For other contents see B158, B173a, B174–B177, B178a, B179, B180a, B181–B182. For missing leaves see D20.

E15a.   Citation: *Journal* [vol. 4] A.ms., 101 sides. Ink (c,r) Pencil (r,p). NNPM (MA 1302:10).

First line: I am glad to have drunk water so long as I prefer the natural sky to an opium eater's heaven—

Collation: 39 leaves of white wove (type 7), 24.9 x 19.6 cm., paged "1–165"; bound, π^2 [A–H^{10}] + 2, pp. [1–168], with 45 leaves missing.

Date: 25 September to 2 December 1850.

Contents: Original entries; text in *J* 2:69–121. For other contents see B183a.

E15b.   Citation: *Journal* [from vol. 4] A.ms., 2 sides. Ink (c,d). NNPM (MA 920).

First line: up are the Carpenter and the Cook. I conversed with the former and the Mate,

Collation: 1 fragment of white wove (type 7), 12.1 x 19.1 cm., pp. [1–2]; mounted, formerly bound in Set No. 516 of the Manuscript Edition.

Date: [16 June 1850].

Contents: Original entry; text resembles J 2:49, 78–79. An edited version is in K. W. Cameron, "Thoreau's Notes on the Shipwreck at Fire Island", *ESQ*, No. 52 (1968), pp. 97–99.

E15c.   Citation: *Journal* [from vol. 4] A.ms., 6 sides. Ink (c). CSmH (HM 13182:II, 52–54).

First line: The feminine is mother of the masculine and the latter still draws nourishment from the breast of the former.

Collation: 3 leaves of white wove (type 7), 25 x 19.2 cm., pp. [1–6], paged "160–61".

Date: [November 1850].

Contents: Original entries; text later used in "Love" (see *W* 6:198–200). For an early version see E13h.

E16.   Citation: *Journal* [vol. 5] A.ms., 256 sides. Ink (c,r) Pencil (r,d). NNPM (MA 1302:11).

Title: Wednesday. Dec. 4th 1850

First line: Fair Haven Pond is now open—and there is no snow.

Collation: 123 leaves of blue wove (type 11), 24.1 x 17.9 cm., paged "1–256"; bound, π^2 [A–Q^8] + 2, pp. [1–264], with 9 leaves missing.

Date: 4 December 1850 to 7 July 1851.

Contents: Original entries; text in *J* 2:121–292. For other contents see B184.

E17.   Citation: *Journal* [vol. 6] A.ms., 169 sides. Ink (c,n) Pencil (r,d). NNPM (MA 1302:12).

Title: Tuesday July 8th 1851

First line: Walked along the clam-shell bank after sundown—a cloudy sky.

Collation: 86 leaves of blue wove (type 5), 24.4 x 19.8 cm., paged "1–163"; bound, π^2 [A–H^{10}] + 6, pp. [1–176], with 2 leaves missing.

Date: 8 July to 20 August 1851.

Contents: Original entries; text in *J* 2:292–408. For other contents see B122a.

E18.   Citation: *Journal* [vol. 7] A.ms., 189 sides. Ink (c,n) Pencil (r,d). NNPM (MA 1302:13).

Title: Aug 21st 1851

First line: To a great extent the feudal system still prevails there (in Canada) and I saw that I should be a bad citizen.

Collation: 97 leaves of blue wove (type 11), 24 x 18.2 cm., paged "3–183"; bound, π^2 [A^{10}, B^8, C^{10}, D–L^8] + 5; pp. [1–194].

Date: 21 August to 7 October 1851.

Contents: Original entries; text in *J* 2:412–3:55. For other contents see B183b.

E19.   Citation: *Journal* [vol. 8] A.ms., 186 sides. Ink (c,n) Pencil (r,d). NNPM (MA 1302:14).

Title: Oct. 7th 51.

First line: 1 pm to river by boat to Corner Bridge A very still warm bright clear afternoon.

Collation: 94 leaves of blue wove (type 10), 24 x 18.7 cm., paged "1–181"; bound, π^2 [A^{10}, B–L^8] + 2, pp. [1–188].

Date: 7 October 1851 to 11 January 1852.

Contents: Original entries; text in J 3:55-184. For other contents see B185.

E20. Citation: *Journal* [vol. 9] A.ms., 243 sides. Ink (c,n) Pencil (r,d). NNPM (MA 1302:15).

Title: Monday Jan 12th '52

First line: G. says that he studied lichens a little while, but he found that if you pursued that study you must give up man.

Collation: 124 leaves of blue wove (type 10), 24.1 x 18.6 cm., paged "1-237"; bound, π^2 [A-P^8] + 2, pp. [1-248].

Date: 12 January to 28 March 1852.

Contents: Original entries; text in J 3:184-260.

E21. Citation: *Journal* [vol. 10] A.ms., 148 sides. Ink (c,n) Pencil (r,d). NNPM (MA 1302:16).

Title: March 29th '52

First line: An Eskimo—one of a littoral people— inquired with surprise of Sir John Richardson, "Are not all lands islands?"

Collation: 76 leaves of blue wove, 25.5 x 19.5 cm., paged "1-143"; bound, π^2 [A^{12}, B-G^{10}] + 2, pp. [1-152].

Date: 29 March to 27 April 1852.

Contents: Original entries; text in J 3:360-474.

E22. Citation: *Journal* [vol. 11] A.ms., 243 sides. Ink (c,n) Pencil (r,d). NNPM (MA 1302:17).

Title: April 28th 1852

First line: I scarcely know why I am excited when in M. Huc's book I read

Collation: 124 leaves of blue wove (type 7), 24.5 x 19.3 cm., paged "1–236"; bound, π^2 [A–M^{10}] + 2, pp. [1–248].

Date: 28 April to 8 July 1852.

Contents: Original entries; text in J 3:474–4:203.

E23. Citation: *Journal* [vol. 12] A.ms., 183 sides. Ink (c,n) Pencil (r,d). NNPM (MA 1302:18).

Title: Friday July 9th '52

First line: 4 AM—to Cliffs—no dew—no dewy cobwebs—The sky looks mistlike no clear blue.

Collation: 94 leaves of blue wove, 24 x 19.3 cm., pp. "1–178"; bound, π^2 [A^{10}, B–L^8] + 2, pp. [1–188].

Date: 9 July to 31 August 1852.

Contents: Original entries; text in J 4:204–330.

E24. Citation: *Journal* [vol. 13] A.ms., 164 sides. Ink (c,n) Pencil (r,d) Blue pencil (d). NNPM (MA 1302:19).

Title: Aug 31st—'52 continued

First line: feather. The broad dense & now lower and flatter border of button bushes—

Collation: 84 leaves of blue wove (type 7), 24.5 x 19.3 cm., paged "1–162"; bound, π^2 [A–H^{10}] + 2, pp. [1–168].

Date: 31 August 1852 to 7 January 1853.

Contents: Original entries; text in J 4:330–456. For other contents see B188.

E25. Citation: *Journal* [vol. 14] A.ms., 84 sides. Ink (c,n) Pencil (d) Blue pencil (d). NNPM (MA 1302:20).

Title: Jan. 8th '53

First line: I see what are probably the mother cells distinctly in the large buds of the poplar—

Collation: 42 leaves of white wove (type 24), 18.2 x 15.5 cm., paged "1–83"; bound, π^1 [A–D^{10}] + 1, pp. [1–84].

Date: 8 January to 8 March 1853.

Contents: Original entries; text in J 4:456–5:12.

E26.   Citation: *Journal* [vol. 15] A.ms., 506 sides. Ink (c,n) Blue pencil (d). NNPM (MA 1302:21).

Title: Wednesday March 9th '53

First line: Rain—dissolving the snow & raising the river. I do not perceive that the early elm or the white maple buds have swollen yet.

Collation: 256 leaves of white wove (type 20), 22.9 x 18.7 cm., paged "1–499"; bound, π^2 [A–V^{12}] + 2, pp. [1–512].

Date: 9 March to 18 August 1853.

Contents: Original entries; text in J 5:12–379. "Pond Kalendar", a record of thaws and freezes for local ponds, appears on the inside front cover.

E27.   Citation: *Journal* [vol. 16] A.ms., 461 sides. Ink (c,r,n) Pencil (r,d,n). NNPM (MA 1302:22).

Title: Friday Aug 19th '53

First line: 9 Am to Sudbury by boat with W.E.C. Cooler weather—

Collation: 234 leaves of white wove, 23.9 x 19 cm., paged "1–459"; bound, [A^8, B–J$^{28/20}$, K^{28}, L^6], pp. [1–468], with 1 leaf missing.

Date: 19 August 1853 to 12 February 1854.

Contents: Original entries; text in J 5:379–6:121. For other contents see D15d.

E28. Citation: *Journal* [vol. 17] A.ms., 468 sides. Ink (c,r,n) Pencil (d,p). NNPM (MA 1302:23).

Title: Monday Feb 13th 54 | 7 Am to Walden—

First line: A warm morning—overcast—the ice does not sing when I strike it with an axe.

Collation: 236 leaves of white wove (type 19), 23.7 x 19.2 cm., paged "1–467"; bound, [A^8, B–J$^{28/20}$, K^{28}, L^8], pp. [1–472]. Paging of [L] is irregular, owing to improper collation when the volume was rebound.

Date: 13 February to 2 September 1854.

Contents: Original entries; text in J 6:121–7:7. For other contents see B190.

E29. Citation: *Journal* [vol. 18] A.ms., 439 sides. Ink (c,r) Pencil (p,n). NNPM (MA 1302:24).

Title: Sunday Sep. 3d '54

First line: Fair weather & a clear atmosphere after // 2 days of mizzling—

Collation: 223 leaves of white wove (type 19), 23.5 x 18.5 cm., paged "1–439"; bound, [A^{16}, B^{20}, C^{24}, D–E^{20}, F^{28}, G^{20}, H–K^{24}] + 3, pp. [1–446].

Date: 3 September 1854 to 12 May 1855.

Contents: Original entries; text in J 7:8–375.

Note: Thoreau's // symbol indicates items appearing in his index of this volume.

E30. Citation: *Journal* [vol. 19] (A.ms., 276 sides. Ink (c,r) Pencil (r) Blue pencil (d). NNPM (MA 1302:25).

Title: May 13th 1855

First line: PM. down river—& to Yel. birch swamp. Yesterday was the first warm day for a week or 2—

Collation: 140 leaves of white laid, 25 x 19 cm.; bound, [A¹⁴⁰], pp. [1–280]. Miscellaneous clippings and notes laid in.

Date: 13 May 1855 to 3 January 1856.

Contents: Original entries; text in *J* 7:375–8:83.

E31.   Citation: *Journal* [vol. 20] A.ms., 270 sides. Ink (c) Pencil (r) Blue pencil (d). NNPM (MA 1302:26).

Title: Account of the Jones Family | The Long Snowy Winter | Jan 4th 1856

First line: A clear cold day—pm. to Walden to examine the ice.

Collation: 140 leaves of blue laid (type 3), 24.8 x 18.4 cm.; bound, [A¹⁴⁰], pp. [1–280]. Miscellaneous clippings and notes laid in.

Date: 4 January to 23 April 1856.

Contents: Original entries; text in *J* 7:83–301.

E32.   Citation: *Journal* [vol. 21] A.ms., 330 sides. Ink (c) Pencil (r) Blue pencil (d). NNPM (MA 1302:27).

Title: Ap. 23 '56

First line: where you go jumping from one to another —The farms are now dotted with the minute reddish staminate flowers ready to open—

Collation: 170 leaves of white laid (type 3), 24.8 x 18.8 cm.; bound, [A¹⁷⁰], pp. [1–340]. Miscellaneous fragments laid in.

Date: 23 April to 6 September 1856.

Contents: Original entries; text in *J* 8:301–9:65.

E33.   Citation: *Journal* [vol. 22] A.ms., 309 sides. Ink (c) Pencil (r) Blue pencil (d). NNPM (MA 1302:28).

Title: The Cold Winter & Warm Feb. | Sunday
Sep. 7' 1856 | At Brattleboro Vt

First line: Am. Climbed the hill behind Mr. Addi-
son Brown's.

Collation: 160 leaves of white laid (type 3), 24.9 x
18.8 cm.; bound, [A¹⁶⁰], pp. [1–320]. Miscellaneous
clippings laid in.

Date: 7 September 1856 to 1 April 1857.

Contents: Original entries; text in J 9:65–315.

E34.   Citation: *Journal* [vol. 23] A.ms., 342 sides. Ink (c)
Pencil (r,d). NNPM (MA 1302:29).

Title: April 2d 1857 | Go to New Bedford

First line: A great change in the weather. I set out
apple trees yesterday—

Collation: 170 leaves of white laid (type 3), 25 x
18.8 cm., paged "2–332"; bound, [A¹⁷⁰], pp. [1–340].
Miscellaneous notes laid in.

Date: 2 April to 31 July 1857.

Contents: Original entries; text in J 9:315–497, but
longer than J 9:485–97.

E35.   Citation: *Journal* [vol. 24] A.ms., 309 sides. Ink (c)
Pencil (r,d). NNPM (MA 1302:30).

Title: Friday July 31st '57 | Continued [underscored]
— | PM. E. Branch of Penobscot [four words under-
scored] River —

First line: We were expecting all the while that the
river would take a final leap to get to smooth water—

Collation: 161 leaves,
     160 of white laid (type 3), 24.9 x 18.8 cm.,
     1 of white laid (anom.);
bound, [A¹⁶⁰] + 1, pp. [1–332], paged "2–322".
Miscellaneous notes and clippings laid in.

Date: 31 July to 25 November 1857.

Contents: Original entries; text in J 9:497–10:206, but longer than 9:497–503. For other contents see B192–B194.

E36. Citation: *Journal* [vol. 25] A.ms., 326 sides. Ink (c) Pencil (r,d). NNPM (MA 1302:31).

Title: The Open Winter | Nov 23d (25th) 1857 continued [underscored]

First line: It is surprising how much—from the habit of regarding writing as an accomplishment—is wasted on form.

Collation: 168 leaves of white laid (type 3), 24.9 x 18.7 cm.; bound, [A¹⁶⁸], pp. [1–336]. Miscellaneous clippings and notes laid in.

Date: 25 November 1857 to 11 June 1858.

Contents: Original entries; text in J 10:206–478.

E37. Citation: *Journal* [vol. 26] A.ms., 65 sides. Ink (c) Pencil (n). NNPM (MA 1302:32).

Title: June 4th '58 continued [underscored]—

First line: The lofty-beaked promontory—which when you were on the summit appeared as far off & almost equal to it—

Collation: 34 leaves of blue wove, 25.9 x 19.5 cm.; bound, [A³⁴], pp. [1–68].

Date: 4 June to 8 July 1858.

Contents: Original entries; text in J 10:478–11:29.

E38. Citation: *Journal* [vol. 27] A.ms., 156 sides. Ink (c) Pencil (r) Blue pencil (d). NNPM (MA 1302:33).

Title: At Camp in Tuckerman's Ravine | Friday July 9th 1858 —

First line: Walked to the Hermit Lake some 40 rods NE.

Collation: 172 leaves,
   170 of white laid (type 2), 25.3 x 20 cm.,
   2 of blue laid (type 3), 24.8 x 19.6 cm.;
bound, π^4 [A^{166}] + 2, pp. [1–344]. Miscellaneous clippings laid in.

Date: 9 July to 9 November 1858.

Contents: Original entries; text in J 11:29–301.

E39a.   Citation: *Journal* [vol. 28] A.ms., 343 sides. Ink (c) Pencil (r,d) Blue pencil (d). NNPM (MA 1302:34).

Title: Nov 9th 1858 continued [underscored]

First line: The newspaper tells me that Uncannoo-muc was was [sic] white with snow for a short time on the morning of the 7th.

Collation: 176 leaves of blue laid (type 4), 24.7 x 19 cm.; bound, [A^{176}], pp. [1–352].

Date: 9 November 1858 to 7 April 1859.

Contents: Original entries; text in J 11:301–12:119. For other contents see F14.

E39b.   Citation: *Journal* [Field notes, vol. 28] A.ms., 2 sides. Ink (c) Pencil (r,d). ViU (6345–e:15).

First line: I have seen one [type of] often larger pinweed

Collation: 1 leaf of white wove (anom.), pp. [1–2].

Date: [December 1858].

Contents: Notes for an entry; text unpublished.

E40a.   Citation: *Journal* [vol. 29] A.ms., 302 sides. Ink (c) Pencil (r) Blue pencil (d). NNPM (MA 1302:35).

Title: Friday Ap. 8th 59

First line: I believe that I rarely hear the nuthatch's note from the elms toward evening,

Collation: 158 leaves,
    156 of white laid (type 2), 25.2 x 19.9 cm.,
    2 of white wove (type 13), 24.6 x 19.4 cm.;
bound, [A^{156}] +2, pp. [1–316].

Date: 8 April to 21 September 1859.

Contents: Original entries; text in J 12:119–339.

E40b.   Citation: *Journal* [Field notes, vol. 29] A.ms., 2 sides. Pencil (c,r) Ink (d). MCon.

Title: Friday 13th

First line: I have been here much longer than I expected Night warbler (perhaps 11th) Apple bloom

Collation: 1 fragment of white wove (type 13), 12.3 x 19.4 cm., pp. [1–2]; in folder marked "Coat Manuscript".

Date: [13–15 May 1859].

Contents: Notes for entries; text resembles J 12:187–88.

E41.   Citation: *Journal* [vol. 30] A.ms., 316 sides. Ink (c) Pencil (r,d) Blue pencil (d). NNPM (MA 1302:36).

Title: Sep. 22 — 1859

First line: A mizzling day—with less rain than yesterday // filling the stream.

Collation: 162 leaves of white wove (type 6), 25.1 x 18.8 cm.; bound, [A^{162}], pp. [1–324].

Date: 22 September 1859 to 13 February 1860.

Contents: Original entries; text in J 12:339–13:145. For other contents see B197.

E42.   Citation: *Journal* [vol. 31] A.ms., 324 sides. Ink (c) Pencil (r,d) Blue pencil (d). NNPM (MA 1302:37).

Title: The early Spring | Feb. 15th 1860

First line: As in the expression of moral truths we admire any closeness to the physical fact

Collation: 166 leaves of blue laid (type 4), 24.6 x 19.2 cm.; bound, [A¹⁶⁶], pp. [1–332]. Miscellaneous notes tipped in.

Date: 15 February to 22 July 1860.

Contents: Original entries; text in J 13:145–415. For other contents see B198.

E43.   Citation: *Journal* [vol. 32] A.ms., 334 sides. Ink (c) Pencil (r,d) Blue pencil (d). NNPM (MA 1302:38).

Title: July 23 — 1860

First line: The button bush is —— just fairly beginning here & there.

Collation: 172 leaves,
     170 of blue laid (type 4), 24.7 x 19.3 cm.,
     2 of white laid (type 5), 24.5 x 19.5 cm.;
bound, [A¹⁷⁰] + 2, pp. [1–344], paged "2–334". Miscellaneous fragments laid in.

Date: 23 July to 22 November 1860.

Contents: Original entries; text in J 13:415–14:260.

E44a.   Citation: *Journal* [vol. 33] A.ms., 106 sides. Ink (c) Pencil (r,d) Blue pencil (d). NNPM (MA 1302:39).

Title: Nov. 23 — 60

First line: Geo. Minott tells me that 60 years ago— wood was only 2 or 3 dollars a cord here.

Collation: 106 leaves of white wove (type 6), 25.1 x 19.2 cm., paged "1–63"; bound, [A¹⁰⁶], pp. [1–212]. Exactly half of the volume, pp. [106–212], is blank.

Date: 20 November 1860 to 3 November 1861.

Contents: Original entries; text in J 14:260–346.

E44b. Citation: *Journal* [Field notes, vol. 33] A.ms., 103
sides. Pencil (c,r,d) Ink (n*). CSmH (HM 13192).

First line: 7 AM May 27—I last evening called on
Mr. Thatcher.

Collation: 54 leaves,
   51 of white laid (type 5, folded), 19.5 x 12.3 cm.,
   2 of white laid (type 2, folded), 20.1 x 16.2 cm.,
   1 of white laid (anom.),
pp. [1–108], paged "1–97".

Date: 11 May to 19 August 1861.

Contents: Notes on the Minnesota journey, never
written into the *Journal.* The text of *FLJ* is corrupt;
a properly edited version is in W. Harding, *Thoreau's
Minnesota Journey* (Geneseo, N.Y.: Thoreau Society,
1962), pp. 1–44.

F.

NOTES AND NOTEBOOKS, 1835–1862

This section of the calendar is unfamiliar territory to most of Thoreau's readers; even to many scholars it represents unexplored ground. Always an inveterate jotter of notes, he refined the habit in college, later compiled extracts as a literary exercise, and finally made notebooks a major part of his life's business. A scrupulous archivist, he stored most of these papers in a large trunk, now in the Thoreau Collection of the Concord Free Public Library. Although the manuscripts are now widely scattered, they once rested in this common locker, a companion to the *Journal* and its custom-built case of yellow pine.

I have arranged this material chronologically, with occasional exceptions; yet it also follows a topical order of its own. Thoreau's "College Notes" (F1–F2) bear the imprint of his early studies; his "Reading Notes" (F3–F8) are the tools of a struggling professional writer; and the late items (F9–F32) reflect the growth of his continuing self-education. This final group divides into three large subsections: "Canada and the Indians", "Surveying and Natural History", and "Nature Notes".

The papers in Section A, Student Writings, are original compositions; these notes derive from Thoreau's reading while at Harvard and shortly thereafter. Consisting mostly of long verbatim extracts and brief comments, the notes provide a valuable record of his early ideas and tastes, both before and after meeting with Emerson in late 1837. The "Index Rerum" (F2) contains both notes and original compositions, indicating that it may have served Thoreau as an experimental prototype for the *Journal*.

F1a. Citation: [College Notes] A.ms., 4 sides. Ink (c). NNPM (MA 920).

Title: Musings.

First line: It was always my delight to monopolize the little Gothic window, which overlooked the kitchen garden, particularly of a Sabbath afternoon,

Collation: 2 leaves of white wove (type 3), 25.2 x 20 cm., pp. [1–4]; mounted, bound.

Date: 20 April 1835.

Contents: Early draft of autobiographical notes; text varies from *HDT*, pp. 152–54.

Note: Professor Channing assigned an autobiographical theme in the fall of 1836, but Thoreau elected other topics at that time (see A16–A20). For later notes of a similar nature see F2d.

F1b. Citation: [College Notes] A.ms., 24 sides. Ink (c) Pencil (c). ViU (6345).

First line: "Retire—the world shut out—thy thoughts call home—

Collation: 12 leaves of white wove, 22.6 x 18.5 cm., pp. [1–24]; mounted, bound.

Date: [Fall] 1835.

Contents: Extracts of English and American authors: E. Young, S. Johnson, W. Godwin, H. Longfellow, F. Cooper, W. Irving. For text see *TM* 1:130–43, passim.

F1c. Citation: [College Notes] A.ms., 3 sides. Ink (c) Pencil (n*). ViU (6345).

Title: Coleridge in Moxen's — Book Says

First line: "When the whole and the parts are seen at once, as mutually producing and explaining each other,

Collation: 2 leaves of gray wove (type 4), 24.3 x 19.5 cm., pp. [1–4]; bound.

Date: December [18]36.

Contents: Notes on Coleridge and Plato, with extracts.

F1d. Citation: [College Notes] A.ms., 2 sides. Ink (c) Pencil (n*). ViU (6345).

Title: Extracts from Philothea.

First line: "The simple fact that the human soul was thought to be of another world,

Collation: 1 leaf of gray wove (type 4), 24.6 x 19.1 cm.; bound.

Date: [Ca. 1836].

Contents: Notes on Plato, with extracts.

F1e. Citation: [College Notes] A.ms., 14 sides. Ink (c). ViU (6345).

Title: The Principal Philosophical Systems, | and their purport—as distinguished | by Degerando in the | "Historie Comparee Des Systems De | Philosophie" [French title underscored]

First line: Five Periods [underscored] | Period 1st— From the origin of philosophy to Socrates.

Collation: 7 leaves of gray wove (type 3), 25 x 20 cm., pp. [1–14]; bound.

Date: [Ca. 1836].

Contents: Notes and translated extracts; text in *TM* 1:248–53.

F1f.   Citation: [College Notes] A.ms., 2 sides. Ink (c) Pencil (c). RPB.

Title: Question: How can $\dfrac{1}{a} = a^{-1}$?

First line: This will be manifest if the student but attend to the manner of forming a series of powers in a retrograde order.

Collation: 1 fragment of white wove, 16.7 x 18.9 cm., pp. [1–2].

Date: 10 July 1837.

Contents: Fair copy of a class exercise.

F2a.   Citation: ["Index Rerum"] A.ms., 77 sides. Ink (c) Pencil (c). CSmH (HM 945).

Title: D. H. Thoreau | Cambridge | Index Rerum

First line: From Hugh Murray's Hist. of Ind. Fam. Lin. "The Macedonian does not seem to have been himself inclined

Collation: 39 leaves,
    37 of white wove, 20 x 16 cm.,

2 of blue laid, 20 x 15.2 cm.,
pp. [1–78], paged "1–38"; bound, π^2 [A–E^{10}, X^2, F^{10}, G^{16}] + 2, pp. [1–164], with 43 leaves missing.

Date: 31 March 1836 to 11 November 1837; 1840; [1856].

Contents: Notes on reading: Murray, Hindu scripture, Cromwell. Original compositions: book reviews and poems. A facsimile text appears in *TM* 1:130–358 passim. For an edited text of the book reviews see W. Glick, "Three New Early Manuscripts by Thoreau", *HLQ* 15 (November 1951):59–71.

F2b.   Citation: [from the "Index Rerum"] A.ms., 2 sides. Ink (c). CSmH (HM 13201:5v).

Title: Education.

First line: value of a systematical plan of, Stew. Phil. V.I. p. 20 et 44.

Collation: 1 leaf of white wove, 21 x 15.5 cm., pp. [1–2].

Date: [After October 1836].

Contents: Notes on reading, arranged in alphabetical order; text in *TM* 1:368–71. For contents of verso see B10c.

F2c.   Citation: [from the "Index Rerum"] A.ms., 2 sides. Ink (c) Pencil (c). CSmH (HM 13201:9v).

Title: Washington.

First line: Compared with Buonopart. Chateaubriand. Voy. en Amerique et Italie. Vol. I. p. 27.

Collation: 1 leaf of white wove, 20 x 15.7 cm., pp. [1–2].

Date: [1836–1837].

Contents: Notes on reading, arranged in alphabetical order; text in *TM* 1:368–71. For contents of verso see B31.

F2d.   Citation: [from the "Index Rerum"] A.ms., 2 sides. Pencil (c) Ink (n). ViU (6345–e, 23).

First line: the cheek, and spoiled my collar at the risk of losing my dinner.

Collation: 1 fragment of white wove, 19.1 x 12.2 cm., pp. [1–2]; mounted.

Date: [After spring 1837].

Contents: Early draft of autobiographical notes.

Note: Thoreau's marginal note reads "Merely for the sake of writing". For earlier notes of a similar nature see F1a.

Reading Notes, 1837–1850

This material corresponds to the chronology of section B, Poems and Translations, and to the early years of sections C, D, and E. Most of these "notes" are extracts only, copied or paraphrased by Thoreau from his reading in literature and philosophy. Very few original comments appear, testifying either to the imitative quality of his early writing or to the *Journal*, which absorbed most of his original efforts. As with the early *Journal* volumes, Thoreau's "Commonplace Books" (F4–F5, F7–F8) bear the cut pages and deletion marks indicating that he "harvested" them for publication. The fact that these are bound notebooks, however, may anticipate the vast, methodical projects that were to follow.

F3.   Citation: [Reading Notes] A.ms., 49 sides. Ink (c, r,d) Pencil (r,d). NNPM (MA 608).

First line: Any book of great authority and genius would seem to our imagination to permeate and pervade all space.

Collation: 25 leaves of white wove (type 21), 20.2 x 16.7 cm., pp. [1–50], paged "2–126"; bound, [A–G¹²], pp. [1–168], with 59 leaves missing.

Date: [1842], dated "1837" to "1842".

Contents: Notes and comments on various books and authors with special emphasis in the later pages on Hindu literature. A facsimile text is in *TC* 3:901–69. For other contents see D1b. For missing leaves see B16d, B17a, B18a, B31, B87, D5e.

F4a.   Citation: [Commonplace Book: 1] A.ms., 164 sides. Ink (c) Pencil (c,r,d). NNPM (MA 594).

Title: Miscellaneous extracts | Cambridge, Mass., Nov. 1836

First line: Hollis 23. William Sewel, a historian and lexicographer, was born in 1654,

Collation: 88 leaves of white wove (type 10), 24.8 x 20.3 cm., paged "5–165"; bound, π^2 [A^{12}, B–G^{10}, H^{12}] + 2, pp. [1–176].

Date: November 1836 to November 1839; [January 1843].

Contents: Extracts, notes on literature and philosophy; facsimile text in *TM* 2:130–358, 374–80, passim. For other leaves see B28b, B29b, B74b.

F4b.　Citation: [from Commonplace Book: 1] A.ms., 2 sides. Ink (c) Pencil (c). NNPM (MA 1720).

First line: Orpheus "Argonautica" — and other poems

Collation: 1 leaf of white wove (type 10), 24.1 x 20.3 cm., pp. [1–2].

Date: [1838–1839].
Contents: List of classical authors and titles; text in *TM* 2:366–67.

F4c.　Citation: [from Commonplace Book: 1] A.ms., 2 sides. Pencil (c). CSmH (HM 13201:7v).

First line: 1st Each ex. to be written on a single piece of paper, not less than half a sheet.

Collation: 1 fragment of white wove (type 10), 12.1 x 20.2 cm., pp. [1–2].

Date: [1839–1840].

Contents: Six rules for preparing class papers. For other contents see B16a.

F4d.　Citation: [from Commonplace Book: 1] A.ms., 1 side. Pencil (c). RPB.

Title: Last Note on Geom. Prog. in Day's Algebra.

First line: (There is a geom. prog. of four numbers, such that the last is 24 more than the second,

Collation: 1 leaf of white wove (type 10), 23.5 x 19.9 cm., pp. [1–2]; bound in copy of F. B. Sanborn, *The Personality of Thoreau* (Boston: C. E. Goodspeed Co., 1901).

Date: 18 January 1840.

Contents: Notes from a mathematical text, probably for classroom preparation.

F5.   Citation: [Commonplace Book: 2] A.ms., 65 sides. Ink (c) Pencil (c). CSmH (HM 957).

First line: —Searo hwit sola | Sumur het cola, —

Collation: 71 leaves of white wove (type 19) 23.8 x 19.3 cm., paged "1–67"; bound, π^2 [A^{10}, B–G$^{6/14}$, H^{10}] + 2, pp. [1–164], with 11 leaves missing.

Date: 30 November 1841 to [ca. 1843].

Contents: Extracts, with notes on English poetry and drama, 1300–1800.

Note: Sophia Thoreau wrote dated entries on books and travel in this volume between 1870 and 1876.

F6a.   Citation: [Reading Notes] A.ms., 4 sides. Ink (c). NBu.

Title: Mortal Glory.

First line: If Rome's great power, and AEgypt's wisdom can

Collation: 2 leaves of white wove (type 11), 24.6 x 19.4 cm., pp. [1–4]; mounted.

Date: [Ca. 1842–1843].

Contents: Extracts of the poetry of Francis Quarles, arranged under topic headings.

Note: Thoreau may have copied F6a–d for *A Week*.

F6b.   Citation: [Reading Notes] A.ms., 2 sides. Ink (c)
        Pencil (c). ViU (6345).

        First line: "The inquiry is into the means of pre-
        cluding the three sorts of pain"—which constitute the
        pain of life—

        Collation: 1 leaf of white wove (type 11), 24.4 x
        19.3 cm., pp. [1–2]; bound.

        Date: [Ca. 1842].

        Contents: Extracts of Hindu scripture, with some
        original sentences.

F6c.   Citation: [Reading Notes] A.ms., 2 sides. Ink (c)
        Pencil (c). NYPL (Ms. Div.).

        Title: The Sankhya Karika.

        First line: The term Karika "designating a collection
        of memorial verse, or apothegmatical stanzas,

        Collation: 1 leaf of white wove (type 11), 24.5 x
        19.3 cm., pp. [1–2].

        Date: [Ca. 1842].

        Contents: Notes and translated extracts from a French
        version of Hindu scripture.

        Note: This copy is a photostat; the original ms. was
        sold in 1949.

F6d.   Citation: [Reading Notes] A.ms., 21 sides. Ink (c)
        Pencil (c,d). RPB.

        Title: Gil Mornice | Old Scot. Ballad in | Gilchrist's
        Scot. Ballads

        First line: —His brow was like the mountain snow

        Collation: 12 leaves of white wove, 17.1 x 10.3;
        wrapped [A¹²], pp. [1–24].

        Date: [1840–1843].

Contents: Extracts and notes on English poetry and drama, 1300–1800. For another description see B. L. St. Armand, "Thoreau Comes to Brown", *BBr* 22 (1968): 126–40.

F7.   Citation: [Commonplace Book: 3] A.ms., 347 sides. Ink (c) Pencil (n,p). DLC (Poetry Archive).

First line: desert still keeps in advance of the immigrant and fills the cavities of the forest for his repast.

Collation: 182 leaves of white wove (type 2), 31.1 x 19.5 cm., paged "3–361"; bound, π^2 [A–M^{16}] + 2, pp. [1–392], with 14 leaves missing.

Date: [December 1840 to November 1848].

Contents: Notes and extracts on English poetry (1450–1650), Greek philosophy, and Hindu scripture. Facsimile text appears in K. W. Cameron, *Thoreau's Literary Notebook in the Library of Congress* (Hartford, Conn.: Transcendental Books, 1964). See also *TM* 1:293 ff. For missing leaves see B10d, B11a, B91b, B96a.

F8.   Citation: [Commonplace Book: 4] A.ms., 222 sides. Ink (c) Pencil (r,d). NYPL (Berg).

Title: Henry D. Thoreau.

First line: The Shepherd's Love for Philliday. (From The Muses Garden.)

Collation: 136 leaves of white wove, 23.8 x 19.2 cm., paged "1–269"; bound, π^2 [A–L^{12}] + 2, pp. [1–272].

Date: [1842–1843], [1850].

Contents: Notes and extracts on English poetry (1300–1600) and Hindu scripture. A facsimile page and description of the ms. appear in *ESQ*, No. 13 (1958), p. 105.

Canada and Indian Notebooks

These twelve notebooks, totaling over 3,000 manuscript pages, are a monumental labor of love. Their principal subject is aboriginal North America: its people, geography, and history. Into these volumes Thoreau wrote nearly a million words of text, recording ideas and facts gathered from more than a decade of careful study. His notebooks contain lengthy verbatim extracts, many pages of translation or paraphrase; and occasionally some passages of original writing. He also laid in various notes and clippings for future reference. The size of his volumes reflects the scope of his interest, expanding from 60 to 600 pages in six years (1850–1856), and then diminishing to less than 50 pages annually after 1857.

Exactly what Thoreau planned to do with all this data is uncertain. The notebook on Canada (F9) contributed to some of his publications, but he never indexed or "harvested" the Indian notebooks (F10a–k). In his own mind that project may have become, like the *Journal*, a task of intrinsic merit. Apparently he thought of them as physical parallels, for between 1853 and 1860 the *Journal* volumes and Indian notebooks are identical in paper and format (see E24–E44). Yet Thoreau may have actually planned to write a book on the Indians. A few inserts in his early volumes resemble a table of contents, and some original passages in volume [6] try to organize and clarify his basic ideas. But nothing like an outline or prospectus of a book survives. As his knowledge grew, his ambition to publish seemed to wane.

Previous descriptions of the Indian notebooks have been somewhat inaccurate, owing to their bulk and the illegibility of Thoreau's hand. Most observers, for example, have assumed that the notebooks have no chronological order. Herbert Cahoon, curator of manuscripts at the Morgan Library, greatly assisted my own studies by locating a complete type transcript of the notebooks, prepared by Professor Arthur Christy of Columbia University in the early 1930s. This extraordinary document, housed in fifteen large spring binders, is a literatim transcript, each page a typed facsimile of a page of Thoreau's manuscript. Professor Christy's footnotes correct spellings, suggest textual emendations, and identify Thoreau's sources. The dates of these sources follow a definite chronological sequence, as Thoreau kept up with new publications in the field, and thus his notebooks can be dated accordingly.

An additional typescript (NNPM: Pamphlets C553), entitled "Bibliography of Thoreau's American Indian Notes", lists in alphabetical order the 221 books and 52 articles identified as Thoreau's sources. Professor Christy was preparing an edition of the notebooks; his letter of 2 March 1932 (NNPM: Curator's File) describes his plans and comments humorously on the task of transcription. But his project found no publisher; during World War II the papers were stored in a basement vault and forgotten. Mr. Cahoon rediscovered them shortly before I began my own investigation.

In the following descriptions I have ignored H. G. O. Blake's numbering system of "1–12", which appears on the labels he affixed to the volumes. The Canada notebook is unique and therefore unnumbered, but the series of Indian notebooks I have numbered [1–11]. Thus my number [4] bears Blake's number "5", and so on.

F9.   Citation: "Canadian Notebook" A.ms., 137 sides. Ink (c) Pencil (r,d). NNPM (MA 595).

Title: Books on Canada at Cam. | Gray's Canada 1 vol.

First line: p.1 Author of Hochelaga makes the St Lawrence 120 miles wide at its mouth—

Collation: 54 leaves of white wove (type 21), 19.8 x 16.5 cm., pp. [1–108]; bound, π^2 [A–G^8] + 2, pp. [1–120], with 6 leaves missing.

13 leaves, laid in,
    2 of white wove (type 16), 24.7 x 19.2 cm.,

1 of white laid, 19.2 x 11.7 cm.,
1 of blue laid (type 1), 24.8 x 19.9 cm.,
4 of blue wove (anom.),
1 fragment of blue wove, 12.5 x 19.5 cm.,
4 of white wove (type 16), 24.6 x 19.3 cm., folded
   and paged "28–41",
1 of white laid (anom.),
pp. [1–26].

Date: 18 November 1850 to [1852] (volume), 4
September 1855 to March 1856 (laid in).

Contents: Notes and extracts on the history, geography, and cartography of Canada and eastern America; later used in *A Yankee in Canada* and *Cape Cod*. Some notes on "hydraulics" were used in *Walden*. For another description see L. Willson, "Thoreau's Canadian Notebook", *HLQ* 22 (1958–59):179–200. A facsimile text appears in *TC* 2:310–411.

F10a.   Citation: "Indian Notebook" [1] A.ms., 84 sides. Ink (c) Pencil (r,d). NNPM (MA 596).

Title: Interesting houses,—localities etc. in Mass. | mentioned in Barber's Hist. Coll.

First line: Bug ate out of a table in Williamstown 73 years after the egg was laid.

Collation: 41 leaves of white wove (type 23), 18.4 x 15.6 cm.; bound, π^1 [A^{16}, B^8, C^{16}] + 1, pp. [1–84], with 1 leaf missing.

Date: [Ca. 1849].

Contents: Notes and extracts from books published 1843–1849; text in A. Christy transcripts, binder 1 (NNPM).

F10b.   Citation: "Indian Notebook" [2] A.ms., 62 sides. Ink (c) Pencil (r,d). NNPM (MA 597).

Title: Facts from Charlevoix's Voyage to America.

First line: The Indians baited their figure 4 beaver traps with "small bits of tender wood newly cut."

Collation: 31 leaves of white wove (type 21), 20.1 x 16.6 cm.; bound, [A³²], pp. [1–64], with 1 leaf missing.

Date: [Ca. 1850].

Contents: Notes and extracts from books published 1845–1848; text in A. Christy transcripts, binder 1 (NNPM).

F10c.   Citation: "Indian Notebook" [3] A.ms., 117 sides. Ink (c) Pencil (r,d). NNPM (MA 598).

Title: At Athenaeum | A. W. Bradford's Am. Antiquities 184[ ], large 8vo. | Drakes' Tragedies of the Wilderness 1–12mo 1841.

First line: Warburton | "The natives [of Newfoundland] met with in the first discovery were Esquimaux;

Collation: 60 leaves of white wove (type 6), 19.8 x 16.5 cm.; bound, π^2 [A–G⁸] + 2, pp. [1–120].

Date: [Ca. 1851].

Contents: Notes and extracts from books published 1846–1851; text in A. Christy transcripts, binder 2 (NNPM).

F10d.   Citation: "Indian Notebook" [4] A.ms., 124 sides. Ink (c) Pencil (r,d). NNPM (MA 599).

Title: Peter Kalm Sep 9th 51 | Continued from last book.

First line: They employ tree-mushrooms very frequently instead of tinder.

Collation: 64 leaves of white wove (type 21), 20.1 x 16.5 cm.; bound, π^2 [A–E¹²] + 2, pp. [1–128].

Date: [Ca. 1851–1852].

Contents: Notes and extracts from books published 1849–1851; text in A. Christy transcripts, binder 3 (NNPM).

F10e.   Citation: "Indian Notebook" [5] A.ms., 167 sides. Ink (c) Pencil (n). NNPM (MA 600).

Title: Arctic Searching Expedition [two words partially underscored] &c by Sir John Richardson 1852.

First line: In harvest time the natives row their canoes among the grass,

Collation: 84 leaves of blue wove, 20 x 16.2 cm.; bound, π^2[A–H^{10}] + 2, pp. [1–168].

Date: [Ca. 1852].

Contents: Notes and extracts from books published 1851–1852; text in Christy transcripts, binder 4 (NNPM).

F10f.   Citation: "Indian Notebook" [6] A.ms., 159 sides. Ink (c) Pencil (n). NNPM (MA 601).

Title: "Relation" for '34 continued.

First line: They join their drums & their songs (chants) I asked the origin of this drum,

Collation: 84 leaves of blue wove (type 7), 24.5 x 19.1 cm., paged "1–69"; bound, π^2 [A–H^{10}] + 2, pp. [1–168]. Pages [106–60] contain inverted text, paged "1–53".

Date: [Ca. 1853].

Contents: Notes and extracts from books published 1852–1853; text in A. Christy transcripts, binder 5 (NNPM).

F10g.   Citation: "Indian Notebook" [7] A.ms., 499 sides. Ink (c) Pencil (r,n). NNPM (MA 602).

Title: Brefeuf's Relation of the Hurons for '36 continues— | about the punishment of murder.

First line: There are two kinds of presents some "as they go first" which are given to the relatives of the dead to appease them;

Collation: 256 leaves of white wove (type 20), 23 x 18.1 cm.; bound, π^2 [A–V^{12}] + 2, pp. [1–512]. Laid in, 1 leaf of blue laid, 24.8 x 19.5 cm., pp. [1–2].

Date: [Ca. 1854].

Contents: Notes and extracts from books published 1853–1854; text in A. Christy transcripts, binders 6 and 7 (NNPM).

F10h. Citation: "Indian Notebook" [8] A.ms., 209 sides. Ink (c) Pencil (r). NNPM (MA 603).

Title: Le Grand Voyage Du Pays Des Hurons &c

First line: "Avec un Dictionaire de la Langue Huronne," par Fr. Gabriel Sagard Theodat. [name underscored]

Collation: 218 leaves of white wove (type 19), 23.7 x 18.8 cm.; bound, π^2 [A^{20}, B–E$^{16/24}$, F^{24}, G^{18}, H–K^{24}] + 2, pp. [1–436].
15 leaves, laid in,
    14 of white wove (anom.),
    1 of blue laid (type 3), 24.8 x 19.6 cm.,
pp. [1–30].

Date: [Ca. 1856].

Contents: Notes and extracts from books published 1855–1856; text in A. Christy transcripts, binders 8 and 9 (NNPM).

F10i. Citation: "Indian Notebook" [9] A.ms., 659 sides. Ink (c) Pencil (r). NNPM (MA 604).

Title: Loskiel Continued [twice partially under-scored]

First line: 129 | Even in forsaken dwellings, the Ind. can discover of what nation the former inhab-itants were,

Collation: 334 leaves of blue laid (type 3), 24.8 x 19.6 cm.; bound, [A–O²⁴], pp. [1–672], with 2 leaves missing.

Date: [Ca. 1856].

Contents: Notes and extracts from books published 1855–1856; text in A. Christy transcripts, binders 10 and 11 (NNPM).

F10j.   Citation: "Indian Notebook" [10] A.ms., 196 sides. Ink (c) Pencil (n). NNPM (MA 605).

Title: Relation for 62 & 63 | by Heirosme Lalemant

First line: The Indians "au dessoubs de Tudoussacq."

Collation: 99 leaves of blue wove (type 4), 24.7 x 19.4 cm.; bound, π² [A–H¹²] + 2, pp. [1–200], with 1 leaf missing.

Date: [Ca. 1857].

Contents: Notes and extracts from books published 1856–1857; text in A. Christy transcripts, 198 pp. unbound (NNC: Christy Collection, No. 15).

F10k.   Citation: "Indian Notebook" [11] A.ms., 348 sides. Ink (c) Pencil (n). NNPM (MA 606).

Title: La Borde [underscored] on the Caraibes | continued

First line: They think they have many souls — the 1st in the heart the 2nd in the head, and the others in all the joints,

Collation: 174 leaves of blue laid (type 4), 24.7 x 18.3 cm.; bound, [A¹⁷⁴], pp. [1–348].

Date: [Ca. 1861].

Contents: Notes and extracts from books published 1857–1861; text in A. Christy transcripts, binders 14 and 15 (NNPM).

Surveying and Natural History Notebooks

Strictly speaking, some of these papers may not seem to qualify as "literary manuscripts". Thoreau's surveying notes and notebooks (F11–F12) document his major source of income in the late years, mostly in rather flat and prosaic terms. Yet surveying made its own contribution to the writer's craft, providing Thoreau with experiences, ideas, and even metaphors of substantial importance.[1] Except for the "Concord River Survey" (F13), a piece that combines careful research and excellent draftmanship, I have omitted the many survey drawings by Thoreau that still survive. A volume of these surveys is under preparation by Mrs. William H. Moss of the Concord Free Public Library. The library has a large collection of surveys, several of which helped me to confirm the dates of certain paper types Thoreau used between 1850 and 1860.

The two large notebooks (F15–F16), sometimes called "Fact Books", mostly contain extracts from Thoreau's reading. Unlike the "Commonplace Books" of his earlier days, however, these notebooks bear no signs of "harvesting". Thoreau certainly used some of this material in his late publications, but by this time he had discontinued the "cut and paste" methods that mutilated so many of his earlier manuscript volumes.

F11.   Citation: [Notes on Surveying] A.ms., 8 sides. Ink (c). MCon.

First line: In certain cases, especially in northern latitudes, even when the secondary maximum & minimum are not formed,

---

1. See Fig. 12, Note.

Collation: 10 leaves of white wove (type 18), 24 x 19.2 cm., pp. [1–20]; in folder marked "Notes for Surveying Plans".

Date: [1849–1851].

Contents: Notes and extracts from books published 1846–1851.

F12.   Citation: [Survey Notebook] A.ms., 133 sides. Ink (c) Pencil (r). MCon.

Title: Field Notes | of | Surveys | made by Henry D. Thoreau | Since | November 1849

First line: Isaac Watts' Woodlot [three words twice underscored]. Nov. 1849

Collation: 76 leaves of blue wove, 19.8 x 16.5 cm., paged "1–111"; bound, π^2 [A–F^{12}] + 2, pp. [1–152]. Several fragments (anom.) laid in.

Date: November 1849 to 2 January 1861.

Contents: Notes, drawings, accounts received; text in *TC* 2:413–549, and published separately as *Thoreau's . . . Record of Surveys* (Hartford, Conn.: Transcendental Books, 1967). For another description see A. F. McLean, Jr., "Thoreau's True Meridian: Natural Fact and Metaphor", *AQ* 20 (1968): 567–79.

F13.   Citation: [Concord River Survey] A.ms., 52 sides. Pencil (c,r) Ink (r,n). MCon.
Title: Statistics of the Bridges over Concord River, between Heards' Bridge | & Billerica Dam, obtained June 22, 23, & 24 1859

First line: June 20 | Name South Bridge | Material Wood

Collation: 34 leaves of white wove (type 12), 24.7 x 19.5 cm., pp. [1–68]; in folder marked "The Concord River Project".

Date: 20 June to 22 July 1859.

Contents: Statistical tables on water levels, rate of flow, and so on, at the various bridges.

Note: MCon also has Thoreau's survey map of the river, over 2 miles long, bearing his additional notes on topography and vegetation.

F14.   Citation: [Notes for River Survey] A.ms., 4 sides. Ink (c). NNPM (MA 1302:34).

Title: "Principes D'Hydraulique" &c | par M. Dubuat | A Paris 1806

First line: vol 1 | p. 82 "We must conclude that the bed, of the figure of a trapezium [sketch]

Collation: 2 leaves of white wove (anom.) laid in [vol. 28] of the *Journal*.

Date: [After 15 August 1859].

Contents: Translated extracts from a French volume on hydrology. Text and facsimile, including the French source, are in K. W. Cameron, "Thoreau's Notes from Dubuat's *Principes*", *ESQ*, No. 22 (1961), pp. 68–76.

F15.   Citation: "Fact Book" A.ms., 354 sides. Ink (c) Pencil (r,d). MH (Harry Elkins Widener Collection).

Title: Halcyon Days

First line: "By some [of the ancients] it was superstitiously supposed that this bird exercised a controlling influence over the winds and waves

Collation: 182 leaves of blue wove (type 12), 20.9 x 17.4 cm., paged "3–353"; bound, π^1 [A–P^{12}] + 1, pp. [1–364]. Laid in, 2 leaves of white wove (anom.), pp. [1–4]; several clippings [1854–1856], and ts. index.

Date: [1853 to 1858].

Contents: Notes and extracts from books published 1851–1858; facsimile text in K. W. Cameron, *Thoreau's Fact Book . . . in the Harvard College Library*, 2 vols. (Hartford, Conn.: Transcendental Books, 1966). For another description see A. Christy, "A Thoreau Fact-Book", *Colophon* 4 (1934): Part 16.

F16.   Citation: [Commonplace book: 5] A.ms., 282 sides. Ink (c,n) Pencil (r,d). NYPL (Berg).

Title: Coleridge's Conversation.

First line: "And these little points [underscored] of business being settled

Collation: 184 leaves of blue wove (type 12), 20.9 x 17.3 cm., paged* "1–280"; bound, π^2[A–P^{12}] + 2, pp. [1–368]. Laid in, miscellaneous items and ts. description of contents.

Date: [1853 to 1860].

Contents: Notes and extracts from books on travel and natural science.

Nature Notes

During the last six years of his life Thoreau spent many hours compiling tables, indexes, and other notes on the natural phenomena described in his *Journal* between 1851 and 1861. These "nature notes" fall into four general categories: the seasons, plant life, animal life, and miscellanea. Exactly why he compiled all this data is uncertain. His notes on fruits and seeds were clearly part of intended publications, and some observers believe that his seasonal notes were for a projected "Calendar" (or "Kalendar"), a book about an archetypal year in the Concord region.

Since he left no clear indication of his motives, we can only speculate about the purpose and order of these materials. In the hope of clarifying their contents, I have conjectured two groupings that Thoreau, with his preference for natural structure, might also have conceived: the "Calendar" notes follow a seasonal cycle, spring to winter (March to February); and the "Plant Life" notes follow an organic cycle (leaves to seeds). The "Animal Life" and "Miscellaneous" notes appear in their chronological order. The first item (F17) actually belongs to a much earlier period, but it appears here for comparison with Thoreau's later studies.

F17.   Citation: [Nature Album] A.ms., 132 sides. Ink (c,r) Pencil (c,r,d). NYPL (Berg).

Title: Order | $1 \frac{rst}{\prime\prime}$ (Rapacious) | Falcon

First line: A female osprey—or Fish Hawk seen flying at the cliff March 27th 1842—

Collation: 66 leaves of white wove (type 1), 32 x 19.9 cm.; bound, $\pi^1[A-F^{16/8}, G^8] + 1$, pp. [1–164], paged* "1–132," with 16 leaves missing. Laid in, several miscellaneous fragments.

Date: September 1836 to 27 March 1842.

Contents: Zoological and botanical album, with plant specimens laid in; dated entries by John, Henry, and Sophia Thoreau. For another description see G. S. Hellman, Boston *Transcript*, 6 January 1909. Reprinted in *TSB* 46 (1954).

Note: Thoreau wrote an amusing preface to his own entries in this album, beginning "It may be as well if first of all I should give some account of my own species and variety. I am about five feet 7 inches in height—. . . . " For other contents by Thoreau see B40b, B41b, B90, C4a. For missing leaves see B9.

F18a.   Citation: [Nature Notes: March] A.ms., 4 sides. Ink (c,r,d) Pencil (r,n). RPB.

Title: On Mar. v 18 p. 295 & 306–319 328–331

First line: 51 | Elm & willow catkin Mar. 23

Collation: 2 leaves of white wove (type 13), 24.7 x 19.6 cm., pp. [1–4].

Date: [After 2 March 1859].

Contents: Notes on March phenomena, 1851–1857, compiled from the *Journal*.

F18b.   Citation: [Nature Notes: March] A.ms., 18 sides. Ink (c) Pencil (r,d). CSmH (HM 13202).

Title: Calendar for March

First line: Sleighing ends 1st. Grey narrow-winged insect about ice.

Collation: 9 leaves,
    6 of white laid (type 5), 24.5 x 19.5 cm.,
    3 of white wove (type 13), 24.6 x 19.4 cm.,
pp. [1–18], foliated* "2–9".

Date: [After March 1860].

Contents: Notes on March phenomena, 1853–1860, compiled from the *Journal*. For contents of versos, see C16b.

Note: Thoreau probably compiled these notes for his *Journal* entry on "The story of March," J 13: 222–29.

F18c.   Citation: [Nature Notes: March] A.ms., 2 sides. Ink (c) Pencil (c). NYPL (Berg: 35B)

Title: 59 March only complete except miscellaneous | & v. under March papers.

First line: Bluebirds in Worcester Feb. 24

Collation: 1 leaf of white laid (anom.), 21.4 x 13.2 cm., pp. [1–2].

Date: [After 3 April 1859].

Contents: Notes on March phenomena, 1859, compiled from the *Journal*.

Note: The numbers assigned to Berg items in this section are accession numbers, not call numbers. They appear on the manuscript folders, but not in the card catalogue of the collection. As a convenience, I have recorded only the last two digits of each number.

F18d.   Citation: [Nature Notes: March] A.ms., 4 sides. Ink (c,r) Pencil (r,d). NNPM (RV 12–C).

First line: River when lowest in Mar.

Collation: 2 leaves of gray laid, 37.8 x 31.3 cm., pp. [1–4], foliated* "44–45."

Date: [1860].

Contents: Notes on March phenomena, 1851–1860, compiled from the *Journal*.

F18e.   Citation: [Nature Notes: March] A.ms., 5 sides. Ink (c,r,d) Pencil (c,r). NYPL (Berg: 04B)

Title: 55

First line: Warm rain 1st (v. 5 '53)

Collation: 3 leaves of white wove (anom.), 20.7 x 13.3 cm., pp. [1–6].

Date: [After March 1860].

Contents: Notes on March phenomena, 1852–1860, compiled from the *Journal.*

F19a.   Citation: [Nature Notes: April] A.ms., 2 sides. Ink (c,n*). CSmH (HM 13198).

Title: April 51

First line: Tortoises drop into brooks Mar 30

Collation: 1 leaf of blue wove (anom.), 21.3 x 12.2 cm., pp. [1–2].

Date: [After 18 January 1854].

Contents: Notes on April phenomena, 1851–1853, compiled from the *Journal.* Text of verso, a court summons, appears in *Corr.,* p. 318.

F19b.   Citation: [Nature Notes: April] A.ms., 18 sides. Ink (c,r,d) Pencil (r,d). CSmH (HM 13203).

Title: General Phenomena for April

First line: 53 | Rain drops on mullein leaves 1st.

Collation: 9 leaves,
    7 of white laid (type 5), 24.5 x 19.5 cm.,
    2 of white wove (type 12), 24.7 x 19.5 cm.,
pp. [1–18]; versos paged "1, 18, 60a, 60b".

Date: [After April 1860].
Contents: Notes on April phenomena, 1851–1860, compiled from the *Journal.* For contents of versos see C16a.

F19c.   Citation: [Nature Notes: April] A.ms., 2 sides. Ink (c) Pencil (n). NNPM (MA RV 12–C).

Title: General Phenomena for April

First line: Ap 1st Walden open ear. of 13 years.

Collation: 1 leaf of gray laid, 37.8 x 31.3 cm., pp. [1–2], foliated* "7".

Date: [Ca. 1860].

Contents: Notes on April phenomena, 1852–1860, compiled from the *Journal.*

F19d. Citation: [Nature Notes: April] A.ms., 4 sides. Ink (c). CtY (Za 9).

Title: Rain in 56 April

First line: Ap. 3' 1st rain for a very long time in west.

Collation: 2 fragments of white laid (anom.), 19.5 x 13, pp. [1–4].

Date: [After 16 April 1860].

Contents: Notes on April weather, 1853–1860, compiled from the *Journal.*

F19e. Citation: [Nature Notes: April] A.ms., 2 sides. Ink (c). NNPM (RV 12–C).

Title: Earliest Flowering of April Flowers

First line: Alnus incana | Mar 30. 51

Collation: 1 leaf of gray laid, 37.8 x 31.3 cm., pp. [1–2], foliated* "8".

Date: [Ca. 1860].

Contents: Notes on April flowers, 1852–1860, compiled from the *Journal.*

F19f. Citation: [Nature Notes: April] A.ms., 4 sides. Ink (c). NNPM (RV 12–C).

Title: Growth — leafing in April & ferns — grass &c &c

First line: Swollen red maple buds at dist. Ap. 1st
52 —

Collation: 2 leaves of white laid (type 5), 24.4 x
19.5 cm., pp. [1–4], foliated* "20".

Date: [Ca. 1860].

Contents: Notes on April vegetation, 1852–1860,
compiled from the *Journal.*

F19f[1]. Citation: [Nature Notes: April] A.ms., 2 sides. Ink
(c). MH-Z.

Title: Birds for April &c in order of earliest arrival of
each ever noticed.

First line: Y.C. wren

Collation: 2 leaves of gray laid, 38 x 32 cm., pp.
[1–4].

Date: [After 16 May 1860].

Contents: Notes on bird sightings, 1852–1860, compiled from the *Journal.*

F19g. Citation: [Nature Notes: April] [see Section H].

F20a. Citation: [Nature Notes: May] A.ms., 12 sides. Ink
(c). NNPM (RV 12–C).

Title: General Phenomena for May

First line: 51 | 18 Turning point betw. summer &
winter & birds in full blast.

Collation: 7 leaves,
    6 of white laid (type 5), 24.4 x 19.5 cm.,
    1 of gray laid, 37.8 x 31.3 cm.,
pp. [1–14], foliated* "21–24".

Date: [Ca. 1860].

Contents: Notes on May phenomena, 1852–1860,
compiled from the *Journal.*

F20b.   Citation: [Nature Notes: May] A.ms., 22 sides. Ink (c,r) Pencil (r,d). NNPM (RV 12–C).

Title: Growth Leafing &c &c for May

First line: 23   60   flags center of E. Musquash

Collation: 11 leaves of white laid (type 5), 24.4 x 19.5 cm., pp. [1–22], foliated* "9–11, 13–19".

Date: [Ca. 1860].

Contents: Notes on May vegetation, 1850–1860, compiled from the *Journal*.

F21a.   Citation: [Nature Notes: June] A.ms., 14 sides. Ink (c,r) Pencil (n). NNPM (RV 12–C).

Title: General Phenomena—with sedges grasses ec. — | for June

First line: June 7 – '51 A gentle straight down rainy day — a fishing day

Collation: 7 leaves,
     4 of white laid (type 5), 24.4 x 19.5 cm.,
     3 of white laid (type 1), 32 x 19.5 cm.,
pp. [1–14], foliated* "25–29".

Date: [Ca. 1860].

Contents: Notes on June phenomena, 1851–1860, compiled from the *Journal*.

F21b.   Citation: [Nature Notes: June] A.ms., 6 sides. Ink (c,r) Pencil (n). NYPL (Berg: 97B).

Title: Growth Leafing &c [for June]

First line: June continued 53——

Collation: 3 leaves of white laid (type 5), 24.5 x 19.4 cm., pp. [1–6].

Date: [Ca. 1860].

Contents: Notes on June foliage, 1853–1860, compiled from the *Journal*.

Note: Notes for July, August, and September do not survive. Thoreau was apparently most interested in the spring, fall, and winter seasons.

F22a.   Citation: [Nature Notes: October] A.ms., 4 sides. Ink (c). NYPL (Berg: 13B).

Title: General Phenomena for October (& Fall of Leaves)

First line: 51 | Twilight much shorter than a month ago—stars brighter at night—1

Collation: 2 leaves of (anom.), misc. size and color, pp. [1–2].

Date: [Ca. 1860].

Contents: Notes on October phenomena and foliage, 1851–1852, compiled from the Journal.

F22b.   Citation: [Nature Notes: October] A.ms., 18 sides. Ink (c) Pencil (n). NNPM (RV 12-C).

Title: General Phenomena for October (& fall of leaf)

First line: 51 continued | A severe frost — Oct. 17th

Collation: 9 leaves of (anom.), misc. size and color, pp. [1–18], foliated* "30–38".

Date: [Ca. 1860–1861].

Contents: Notes on October phenomena and foliage, 1851–1861, compiled from the Journal. For contents of versos see K. W. Cameron, A Companion to Thoreau's Correspondence (Hartford, Conn.: Transcendental Books, 1964), pp. 197–235.

F22c.   Citation: [Nature Notes: October] A.ms., 2 sides. Ink (c) Pencil (r). CtY (Za 14).

Title: General Phenomena for October

First line: Rain Lowest

Collation: 2 leaves of white wove, 35.5 x 21.5 cm., pp. [1–4].

Date: [After 24 December 1861].

Contents: Notes on October phenomena, 1852–1861, compiled from the *Journal*.

F22d. Citation: [Nature Notes: October] A.ms., 1 side. Ink (c) Pencil (r). VtMiM.

Title: 59

First line: Oct 23 — 59   wood hulls coupled

Collation: 1 fragment of white laid (type 5), 12.2 x 19.1 cm., pp. [1–2].

Date: [After 13 November 1861].

Contents: Notes on autumnal phenomena, 1859–1861 compiled from the *Journal*. For contents of verso see *Corr.*, p. 629.

F23a. Citation: [Nature Notes: November] A.ms., 2 sides. Ink (c,r,d) Pencil (r,d). CtY (Za 1).

Title: General Phenomena for November (& Fall of Leaf)

First line: 51   Crickets sound faintly

Collation: 1 leaf of blue wove (anom.), pp. [1–2].

Date: [After 18 April 1855].

Contents: Notes on November phenomena and foliage, 1850–1851, compiled from the *Journal*. Verso contains business a.l.s. to John Thoreau.

F23b. Citation: [Nature Notes: November] A.ms., 4 sides. Ink (c,r) Pencil (r). MH (MS Am 278.5.20 [2]).

Title: General Phenomena for Nov. with Fall of |
Leaf & Nov. Flowers

First Line: A flock of larks singing

Collation: 2 leaves of white wove (anom.), pp. [1–4].

Date: [Ca. 1858].

Contents: Notes on November phenomena, 1853
and 1858, compiled from the *Journal*. Versos contain
business a.l.s. to John Thoreau, 1854–1855.

F23c. Citation: [Nature Notes: November] A.ms., 32
sides. Ink (c,r) Pencil (c,r,d). NYPL (Berg: 13B).

Title: General Phenomena for Nov. (with Fall of
leaf | & Nov. flowers)

First line: 53 continued | Gossamer Day — (but
not as perfect as Oct 31st) 19th

Collation: 16 leaves of (anom.). misc. color and
size, pp. [1–32], paged "5–22".

Date: [Ca. 1861].

Contents: Notes on November phenomena, 1853–
1861, compiled from the *Journal*. Versos contain business a.l.s. to John Thoreau, 1853–1858. For other
contents see K. W. Cameron, *A Companion to Thoreau's Correspondence*, pp. 197–235.

F23d. Citation: [Nature Notes: November] A.ms., 8 sides.
Ink (c,r) Pencil (c,r,d). NYPL (Berg: 13B).

Title: [Miscellaneous Notes] incl. November Flowers

First line: Nuthatch | Crow's nest

Collation: 8 leaves of (anom.), misc. color and size,
pp. [1–16], foliated* "41–50".

Date: [Ca. 1861].

Contents: Notes on November flowers, 1853–1861, compiled from the *Journal*. Versos contain business a.l.s. to John Thoreau, 1853–1858.

F23e.   Citation: [Nature Notes: November] A.ms., 12 sides. Ink (c) Pencil (r,n). NNPM (RV 12-C).

Title: Fall of Leaf

First line: Bay-berry

Collation: 6 leaves of white wove, 35.3 x 21.5 cm., pp. [1–12], foliated* "41–43".

Date: [Ca. 1861]

Contents: Complete tabulation of notes on November foliage, 1851–1861.

F23f.   Citation: [Nature Notes: November] A.ms., 4 sides. Ink (c) Pencil (r). NNPM (RV 12-C).

Title: General Phenomena for November

First line: River Lowest Nov 9 fallen more than 1 foot since last observed

Collation: 2 leaves of white wove, 35.5 x 21.5 cm., pp. [1–4], foliated* "39–40".

Date: [Ca. 1861].

Contents: Notes on November phenomena, 1851–1861, compiled from the *Journal*.

F24a.   Citation: [Nature Notes: December] A.ms., 1 side. Ink (c,r) Pencil (n). CSmH (HM 954).

Title: All Phenomena for December

First line: Snow more than a foot deep 13th

Collation: 1 leaf of (anom.), pp. [1–2].

Date: [After 8 November 1855].

Contents: Notes on December phenomena, 1852 only, compiled from the *Journal*. Verso contains business a.l.s. to John Thoreau.

F24b.   Citation: [Nature Notes: December] A.ms., 24 sides. Ink (c,r,d) Pencil (r). VtMiM.

Title: All Phenomena of December —

First line: '50 | Hemisphere of green moss on Fair Haven open, a week ago frozen, 2

Collation: 12 leaves of (anom.), misc. size and color, pp. [1–24]; in folder marked "Fragments".

Date: [Ca. 1860].

Contents: Notes on December phenomena, 1850–1859, compiled from the *Journal*. Versos contain business a.l.s. to John Thoreau, 1855–1856.

F24c.   Citation: [Nature Notes: December] A.ms., 8 sides. Ink (c) Pencil (r). CtY (Za 13).

Title: All Phenomena for December

First line: A Thaw (not Jan.) | Wild Apples Thawed | River Open Again

Collation: 4 leaves of white wove, 35.5 x 21.5 cm., pp. [1–8].

Date: [After 24 December 1861].

Contents: Notes on December phenomena, 1850–1861, compiled from the *Journal*.

Note: This set of notes is the latest and fullest to survive. Thoreau includes observations on natural and social events (sleighing, skating, and so on); indicating perhaps that he had a seasonal "Calendar" in mind.

F25a. Citation: [Nature Notes: January] A.ms., 24 sides. Ink (c,r) Pencil (r,d). CSmH (HM 954).

Title: All Phenomena for January

First line: Farmer brings me a red-shouldered hawk 12–59

Collation: 18 leaves,
   16 of (anom), misc. size and color,
   2 of blue laid (type 3), 24.8 x 19.5 cm.,
pp. [1–36].

Date: [Ca. 1861].

Contents: Notes on January phenomena, 1851–1861, compiled from the *Journal*. Versos contain business a.l.s. to John Thoreau, 1854–1857. For other contents see *Corr.*, p. 635. An unpublished a.l.s., L. Johnson & Co. to HDT, 11 March 1856, appears on p. [15].

F25b. Citation: [Nature Notes: January] A.ms., 4 sides. Ink (c,r) Pencil (r,n). CSmH (HM 954).

Title: Phenomena for Jan. All the Jans.

First line: Alder cat. frozen stiff 5.51

Collation: 2 leaves of (anom.), misc. size and color, pp. [1–4].

Date: [Ca. 1861].

Contents: Notes on January phenomena, 1851–1856, compiled from the *Journal*. Versos contain business a.l.s. to John Thoreau, 1854–1855.

F26. Citation: [Nature Notes: February] A.ms., 4 sides. Ink (c,r,d) Pencil (r). NYPL (Berg:97B).

Title: General Phenomena

First line: 58 | Feb. 20 The most misty day of the winter.

Collation: 2 leaves of white laid (type 5), 24.5 x 19.4 cm., pp. [1–4].

Date: [Ca. 1860].

Contents: Notes on February phenomena, 1858–1860, compiled from the *Journal.*

F27a.   Citation: [Nature Notes: Leaves] A.ms., 12 sides. Ink (c,r) Pencil (r,d). NNPM (RV 12-C).

Title: Leafing of trees & shrubs

First line: White pine

Collation: 6 leaves,
  4 of white laid (type 5), 24.4 x 19.5 cm.,
  1 of gray laid, 37.8 x 31.3 cm.,
  1 of white laid, 32 x 32.3 cm.,
pp. [1–12], foliated* "1–6".

Date: [Ca. 1860].

Contents: Notes on foliage, 1852–1860, compiled from the *Journal.*

F27b.   Citation: [Nature Notes: Leaves] A.ms., 7 sides. Ink (c,d) Pencil (d,p). VtMiM.

Title: Verdure

First line: Mar. 1 — open moss at springs

Collation: 4 leaves of white laid (type 5), 24.5 x 19.4 cm., pp. [1–8], paged "1–4, 7–9".

Date: [Ca. 1860].

Contents: Notes on foliage, 1853–1860, compiled from the *Journal.*

F27c.   Citation: [Nature Notes: Leaves] A.ms., 3 sides. Ink (c) Pencil (r). NNPM (RV 12-C).

Title: Leafing of Trees in 60

First line: as I remember May 6 — (not named before)

Collation: 2 leaves of (anom.), a letter and envelope, pp. [1–4], foliated* "12".

Date: [After 2 May 1860].

Contents: Notes on foliage, 1860, compiled from the *Journal.* For contents of verso see *Corr.*, p. 578.

F27d.   Citation: [Nature Notes: Leaves] A.ms., 10 sides. Pencil (c,r,d). NYPL (Berg: 99B).

Title: Indigenous trees [twice underscored] in Concord

First line: Black spruce | Hemlock | Maple (3 kinds) | Alder (2 kinds)

Collation: 5 leaves of (anom.), misc. size and color, pp. [1–10].

Date: [Ca. 1860].

Contents: Notes on foliage, 1860, compiled from the *Journal.* Written on 1 envelope and 4 fragments of business a.l.s.

Note: For April, May, June growth and leafing see F19f, F20b, F21b; for October, November fall of leaf see F22a, F23a–c, F23e.

F28a.   Citation: [Nature Notes: Flowers] A.ms., 42 sides. Ink (c,r) Pencil (r). NYPL (Berg: 65B).

Title: The Flowering of Plants, accidentally observed in '51, with | considerable care in '52; the Spring of '51 being 10 days, | and more earlier than that of '52. The names those used by Gray. | X observed in good season The XX before the names refer to '52 | XXX very early — in '52.

First line: XX Sympolcarpus Foetidus

Collation: 24 leaves of white wove (type 19), 23.8 x 19.3 cm., pp. [1–48], with ts. note by L. S. Livingston.

Date: [Ca. 1855].

Contents: Notes on flowers, 1851–1854, compiled from the *Journal*.

F28b. Citation: [Nature Notes: Flowers] A.ms., 68 sides. Ink (c,r) Pencil (r,d). CSmH (HM 954).

Title: Order of Flowers accidentally [partially underscored] observed | in '51   Only of use as an index

First line: Skunk Cabbage? Feb 13

Collation: 34 leaves,
    25 of blue laid (type 1), 24.8 x 19.8 cm.,
    9 of white wove (type 19), 23.7 x 19.3 cm.,
pp. [1–68].

Date: [Ca. 1855 and 1860].

Contents: Notes on the appearance of flowers, 1851–1852 and 1855–1858, compiled from the *Journal*.

F28c. Citation: [Nature Notes: Flowers] A.ms., 88 sides. Pencil (c). NYPL (Berg: 78B).

Title: A. | Mar. | Apr. I

First line: A. Stellaria media——commonly every month.

Collation: 44 leaves of white wove (type 13), 24.5 x 19.5 cm., pp. [1–88]; most are cut into half leaves and divided into 9 booklets, each wrapped with a whole leaf; paged* "1–78".

Date: [Ca. 1860].

Contents: Notes on flowers, 1851–1860, compiled from the *Journal*.

F28d. Citation: [Nature Notes: Flowers] A.ms., 1 side.
Ink (c,r) Pencil (lines). M. Ferguson, West Concord,
Mass.

Title: 51 2 3 4 5 6 7 8 9 60

First line: Stellaria media Ap. 26

Collation: 1 leaf of white laid (type 5), 24.5 x 19.2
cm., pp. [1–2], paged "17"; mounted, bound in Set
No. 586 of the Manuscript Edition.

Date: [After 18 April 1860].

Contents: Notes on flowers, 1851–1860, compiled
from the *Journal*.

F28e. Citation: [Nature Notes: Flowers] A.ms., 1 side.
Pencil (c,r). NYPL (Berg).

First line: Atonzene American vine

Collation: 1 fragment of white laid (type 5), 12.2 x
19.4 cm., pp. [1–2], laid in Thoreau's copy of Asa
Gray, *Manual of the Botany of the Northern United
States*, 2d ed. (New York: G. P. Putnam & Co.,
1856).

Date: [Ca. 1862].

Contents: A final checklist of flowers, compiled from
previous listings.

Note: Thoreau probably composed this list shortly
before his death. Under his signature on the book's
front flyleaf he wrote: "Sep. 11 - 61 I have collected
a little over 900 (910) flowers — not counting sedges
grasses &c".

F29a. Citation: [Nature Notes: Fruits] A.ms., 4 sides. Ink
(c) Pencil (r,d). ViU (6345:13).

Title: Huckleberry

First line: Fall of 50 At Patchogue I saw a hundred
bushels of huckleberries in one field.

Collation: 2 leaves of white wove (type 13), 24.5 x 19.5 cm., pp. [1–4], paged "7, 9".

Date: [Ca. 1858].

Contents: Notes on huckleberries, 1850–1854, compiled from the *Journal*.

F29b.   Citation: [Nature Notes: Fruits] A.ms., 10 sides. Ink (c,r,d) Pencil (c,r,d). NYPL (Berg:70B).

Title: Huckleberries

First line: July 3 53 Vac. vacillanus

Collation: 5 leaves,
   2 of white laid (type 1), 31.3 x 19.2 cm.,
   3 of white wove (type 13), 24.7 x 19.5 cm.,
pp. [1–10].

Date: [Ca. 1859].

Contents: Notes on huckleberries, 1853–1858, compiled from the *Journal*.

F29c.   Citation: [Nature Notes: Fruits] A.ms., 4 sides. Ink (c,r,d) Pencil (r). VtMiM.

Title: Grapes

First line: Fall of 50   Now you can scent the ripe grapes far off on the banks, as you row along.

Collation: 2 leaves of white wove (type 13), 24.6 x 19.5 cm., pp. 1–4.

Date: [Ca. 1858].

Contents: Notes on grapes, 1850–1856, compiled from the *Journal*.

F29d.   Citation: [Nature Notes: Fruits] A.ms., 2 sides. Ink (c,d) Pencil (c). W. E. Stockhausen, New York, N.Y.

Title: Grapes

First line: These grapes are much shrivelled, but they have a very agreeable spicy acid taste,

Collation: 1 leaf of white wove (type 13), 24.9 x 19.6 cm., pp. [1–2].

Date: [Ca. 1859].

Contents: Notes on grapes, 1857–1859, compiled from the *Journal*.

F29e. Citation: [Nature Notes: Fruits] A.ms., 35 sides. Ink (c,r,d) Pencil (r,n). NYPL (Berg: 69B).

First line: July 13 56   along walls . . . honest and wholesome—see where the mowers have plucked them.

Collation: 19 leaves of white laid (type 1), 31.3 x 19.2 cm., pp. [1–38], paged* "43–44, 48–51, 150–51, 157, 177, 187, 197, 201–4, 271, 284, 293".

Date: [Ca. 1859].

Contents: Notes on wild fruit, 1853–1859, compiled from the *Journal*. Arranged by species and days of the month.

F29f. Citation: [Nature Notes: Fruits] A.ms., 4 sides. Ink (c,r) Pencil (r,d). CSmH (HM 954).

Title: Fruits for 54

First line: June 9   Strawberry

Collation: 2 leaves of white wove (type 13), 24.9 x 19.6 cm., pp. [1–4].

Date: [Ca. 1859].

Contents: Notes on wild fruit, 1854, compiled from the *Journal*. Arranged by species and days of the month. For other contents see C16d.

F29g. Citation: [Nature Notes: Fruits] A.ms., 2 sides. Ink (c) Pencil (d,n). ViU (6345-2:25).

Title: In Pliny

First line: Pliny complains that Vergil has "named only 15 varieties of the grape . . . & 3 of the pear."

Collation: 1 leaf of white laid (anom.), 12.5 x 19.9 cm., pp. [1–2].

Date: [Ca. 1859].

Contents: Notes and extracts from Pliny on the subject of wild fruit.

F29h.   Citation: [Nature Notes: Fruits] A.ms., 626 sides. Ink (c,d,r) Pencil (c,r,d). NYPL (Berg:69B).

Title: [p. "399"] I am going to play a rustic strain on my | slender reed—but | I trust that I do not sing unbidden | things

First line: [p. "399"] Many public speakers are accustomed, as I think foolishly, to talk about what they call little things [two words underscored]

Collation: 313 leaves of white laid (type 5), 24.6 x 19.5 cm., pp. [1–626], paged* "1–600".

Date: [1859–1861].

Contents: Notes on wild fruit, compiled from the *Journal* and arranged by species; numerous tables and indexes; and several portions of lecture/essay draft.

Note: Thoreau apparently worked several months on this project without completing it. The manuscripts are quite disorderly; a text assembled by the late Leo Stoller is *Huckleberries* (Iowa City: Windhover Press, University of Iowa, 1971).

F29i.   Citation: [Nature Notes: Fruits] A.ms., 2 sides. Ink (c). J. Osterlee, New York, N.Y.

First line: sunny & still, and the smooth water through which we studied the bottom of the meadow, reminded us of spring.

Collation: 1 leaf of white laid (type 5), 24.6 x 19.6 cm., pp. [1–2]; mounted, bound.

Date: [1859–1860].

Contents: Portion of "wild fruits" project, belonging to the lecture/essay draft. For an early version see *J* 11:165.

F29j.   Citation: [Nature Notes: Fruits] A.ms., 10 sides. Ink (c,r) Pencil (c,r). NYPL (Berg: 31B).

First line: Most of us are still related to our native fields as the navigator to undiscovered islands in the sea.

Collation: 5 leaves of white laid (type 5), 24.6 x 19.6 cm., pp. [1–10], with ts. copy.

Date: [After 20 September 1860].

Contents: Portion of "wild fruits" project, belonging to a late part of the lecture/essay draft.

F30.   Citation: [Nature Notes: Seeds] A.ms., 338 sides. Ink (c,r,d) Pencil (c,r,d). NYPL (Berg: 70B).

Title: The Dispersion of Seeds

First line: Pliny, whose work embodies the natural science of his time, tells us that some trees bear no seed.

Collation: 193 leaves,
    165 of white laid (type 5), 24.6 x 19.6 cm.,
    38 of (anom.), misc. size and color,
pp. [1–386], paged* "1–410".

Date: [1859–1861].

Contents: Notes, *Journal* extracts, and portions of lecture/essay draft. For other contents see *Corr.*, pp. 487, 586–87 (with facsimile), 588–89, 601–2. There are also 3 unpublished a.l.s. to HDT, all dated 1860.

Note: This project, divided into chapters, appears to be a massive revision and expansion of "The Succession of Forest Trees" (C19) into a book-length ms.

F31a.   Citation: [Nature Notes: Animals] A.ms., 8 sides. Ink (c,r) Pencil (r). CtY (Za 11).

Title: Insects &c   51   52   53   54

First line: Grubs stretch under leaves

Collation: 4 leaves of white wove (type 19), 23.7 x 19.3 cm., pp. [1–8].

Date: [After 15 December 1854].

Contents: Notes on insects, 1851–1854, compiled from the *Journal*.

F31b.   Citation: [Nature Notes: Animals] A.ms., 8 sides. Ink (c,r) Pencil (n). CSmH (HM 954).

Title: Quad—Reptiles—Fishes etc. for 57

First line: Feb 18   A frog out by a ditch.

Collation: 4 leaves of blue laid (type 1), 24.8 x 19.8 cm., pp. [1–8].

Date: [Ca. 1858].

Contents: Notes on animal life in the Concord area, 1855–1857, compiled from the *Journal*.

F31c.   Citation: [Nature Notes: Animals] A.ms., 6 sides. Ink (c,r) Pencil (c,r). MH-Z.

First line: A small bird

Collation: 6 leaves of white wove (type 19), 24 x 19.4 cm., pp. [1–12], opened to form 3 double sheets.

Date: [After 4 June 1855].

Contents: Notes on bird sightings, 1851–1855, compiled from the *Journal*.

F31c[1]. Citation: [Nature Notes: Animals] A.ms., 20 sides. Ink (c,r) Pencil (r, n). CSmH (HM 954).

Title: Birds in 55

First line: + Jan 31   A large hawk

Collation: 10 leaves of blue laid (type 1), 24.8 x 19.8 cm., pp. [1–20].

Date: [Ca. 1853].

Contents: Notes on birds in the Concord area, 1855–1858, compiled from the *Journal*.

F31d. Citation: [Nature Notes: Animals] A.ms., 1 side. Ink (c) Pencil (r). ICarbS.

Title: Quadrupeds

First line: Mephitis Americana

Collation: 1 leaf of blue laid (anom.), 25.1 x 19.9 cm., pp. [1–2].

Date: [After 19 June 1859].

Contents: Notes on mammals observed in the Concord area, March to November, 1853–1859; compiled from the *Journal*. Verso contains business a.l.s. to John Thoreau, dated 18 May 1858.

F31e. Citation: [Nature Notes: Animals] A.ms., 15 sides. Ink (c,r) Pencil (c,r,d). NYPL (Berg: 13b).

First line: 76 Warbling vireo   Apr. 27

Collation: 8 leaves,
    6 of white wove (type 13), 24.5 x 19.5 cm.,
    2 of blue laid (type 3), 25.1 x 19.8 cm.,
    pp. [1–16], paged* "23–40".

Date: [Ca. 1860].

Contents: Notes on birds, reptiles, and insects in the Concord area, 1852–1860, compiled from the *Journal*.

F31f. Citation: [Nature Notes: Animals] A.ms., 4 sides. Ink (c) Pencil (r). MH (MS Am 278.5.20 [3]).

Title: Fishes Shell-fish, Leeches, &c

First line: Trout Salnus fontinalis (dark & light colored—) March 6-

Collation: 2 leaves of (anom.), misc. size and color, pp. [1–4].

Date: [Ca. 1860].

Contents: Notes on aquatic life, 1854–1860, compiled from the *Journal*.

F31g. Citation: [Nature Notes: Animals] A.ms., 3 sides. Pencil (c,r). MConA.

Title: [1r]Birds found both in Europe & America | (Decidedly) ac. to Wilson & co.

First line: [2r] 16 Ledum

Collation: 2 leaves,
    1 of white wove, 25.1 x 19.4 cm.,
    1 fragment of white wove, 12 x 10.9 cm.,
pp. [1–4]; tipped in Thoreau's copy of Alexander Wilson, *American Ornithology* (New York: H. S. Samuels, 1852), following p. 746.

Date: [1860].

Contents: Notes on birds and plants, compiled from reference sources.

F32a. Citation: [Nature Notes: Miscellaneous] A.ms. 80 sides. Ink (c,r,d) Pencil (r,d). CSmH (HM 954).

Title: Miscellaneous Phenomena since| Nov. 24th '52

First line: Nov 27th Some acorns sprouted—

Collation: 42 leaves,
   23 of blue laid (type 3), 24.8 x 19.5 cm.,
   19 of (anom.), misc. size and color,
pp.[1–84].

Date: [Ca. 1858].

Contents: Notes on weather, vegetation, and animal life in the Concord area, 1852–1858, compiled from the *Journal*. For other contents see *Corr.*, pp. 326–27, 345–46, 348–49, 352–53, 462. Several versos contain business a.l.s. to John Thoreau, 1856–1857.

F32b.   Citation: [Nature Notes: Miscellaneous] A.ms., 12 sides. Ink (c,r) Pencil (c,r). MH (bMS AM 278.5 [7]).

First line: Savage Hist—full of incidents but not signif. XII-90.

Collation: 6 leaves,
   1 fragment of white wove (type 16), 12.3 x 19.3 cm.,
   2 fragments of (anom.), misc. size and color,
   2 leaves of white wove (type 12), 24.5 x 19.2 cm.,
   1 leaf of blue laid (type 2), 24.7 x 19.7 cm.,
pp. [1–12].

Date: [1855–1858].

Contents: Notes on plant and animal life, 1855–1858, compiled from the *Journal*. For other contents see *Corr.*, p. 349.

F32c.   Citation: [Nature Notes: Miscellaneous] A.ms., 2 sides. Ink (c,r,d) Pencil (c,r,d). MH (Houghton-Mifflin Papers).

Title: C.P.B. No. 1

First line: Pigs eat corn & sunflower seeds p. 5

Collation: 1 leaf of white wove (anom.), pp. [1–2].

Date: [After 16 July 1860].

Contents: Notes on weather and plant life, 1860, compiled from the *Journal*. Verso contains business a.l.s. to John Thoreau.

F32d. Citation: [Nature Notes: Miscellaneous] A.ms., 8 sides. Ink (c) Pencil (r,d). NNPM (RV 12-C).

First line: Ferns sour lemon Snakes

Collation: 4 leaves of (anom.), misc. size and color, pp. [1–8], foliated* "46–49".

Date: [After March 1861].

Contents: Notes and tables on weather, plants, and animals in the Concord area, 1850–1861, compiled from the *Journal*. For other contents see *Corr.*, p. 577. Versos also contain business a.l.s. to John Thoreau, 1854–1856, and to HDT, dated 20 April 1860.

F32e. Citation: [Nature Notes: Miscellaneous] A.ms., 8 sides. Ink (c) Pencil (r,n). NYPL (Berg:69B).

Title: [Miscellaneous Notes] incl. Nov. Flowers

First line: Nuthatch | Crow's nest

Collation: 4 leaves of (anom.), misc. size and color, pp. [1–8].

Date: [Ca. 1861].

Contents: Notes on birds, plants, and so forth, in the Concord area, 1853–1861; compiled from the *Journal*. For other contents see *Corr.*, p. 321. Some versos contain business a.l.s. to John Thoreau, and there is an unpublished a.l.s. to HDT, dated 4 December 1854.

G.

"MOONLIGHT" AND "THE MOON", 1854–1860

The following papers require some additional remarks of introduction, because most of them have long been misidentified as "*Journal* fragments," and because their two published versions, "Night and Moonlight" (*W* 5:323–33) and *The Moon* (Boston: Houghton Mifflin Co., 1927), are the garbled efforts of nonauthorial hands. I have prepared a fuller history for publication elsewhere,[1] and I hope eventually to re-edit the text; so I offer here only a compromise arrangement of the papers with a few notes of explanation.

Thoreau began this project in late August of 1854 by first constructing an elaborate index (G1) of all his *Journal* entries pertaining to "moonlight" in volumes "3–18", 1850–1854. In early September he began to write transcripts (G13–G14), revising as he copied, of selected *Journal* entries. These he arranged in a general *monthly* order, ignoring their exact year of origin. This peculiar "mensal" arrangement, the numerous textual variants, and the type of paper—all indicate that these papers are not "*Journal* fragments" but later, much revised copies of certain *Journal* entries.

In late September and early October Thoreau then wrote a lecture draft (G15a–s) entitled "Moonlight (Introductory to an Intended Course of Lectures)," which he read to a small gathering of friends in Plymouth, Massachusetts, on 8 October 1854. Unhappy over the failure of two subsequent lectures in November and December, he announced to the *Journal*, "I would rather write books than lectures" (*J* 7:79). Accordingly, he returned to "Moonlight" and began to redraft its opening sections under a new title, "The Moon". How far he proceeded with this revision is uncertain, since only six leaves survive (G16a–c). By January of 1855, however, he had abandoned the entire project for a new "course of lectures" entitled "Cape Cod" (see D23).

The "moonlight" papers lay dormant for several years, until Thoreau again worked on them briefly in late 1859 and early 1860. On various scraps of paper, including handbills announcing the memorial services for John Brown, he wrote some new indexes, notes from his reading, and a partial transcript of the

1. "Successor to *Walden?* Thoreau's 'Moonlight—An Intended Course of Lectures,'" *Proof* 2 (1972):89–115.

Journal entry for 1 September 1859 (G16d–f). At this time he may have shaped his old lecture into an essay version, "Night and Moonlight", but the history of that text is obscure. Thoreau makes no mention of a "moonlight" essay in his correspondence with Ticknor and Fields. The four essays they published posthumously in the *Atlantic Monthly* were all on hand by 6 April 1862, before Thoreau's death, and for all of these essays—"Walking", "Autumnal Tints", "Wild Apples", and "Life Without Principle"—rough drafts survive. "Night and Moonlight" did not appear until November 1863, a full eighteen months after Thoreau's death, and its rough draft has not survived. In all probability Thoreau never again touched the papers after early 1860; someone else—either Sophia Thoreau or Ellery Channing—prepared "Night and Moonlight" for publication. Later, some of the transcripts and lecture sheets came to the hands of F. H. Allen, who published them in 1927 as *The Moon*.

In view of these findings I have chosen to omit "Night and Moonlight" from section C of the calendar and instead group all of the "moonlight" papers here in their probable order of composition: index, transcripts, "Moonlight", and "The Moon". Since I have not yet fully determined the order of Thoreau's text, however, I have arranged the papers according to the two published texts. This may seem an odd compromise, since neither text is authorial, but the arrangement will at least permit readers to locate printed versions that resemble the original manuscripts.

G1.   Citation: [Moonlight] A.ms., 18 sides. Ink (c) Pencil (r,d). NYPL (Berg).

First line: Flute of evening   no 3-15

Collation: 9 leaves of (anom.), pp. [1–18], paged* "50–53, 16–19, 60–65, 54–57, 75–76" in groups marked E, C, I, F, H, J.

Date: [After 7 September 1854].

Contents: Index of entries pertaining to moonlight walks in *Journal* volumes 3 to 18, 1850–1854.

G2a.   Citation: [Moonlight] A.ms., 4 sides. Ink (c) Pencil (c,r). NYPL (Berg).

First line: I have heard described by an entomologist a larger & brilliant kind of glow worm sometimes found here about an inch long——

Collation: 3 leaves of (anom.), pp. [1–6], paged* "58–59, 66–68" in groups marked G, J.

Date: [August–September 1854].

Contents: Notes from books and other sources pertaining to moonlight walks. For an earlier version of leaf 1 see *J* 4:259–60.

G2b.   Citation: [Moonlight] A.ms., 2 sides. Ink (c,r) Pencil (r,d,n). MConL (on loan from Middlesex School).

First line: Why not walk a little way in its light?

Collation: 1 fragment of blue wove (anom.), pp. [1–2]; mounted, framed.

Date: [August–September 1854].

Contents: Note for lecture; for an early version see *J* 4:486.

G3a.   Citation: [Moonlight: January] A.ms., 2 sides. Ink (c,r) Pencil (r). ICarbS.

First line: indistinct and infinitely remote in the summer, imparting the impression of unfathomability

Collation: 1 fragment of white wove (type 12), 3.5 x 19.3 cm., pp. [1–2]; pasted to inside front board of *A Week on the Concord and Merrimack Rivers* (Boston: J. Munroe and Company, 1849).

Date: [August–September 1854].

Contents: Revised *Journal* entry for 1 January 1852. For an early version see *J* 3:172; for a late version see *W* 5:324.

Note: For a missing portion see G3b.

G3b.   Citation: [Moonlight: January] A.ms., 1 side. Ink (c). MConL.

First line: quite eclipse the more remote. The sky has fallen many degrees.

Collation: 1 fragment of white wove (type 12), 6.3 x 19.3 cm., pp. [1–2]; tipped in *A Week on the Concord and Merrimack Rivers* (Boston: J. Munroe and Co., 1849).

Date: [August–September 1854].

Contents: Revised *Journal* entry for 1 January 1852. For an early version see *J* 3:172.

Note: This fragment is a missing portion of G3a.

G4.   Citation: [Moonlight: February] A.ms., 8 sides. Ink (c) Pencil (r,d). RPB.

Title: Feb. 3ᵈ '52 | To Cliffs at 6 pm through deep snow— | the moon nearly full.

First line: The sun had set without a cloud in the sky, a rare occurrence;

Collation: 4 leaves of white wove (type 12), 24.7 x 19.5 cm., pp. [1–8].

Date: [August–September 1854].

Contents: Revised *Journal* entries for 3, 4, 27 February 1852. For early versions see *J* 3:272–78, 322–23. For a late version see *W* 5:323.

G5.   Citation: [Moonlight: March] A.ms., 4 sides. Ink (c,r) Pencil (r,d). NYPL (Berg).

Title: March 7 52 | To the Deep Cut & high field—at 9pm by a full moon.

First line: The ground is thinly covered with a crusted snow

Collation: 2 leaves of white wove (type 12), 24.5 x 19.3 cm., pp. [1–4], paged* "6–9" in group marked B.

Date: [August–September 1854].

Contents: Revised *Journal* entries for 7, 28 March 1852. For early versions see *J* 3:339–41; 359–60.

G6.   Citation: [Moonlight: April] A.ms., 6 sides. Ink (c,r) Pencil (r,d). NYPL (Berg).

Title: April 1st '53 | Starlight by river up Assabet

First line: Now at early starlight I hear the snipe's hovering note as he circles over Nawshawtuct Meadow.

Collation: 3 leaves of white wove (type 12) 24.5 x 19.3 cm., pp. [1–6], paged* "10–15" in group marked B.

Date: [August–September 1854].

Contents: Revised *Journal* entries for 1, 3, 23 April 1852–1853. For early versions see *J* 3:387–89; 5:81–83, 112.

G7.   Citation: [Moonlight: May] A.ms., 4 sides. Ink (c,r,d) Pencil (r,d). CSmH (HM 931).

Title: Miscellaneous | At Sundown on river — May 9th '53

First line: I love to paddle now at evening when the water is smooth, and the air begins to be warm.

Collation: 2 leaves of white wove (type 12), 24.5 x 19.3 cm., pp. [1–4]; bound.

Date: [Before 8 October 1854].

Contents: Revised *Journal* entries for 9, 17 May 1853; text in *The Moon*, pp. 26–28. For early versions see *J* 5:131–32, 166–70.

G8a.   Citation: [Moonlight: June] A.ms., 24 sides. Ink (c,r) Pencil (r,d). NYPL (Berg).

Title: June 9" 54   Up Assabet

First line: It is twilight & the river is covered with dusty lint.

Collation: 12 leaves of white wove (type 12), 24.5 x 19.3 cm., pp. [1–24].

Date: [August–September 1854].

Contents: Revised *Journal* entries for 9–18 June 1851–1854.

G8b.   Citation: [Moonlight: June] [see Section H]

G8c.   Citation: [Moonlight: June] A.ms., 4 sides. Ink (c,r,d). ViU (6345–e).

First line: frigerators—but I soon again rose out of this cool basin, and felt a puff of warm air,

Collation: 2 leaves of white wove (type 12), 24.5 x 19.3 cm., pp. [1–4] mounted.

Date: [August–September 1854].

Contents: Portions of revised *Journal* entries for 18, 20 June 1853; for early versions see *J* 5:279–86. A facsimile copy appears in K. W. Cameron, "Manuscript Pages from Thoreau's *Night and Moonlight*", *ESQ*, No. 35 (1964), pp. 82-85.

G9a.   Citation: [Moonlight: July] A.ms., 4 sides. Ink (c,r) Pencil (n). MHarF.

Title: July 4th '52   3AM   to Conantum. | prob. full

First line: Before rising I hear an occasional crowing of cocks in distant barns,

Collation: 2 leaves of blue wove, 25 x 19.3 cm., pp. [1-4]; mounted, framed.

Date: [August-September 1854].

Contents: Revised *Journal* entries for July 1851 and 1852. For early versions see *J* 2:286-92, and 4:179-85.

G9b.   Citation: [Moonlight: July] A.ms., 2 sides. Ink (c,r) Pencil (r,n). RPB.

Title: Full moon by about | 8 pm. to Assab. Bath

First line: There is a wind making it cooler & keeping off fog.

Collation: 1 leaf of white wove (type 12), 24.7 x 19.4 cm., pp. [1-2].

Date: [August-September 1854].

Contents: Revised *Journal* entries for July 1851 and 1854. For early versions see *J* 2:297-98, and 6:387-88. For late copies see *The Moon*, pp. 39 and 43.

G9c.   Citation: [Moonlight: July] A.ms., 11 sides. Ink (c,r) Pencil (r,d). VtMiM.

Title: July 8th '51

First line: Walked along the Clam Shell bank after sundown. (Moon full about the 12th) A cloudy sky.

Collation: 9 leaves of white wove (type 12), 24.5 x 19.3 cm., pp. [1–18]; in folder marked "Journal".

Date: [August–September 1854].

Contents: Revised *Journal* entries for July 1851–1853. For early versions see *J* 2:292–93, 323–29; 4:223, 240–45, 254–64; 5:319–22.

G9d.   Citation: [Moonlight: July] A.ms., 6 sides. Ink (c) Pencil (r). NYPL (Berg).

First line: July 11 51   Already I had perceived the peculiar dry scent of corn which has begun to show its tassels,

Collation: 3 leaves of white wove (type 12), 24.5 x 19.3 cm., pp. [1–6], paged* "69–74" in group marked J.

Date: [August–September 1854].

Contents: Revised *Journal* entries for July 1851 and 1853. For early versions see *J* 2:298–302, and 5:319–22, 327.

G9e.   Citation: [Moonlight: July] A.ms., 4 sides. Ink (c,r) Pencil (r). CSmH (HM 933).

First line: Having reached the dry pastures again I am surrounded by a flood of moonlight.

Collation: 2 leaves of white wove (type 12) 24.4 x 19.3 cm., pp. [1–4]; bound.

Date: [Before 8 October 1854].

Contents: Revised *Journal* entries for July 1851–1854. For early versions see *J* 2:12, 302–4. For a late version see *The Moon*, pp. 30–33.

G10a.   Citation: [Moonlight: August] A.ms., 2 sides. Ink (c,r) Pencil (r,d). VtMiM.

Title: Aug 1st 54   1st ¼ | Eve. on Conantum.

First line: 15 to 30 ms after sunset—— A few sparrows sing as in the morning or the spring,

Collation: 1 leaf of white wove (type 12), 24.5 x 19.2 cm., pp. [1–2].

Date: [August–September 1854].

Contents: Revised *Journal* entries for August 1851 and 1854. For early versions see *J* 2:370–75, and 6:416–19.

G10b.   Citation: [Moonlight: August] A.ms., 2 sides. Ink (c) Pencil (r,d). NYPL (Ms. Division, Misc. Papers).

Title: Aug. 8 51

First line: made nothing of it. It is easy to see how by yielding to such feelings as those,

Collation: 1 leaf of white wove (type 12), 24.5 x 19.3 cm., paged* "1–2."

Date: [August–September 1854].

Contents: Revised *Journal* entry for 8 August 1851. For an early version see *J* 2:378–82. For a late version, see *W* 5:327.

G10c.   Citation: [Moonlight: August] A.ms., 9 sides. Ink (c,d) Pencil (r,d). CtY (Za 3–4).

Title: Aug 12 51

First line: The great story of the night is the moon's adventures with the clouds.

Collation: 5 leaves of white wove (type 12), 24.4 x 19.2 cm., pp. [1–10]; in slipcase with ts. transcript.

Date: [August–September 1854].

Contents: Portions of revised *Journal* entries for August 1851 and 1852. For early versions see *J*

2:383–85; 4:145, 312–13. For late versions see *W* 5:329–30, and *The Moon*, p. 47.

G11.   Citation: [Moonlight: September] A.ms., 29 sides. Ink (c) Pencil (r). NYPL (Berg).

Title: September

First line: Rees says "It is remarkable that the moon during the week in which she is full in harvest

Collation: 15 leaves of white wove (type 12), 24.5 x 19.3 cm., pp. [1–30], paged* "20–49" in group marked D.

Date: [August–September 1854].

Contents: Notes and revised *Journal* entries for September 1851–1853. For early versions see *J* 2:463–64, 473–79, 482–87; 4:341, 374–75; 7:10–12, 19–24.

G12.   Citation: [Moonlight: October] A.ms., 16 sides. Ink (c,r) Pencil (r,d). VtMiM.

Title: Oct 1st 51 | To Conantum—at Starlight. The | Moon not quite half full.

First line: The twilight is much shorter than a month ago, probably because the atmosphere is clearer

Collation: 9 leaves of white wove (type 12), 24.5 x 19.2 cm., pp. [1–18]; in folder marked "Journal".

Date: [August–September 1854].

Contents: Revised *Journal* entries for October 1851–1853. For early versions see *J* 3:38–40, 46–52; 4:402–4; 5:396–98.

G13.   Citation: [Moonlight: November] A.ms., 8 sides. Ink (c,r) Pencil (r,d). VtMiM.

Title: Nov. 12th 51 | To Conantum 7^{pm}

First line: It is a still cold night. There is the light of the rising moon in the east.

Collation: 4 leaves of white wove (type 12), 24.5 x 19.2 cm., pp. [1–8]; in folder marked "Journal".

Date: [August–September 1854].

Contents: Revised *Journal* entries for 12 and 14 November 1851–1853. For early versions see *J* 3:109–10; 5:497–500, 503–5.

G14.   Citation: [Moonlight: December] A.ms., 1 side. Ink (c,r) Pencil (r). CSmH (HM 933).

First line: Dec. 8' 50 This evening for the first time the new moon is reflected from the frozen snow crust.

Collation: 1 leaf of white wove (type 12), 24.4 x 19.3 cm., pp. [1–2]; bound.

Date: [Before 8 October 1854].

Contents: Revised *Journal* entries for December, 1850–1853. For early versions see *J* 2:123; 6:4, 14–15, 19–20.

G15a.   Citation: [Moonlight] A.ms., 1 side. Pencil (c). VtMiM.

Title: Moonlight | (Introductory to an Intended Course of Lectures)

First line: Chancing to take a memorable walk by moonlight some years ago,

Collation: 1 leaf of white wove (type 12), 24.6 x 19.4 cm., pp. [1–2]; in folder marked "Fragments".

Date: [Before 8 October 1854].

Contents: Portion of lecture draft; text in *W* 5:323.

G15b.   Citation: [Moonlight] A.ms., 3 sides. Pencil (c,r,d). NYPL (Berg).

First line: light, at first revealing displaying them in all their hugeness & blackness,

Collation: 2 leaves of white wove (type 12), 24.6 x 19.3 cm., pp. [1–4], paged "8". Also paged* "72–74".

Date: [Before 8 October 1854].

Contents: Portion of lecture draft; text in W 5:329–30. For a later version see G10c.

G15c.   Citation: [Moonlight] A.ms., 2 sides. Ink (c,r) Pencil (r,n). TxU.

First line: the least tincture of a blush or sanguine complexion." but we are intellectually & morally albinoes—

Collation: 1 leaf of white wove (type 12), 24.6 x 19.4 cm., pp. [1–2]; mounted, bound in Set No. 487 of the Manuscript Edition.

Date: [Before 8 October 1854].

Contents: Portion of lecture draft; text partly in W 5:326–27, 331. For early versions see J 4:12–13, and The Moon, p. 5.

G15d.   Citation: [Moonlight] A.ms., 2 sides. Ink (c) Pencil (r,d). MCon.

First line: Moonlight is the best restorer of antiquity.

Collation: 1 leaf of white wove (type 12), 24.6 x 19.5 cm., pp. [1–2].

Date: [Before 8 October 1854].

Contents: Portion of lecture draft; text varies from The Moon, p. 5. For early versions see J 1:88,181. For a late version see W 5:331–32.

G15e. Citation: [Moonlight] A.ms., 8 sides. Ink (c) Pencil (r,d). ViU (6345–e).

First line: The note of the whippoorwill which I hear suggests how far apart are the woods and the town.

Collation: 5 leaves of white wove (type 12), 24.4 x 19.3 cm., pp. [1–10]; with ts. copy.

Date: [Before 8 October 1854].

Contents: Portion of lecture draft; text in *The Moon*, p. 14. For early versions see *J* 2:236–37, 378–80; 6:95–96. For a late version see *W* 5:327. A facsimile appears in K. W. Cameron, "Two Thoreau Journal Fragments of 1851", *ESQ*, No. 5 (1956), pp. 2–12.

G15f. Citation: [Moonlight] A.ms., 1 side. Ink (c) Pencil (n*). RPB.

First line: About villages you hear the barking of dogs instead of the howl of wolves.

Collation: 1 leaf of white wove (type 12), 24.6 x 19.6 cm., pp. [1–2].

Date: [Before 8 October 1854].

Contents: Portion of lecture draft; text in *The Moon*, pp. 17–18. For early versions see *J* 3:47; 5:278.

G15g. Citation: [Moonlight] A.ms., 1 side. Ink (c,r). William A. Strutz, Bismarck, N.D.

First line: After whatever revolutions in my moods & experiences, when I come forth at evening

Collation: 1 leaf of white wove (type 12), 24.6 x 19.5 cm., pp. [1–2].

Date: [Before 8 October 1854].

Contents: Portion of lecture draft; text in *The Moon*, pp. 18–19. For an early version see *J* 4:402–3.

Note: A ts. copy of this item is at InU (Am. Lit. Mss.).

G15h.   Citation: [Moonlight] A.ms., 2 sides. Ink (c) Pencil (r,d). ViU (6345–e).

First line: If we contemplate serious walking, it is indispensable that we walk alone,

Collation: 2 leaves (pasted together as one),
  1 fragment of white wove (type 12), 12.5 x 18.4 cm.,
  1 leaf of white laid (anom.), 12.3 x 18.4 cm., pp. [1–4].

Date: [Before 8 October 1854].

Contents: Portion of lecture draft; text in *The Moon*, p. 19. For early versions see J 2:302; 3:39–40; 4:262. Rectos contain unpublished a.l.s. to Michael Flannery, 12 October 1853 (see *Corr.*, p. 295); and "L.H.A." to Thoreau, undated.

G15i.   Citation: [Moonlight] A.ms., 4 sides. Ink (c,r) Pencil (r,d). RPB.

First line: is not black when the air is clear. but blue still—

Collation: 2 leaves of white wove (type 12), 24.6 x 19.6 cm., pp. [1–4].

Date: [Before 8 October 1854].

Contents: Portion of lecture draft; text in *The Moon*, pp. 20–25. For early versions see J 2:35, and 4:469–70. For a late version see *W* 5:333.

G15j.   Citation: [Moonlight] A.ms., 2 sides. Ink (c) Pencil (r). MH (MS Am 278.5.20 [4]).

First line: When I get into the road though far from the town, I feel the sand under my feet

Collation: 1 leaf of white wove, 24.5 x 19 cm., pp. [1–2].

Date: [Before 8 October 1854].

Contents: Portion of lecture draft; text in *The Moon*, pp. 24–25.

G15k.   Citation: [Moonlight] A.ms., 1 side. Ink (c) Pencil (r). RPB.

First line: I rarely walk by moonlight without hearing the sound of a flute or a horn,

Collation: 1 fragment of white wove (type 12), 12.6 x 19.6 cm., pp. [1–2].

Date: [Before 8 October 1854].

Contents: Portion of lecture draft; text varies from *The Moon*, p. 30. For early versions, see *J* 2:302–4; 4:108.

G15l.   Citation: [Moonlight] A.ms., 4 sides. Ink (c) Pencil (r,d). TxU.

First line: What should we think of a bird which had the gift of song,

Collation: 3 leaves of white wove (type 12), 24.5 x 19.5 cm., pp. [1–6].

Date: [Before 8 October 1854].

Contents: Portion of lecture draft; text in *The Moon*, pp. 30–34. For early versions see *J* 2:12, 259; 4:114.

G15m.   Citation: [Moonlight] A.ms., 2 sides. Ink (c,r) Pencil (n*). RPB.

First line: even with a not reflected light. Such is a worthy disciple.

Collation: 1 leaf of white wove (type 12), 24.6 x 19.4 cm., pp. [1–2].

Date: [Before 8 October 1854].

Contents: Portion of lecture draft; text in *The Moon*, pp. 39–41. For early versions see *J* 2:260, 298–99, 475, 479. For late versions see *W* 5:323, 327.

G15n. Citation: [Moonlight] A.ms., 6 sides. Ink (c,r) Pencil (r,d,n). RPB.

First line: it smells. Kalm, who travelled in this country a hundred years ago, says of the milkweed (Asclepius hynaea),

Collation: 3 leaves of white wove (type 12) 24.7 x 19.4 cm., pp. [1–6].

Date: [Before 8 October 1854].

Contents: Portion of lecture draft; text varies from *The Moon*, pp. 38–40, 43–44. For early versions see *J* 2:298–301, 463. For a late version see *W* 5:327.

G15o. Citation: [Moonlight] A.ms., 4 sides. Ink (c,r) Pencil (d,n*). ICarbS.

First line: As I look down from this height on yonder pond, or expansion of the river——

Collation: 3 leaves of white wove (type 12), 24.6 x 19.4 cm., pp. [1–6].

Date: [Before 8 October 1854].

Contents: Portion of lecture draft; text in *The Moon*, pp. 41–42. For an early version see *J* 2:476–78.

G15p. Citation: [Moonlight] A.ms., 3 sides. Ink (c). TxU.

First line: The northern lights now as I descend the hill have become a crescent of light

Collation: 2 leaves of white wove (type 12), 24.5 x 19.6 cm., pp. [1–4].

Date: [Before 8 October 1854].

Contents: Portion of lecture draft; text in *The Moon*, pp. 44–45. For early versions see *J* 2:479, 482.

G15q.   Citation: [Moonlight] A.ms., 1 side. Ink (c) Pencil (n). RPB.

First line: I think of the inhabitants of Arctic Regions—for I feel related

Collation: 1 fragment of white wove (type 12), 12.5 x 16.4 cm., pp. [1–2].

Date: [Before 8 October 1854].

Contents: Portion of lecture draft; text in *The Moon*, p. 46. For an early version see *J* 4:320. For a late version see *W* 5:326.

G15r.   Citation: [Moonlight] A.ms., 1 side. Ink (c) Pencil (n*). ICarbS.

First line: slumbers to fragrant morning thoughts Why should I fear to tell that it is Knights' factory bell at Assabet

Collation: 1 fragment of white wove (anom.), pp. [1–2].

Date: [Before 8 October 1854].

Contents: Portion of lecture draft; text in *The Moon*, p. 59. For an early version see *J* 2:485. Verso contains undated a.l.s. to Thoreau; see *Corr.*, pp. 653–64. A transcribed text is in Stoller, p. 11.

G15s.   Citation: [Moonlight] A.ms., 1 side. Ink (c,r) Pencil (r,d). NYPL (Berg).

Title: So I come home to bed.

First line: After I have spent the greater part of a night abroad in the moonlight

Collation: 1 leaf of white wove (type 12), 24.5 x 19.1 cm., pp. [1–2], paged* "49".

Date: [Before 8 October 1854].

Contents: Portion of lecture draft; text in W 5:331 and *The Moon*, pp. 59–60. For an early version see J 2:495.

G16a. Citation: [The Moon] A.ms., 8 sides. Ink (c,r) Pencil (r,d) NYPL (Ms. Div.: Harkness Gift).

Title: The Moon

First line: My friends wonder that I love to walk alone in solitary fields & woods by night.

Collation: 4 leaves of white wove (type 19), 24 x 19.1 cm., pp. [1–8]; mounted, bound.

Date: [After 8 October 1854 (r)].

Contents: Portion of book draft; text in *The Moon*, pp. 1–6. For early versions see J 2:62–63; W 5:326, 329, 331–32.

Note: These leaves originally belonged to draft G of *Walden* (D18), composed in [1853–1854]. On p. [1] Thoreau canceled an earlier paragraph on architecture and interlined "The Moon", his working title for this later version of "Moonlight".

G16b. Citation: [The Moon] A.ms., 1 side. Ink (c). ViU (6345-e).

First line: My friends wonder that I love to walk in solitary fields and woods by night.

Collation: 1 leaf of white wove (type 19), 23.7 x 19.1 cm., pp. [1–2], paged "71".

Date: [After 8 October 1854].

Contents: Portion of book draft; text varies from *The Moon*, p. 1. For early versions see *J* 2:62–63; *W* 5:326.

G16c.   Citation: [The Moon] A.ms., 2 sides. Ink (c) Pencil (r). VtMiM.

First line: No wonder that there have been astrologers—that some have conceived that they were personally related to particular stars.

Collation: 1 leaf of white wove (type 19), 23.8 x 19 cm., pp. [1–2], paged "75"; mounted, bound in Set No. 490 of the Manuscript Edition.

Date: [After 8 October 1854].

Contents: Portion of book draft; text in *W* 5:328. For an early version see *The Moon*, p. 7.

G16d.   Citation: [The Moon] A.ms., 3 sides. Ink (c) Pencil (r). NYPL (Berg).

First line: 5 -24 Lee Farm full May 16 '51

Collation: 3 leaves of (anom.), pp. [1–6], in group marked A.

Date: [After 2 December 1859].

Contents: Notes, index of selected *Journal* entries. Versos contain printed announcement of memorial services for John Brown.

G16e.   Citation: [The Moon] A.ms., 1 side. Ink (c). Vt MiM.

Title: The Wolf

First line: AElian says "He is the sharpest sighted of animals and sees even by night

Collation: 1 fragment of white laid (type 5), 13.3 x 19.3 cm., pp. [1–2]; in folder marked "Fragments".

Date: [Ca. December 1859].

Contents: Note for book draft.

G16f.   Citation: [The Moon] A.ms., 2 sides. Ink (c). DLC (Batchelder Autograph Coll.: Vol. XI, No. 1591).

Title: Saint Pierre Studies of Nature vol. 2 | p. 283.

First line: "On a fine summer's night, when the sky is serene, clouded only with some light vapors,

Collation: 1 leaf of white laid (type 5), 24.5 x 19.5 cm., pp. [1–2]; mounted, bound.

Date: [Ca. December 1859].

Contents: Note for book draft.

G17.   Citation: [Moonlight] [see Section H]

H.

CHECKLIST OF UNLOCATED MANUSCRIPTS

This final section lists several manuscripts that, for various reasons, I could not locate before the Calendar went to press. Each item has an assigned section and number, according to its alleged contents and date. In most cases enough information survives to permit conjectural collations; but without stronger evidence the descriptions have to remain incomplete.

This checklist derives from my survey of all manuscripts listed in the annual volumes of *American Book Prices Current*, 1904 to date. As of 1970, the volumes listed sales of 63 sets of the Manuscript Edition. The sets are not identified by number, so I could not check them against my Calendar descriptions, which total 57. At least 32 other single leaves, probably cut from the Manuscript Edition, appear in the Calendar (see Indexes). Of the three to four hundred leaves originally dispatched, about 80 percent are still unrecorded.

H1.   Citation: [College Theme]
[A27a]

       Title: Atticus as an Example

       First line: One cannot safely imitate the actions, as such, even of the wise and good.

       Date: [Theme No. 55, 16–30 June 1837].

       Contents: Class exercise; text in *LHDT*, pp. 183–85, as "Titus Pomponius Atticus, as an example".

       Note: This theme brings Thoreau's total to twenty-four, the required number for graduation.

H2.   Citation: "The morning in our prime" A.ms., 4 sides.
[B5a]   Parke-Bernet Sale No. 2054, Item 272, 17 October 1961.

       First line: The morning in our prime

       Date: 2 July 1837.

       Contents: Fair copy of 3 lines; text in *American Book Prices Current 1962* (New York: American Book-Prices Current, 1963), p. 767.

H3.   Citation: "I love a careless streamlet"
[B5b]

       First line: I love a careless streamlet

       Date: 11 July 1837

       Contents: Fair copy of 5 stanzas, 20 lines; text in *CP*, p. 87. Not in Berg Collection, as *CP* states, p. 302.

H4.   Citation: "Delay in Friendship"
[B87b]

       Title: Delay in Friendship

       First line: The blossoms on the tree

       Date: [1841].

Contents: Fair copy of 7 stanzas, 28 lines; text in *CP*, pp. 394, 404.

Note: At the Wakeman sale this item (No. 977) was dated "June 16 1837." *CP* lists the ms. source as "XX," an unexplained location symbol.

H5. Citation: "Methinks that by a strict behavior" MH.
[B129b]
First line: Methinks that by a strict behavior

Contents: Fair copy of 3 lines; text in *CP*, p. 139.

Note: The *CP* listing of this ms. (p. 311) may be an error. See also H6.

H6. Citation: "I have rolled near some other spirits path"
[B130b] MH.
First line: Oft in my passage through this star-lit clime

Contents: Late draft of 5 lines; text in *CP*, pp. 140, 311.

Note: The *CP* listing of this ms. (p. 311) may be an error. See also H5.

H7. Citation: "For though the [eaves] were rabitted"
[B168b] MH.
First line: For though the eaves were rabitted,

Contents: Late draft of 2 stanzas, 8 lines; text in *CP*, p. 189.

Note: The *CP* listing of this ms. (p. 323) may be an error.

H8. Citation: "Walking" A.ms., 2 sides. Paul C. Richards,
[C11m] Catalogue 26, January 1968.
Title: Walking

First line: I have met with but 1 or 2 persons in the course of my life

Date: [Before 23 April 1851].

Contents: Portion of lecture draft; text varies from W 5:203.

[Item H9 eliminated in press.]

H10.   Citation: "Life Without Principle" A.ms., 2 sides.
[C15y] Ink (c) Pencil (c). Swann Galleries, sold 30 October 1969 to Paul C. Richards.

First line: I see advertisements for active young men, as if activity were the whole of a young man's capital

Date: [Before 6 December 1854].

Contents: Portion of lecture draft; text varies from W 4:460–61.

H11.   Citation: "Life Without Principle" Parke-Bernet
[C15z] Sale No. 2145, Item 207, 27 November 1962.

First line: We are already little men.

Date: [Before 6 December 1854].

Contents: Portion of lecture draft, dropped from the essay text.

H12.   Citation: "Autumnal Tints" A.ms., 2 sides. PiP.
[C20h]

First line: I once thought that it would be a fine thing to get a specimen leaf

Date: [Before 22 February 1859].

Contents: Portion of lecture draft; text varies from W 5:251.

Note: The Darlington Memorial Library reported this manuscript to the Thoreau Edition in 1965, but since then it has apparently disappeared. Presumably, it was removed from the library's Manuscript Edition.

H13.   Citation: "Autumnal Tints" A.ms., 2 sides. Parke-
[C2ou]   Bernet Sale 1889, Item 430, 25 March 1959.

First line: To walk amid these upright branching casks of purple wine,

Collation: 1 leaf, pp. [1–2], paged "13"; mounted, bound in the Manuscript Edition.

Date: [1859–1860].

Contents: Portion of essay draft; text varies from W 5:255. A facsimile is in ESQ, No. 35 (1964), p. 84.

H13[1].   Citation: Cape Cod A.ms., 2 sides. Ink (c) Pencil
[D23c[1]]   (r,d). Literary Heritage, Catalogue 13 (Stoughton, Mass.: Spring, 1970), p. 44.

First line: At length we stopped for the night at Higgins' Tavern in Orleans,

Date: [1849].

Contents: Portion of early draft; text varies from W 4:29–30. For a late version see D23c.

H14.   Citation: [Nature Notes: April] Parke-Bernet Sale
[F19g]   2155, Item 443, 15 January 1963.

Date: [1859–1860]

Contents: Notes on April phenomena (trees, plants, birds, insects), dated April 9–16, for various years.

H15.   Citation: [Moonlight: June] A.ms., 2 sides. Ink (c,
[G8b]   r). Parke-Bernet Sale 1920, Item 324, 27–28 October 1959.

First line: There is no wind. It is commonly still at night—a season of rest.

Date: [August–September 1854].

Contents: Portion of a revised *Journal* entry for 18 June 1853. For an early version see *J* 5:278. A facsimile of the recto appears in *ESQ* No. 35 (1964), p. 85.

H16.   Citation: [Moonlight] A.ms., 4 sides. Charles Ham-
[G17]   ilton Autographs, Inc., Sale No. 16, Item 432, 13 December 1966.

Contents: Revised copy of *Journal* entry, unidentified, describing "the woods near Hubbard's Grove".

H17.   Citation: [On Death] A.ms., 2 sides. Ink (c) Pencil (r). Charles Hamilton Autographs, Inc., Sale No. 19, Item 409, 24 May 1967.

Collation: 2 leaves, with a.l.s. F. H. Allen to S. H. Wakeman, ca. 1912.

Contents: Attributed to the *Journal*, but possibly a portion of essay draft or *A Week*.

APPENDIXES

In the 1906 edition of Thoreau's *Journal*, F. H. Allen provided hundreds of cross references to the six-volume set of *Writings*, a collection of Thoreau's published and posthumously edited works. Because the *Writings* appeared first, they could not contain cross references to the *Journal*. The following tables reverse the order of Allen's cross references, correlating them with the consecutive pagination of *Writings*. Readers interested in checking early versions of a page in *Writings* can thus simply look up that page number in these tables. Allen's cross references are by no means complete, and the 1906 edition will soon be superseded; but these tables should prove useful for the time being.

VOLUME I

A Week on the Concord and Merrimack Rivers

Page	Journal	Page	Journal
xx	1:287	50	1:213, 259
xxi	1:287	54	1:245, 256, 296
9	1:59	56	1:273; 6:293
12	1:136, 137, 264	57	1:394, 6:293
13	1:137	58	1:392; 393
17	1:136, 138	61	1:392
19	1:138	65	1:33, 391
33	1:474	66	1:32
34	1:354, 474	77	1:309
35	1:354	78	1:55, 309
37	1:138, 141	79	1:58, 165, 243
38	1:88, 141	81	1:442
39	1:89, 90, 147	93	1:12, 114–15, 151
40	1:147, 227	94	1:56, 151
43	1:90	95	1:61
44	1:140	96	1:33, 59
45	1:140, 142, 144, 225, 441	98	1:313
48	1:283	99	1:313

VOLUME 4

Cape Cod and Miscellanies

Cape Cod

"The Service"

The Service
(Ed. F. B. Sanborn [Boston, 1902])

VOLUME 5

Excursions

A Yankee in Canada

"Natural History of Massachusetts"

"A Walk to Wachusett"

"A Winter Walk"

Page	Journal		Page	Journal
197	1:292		358	12:400, 445
225	6:71		359	12:400, 445
226	6:71		360	12:400
264	7:474		365	13:4
265	7:474		366	13:4
270	8:18		367	13:4
283	9:134		368–72	14:8
286–91	9:134		376	14:290
349	11:402		380	14:339
350	11:435		383–93	14:339
351	11:435			

Tables of Paper Types

The following tables present a rationale for identifying distinct paper "types" in Thoreau's manuscripts and for using those types to establish his dates of composition.

The *descriptive tables* identify all examined paper according to five factors: color (white, blue, gray, green), substance (wove or laid), maximum dimensions (length times width), lineation (abbreviated *v* for vertical margin, *h* for horizontal spacing) and stationer's mark (shape: figures, lettering). The list is inclusive, with type numbers assigned to paper appearing in more than one location or group of manuscripts. The sequence follows a descending order of magnitude, by color, quantity, and maximum dimensions. None of the paper types duplicates any of the others, as the various factors indicate. Some ambiguity persists, however, in the "Gray Wove" section, where certain specimens of (type 1–4) resemble similar types of white or blue paper. Discoloration may account for this similarity, since the hue of some papers can either fade or darken with age. Rather than force these anomalies into other categories, I have left them identified as Gray Wove.

The *chronological tables* arrange all of the major paper types in their dated order. The dates and contents listed here are only approximate; fuller descriptions appear in the various sections of this Calendar. Most of the dates are conjectured from physical or textual evidence and verified by the bibliographical history of Thoreau's composition, revision, and publication. Abbreviations for paper types are as follows:

Color	Wove	Laid
white	ww	wl
blue	bw	bl
gray	gyw	gyl
green	gnw	gnl

DESCRIPTIVE TABLES

White Wove

Type	Dimensions (cm.)	Lineation	Stationer's Mark
	40.7 x 19.2		
	35.5 x 21.5	v,h	
I	32 x 19.9		Bird: ALLEN [as watermark]
Ia	31.9 x 19.5		
2	31.1 x 19.5	v,h	
	25.4 x 20.1	h	
3	25.3 x 20.1		Rectangle: eagle, arrow, laurel R. HUBBARD | NORWICH CONN.
4	25.2 x 20.1	h	Oval: crossed leaves LAWRENCE & COMPANY
5	25.1 x 20.1	h	Oval: H & E GOODWIN
6	25.1 x 19.2	h	Oval: wreath, lyre
7	25 x 19.6	h	
8	25 x 19.5		
9	24.9 x 20		Circle
10	24.8 x 20.3	h	Bird: ALLEN [as watermark]
11	24.7 x 19.7	h	Octagon: wreath AMES
12	24.7 x 19.5	h	Oval: wreath G & Co.
13	24.6 x 19.6	h	Oval: wreath, plant, vase
14	24.6 x 19.1		Oval: crossed flowers LAWRENCE
15	24.5 x 20		
16	24.5 x 19.4	h	Circle: thistle
17	24.3 x 19.1	h	
17a	24.2 x 19.6		
18	24.1 x 19.3	h	Circle: anchor GOODWIN HARTFORD
19	24 x 19.3	h	Oval: wreath G & Co.
	23.9 x 19	h	
20	23 x 18.7	h	Oval: wreath G & Co.
	22.6 x 18.5	h	
	21.6 x 16.5		
	20.7 x 17.5	h	
21	20.2 x 16.7	v,h	
	20.1 x 16.6	h	
	20 x 16	h	
22	19.3 x 16.6		
23	18.4 x 16.5	v,h	
24	18.4 x 15.2		
25	11.2 x 9.3	h	
	10.4 x 8.5	h	

White Laid

Type	Dimensions (cm.)	Lineation	Stationer's Mark
1	31.3 x 19.2		
2	25.3 x 20.2	h	Oval: wreath, flowers, scroll
	25 x 19	h	Lyre [as watermark]
3	25 x 18.8	h	
4	24.8 x 19.2	h	
5	24.5 x 19.5		Oval: scroll SUPERFINE LETTER
6	20.1 x 16.5		

Blue Wove

	25.9 x 19.5	h	
	25.5 x 19.5	h	
1	25.2 x 20	h	Circle: flower
	25.1 x 20	h	Oval: scroll W.C. & Co.
2	25 x 20.2	h	Circle: anchor
3	24.8 x 19.9	h	Octagon: flower DAVIS BOSTON
4	24.7 x 19.4	h	
5	24.5 x 19.8	h	
6	24.5 x 20		Oval: scroll TS & Co.
7	24.5 x 19.3	v,h	
8	24.4 x 19.3	h	Circle: anchor GOODWIN HARTFORD
9	24.3 x 19.1	h	Circle: anchor H & E GOODWIN
	24 x 19.3	h	
10	24.1 x 18.6	v,h	
11	24.1 x 18.2	v,h	
12	20.9 x 17.4	h	
	20 x 16.2	h	
	19.8 x 16.5	h	

Blue Laid

	25.2 x 19.3	h	Circle: flower
1	24.9 x 19.9	h	Octagon: scroll, flowers Wm. S
2	24.9 x 19.8	h	Rectangle: heraldic crest DIEU ET ROIR | LONDON
3	24.8 x 19.6	h	Octagon: crossed flowers S [also watermark: crown, scroll, crest]

Type	Dimensions (cm.)	Lineation	Stationer's Mark
4	24.7 x 19.3		Rectangle: galleon, anchor, caduceus

Gray Wove

1	25 x 20.2		
2	25 x 20		
3	24.9 x 19.9		
4	24.9 x 19.8		
5	24.5 x 19.4		
6	24.2 x 19	h	Oval: leaves PRENCE & Co.

Green Wove

1	25.4 x 20.3		
2	24.5 x 19.7		

Green Laid

1	37.8 x 31.3

Chronological Tables

Date	Contents	Paper	Items*
1834–1835	Themes	ww (15)	A2–A8, A10
1835	Notes	ww 22.6 x 18.5	F1
1835–1836	Themes, Notes	ww (3)	A11–A21, F1
1836–1837	Index Rerum	ww 20 x 16	F2
1836–1837	Themes, Notes	gyw (4)	A22–A34, F1, F4
1836–1839	Notebook	ww (10)	F4
1836–1842	Nature Album	ww (1)	F17
1837–1840	Journal	ww (9)	E1
1838–1840	Essays, A Week	gyw (3)	C2, D5, D7, F1
1840–1842	Notebook	ww (2)	F7
1840–1841	Journal	ww (8)	E2
1841	Journal	ww (25)	E3–E4
1841	Journal	ww 10.4 x 8.5	E5
1841	Journal	ww (23)	E6
1841	Journal	ww 21.6 x 16.5	E7
1841–1842	Journal	ww 20.7 x 17.5	E8
1841–1842	Prometheus	ww (11)	B17
1841–1843	Notebook	ww (19)	F5
1842	Prometheus	ww 25.4 x 20.1	B17
1842–1843	Poems, Essays	bw (2)	C5, E6
1842–1843	Journal	ww (17a)	E9–E10
1843	Poems, A Week	gyw (1)	D5–D6
1843	Notebook	ww (10)	F4
1843–1844	Essays, A Week	ww (11)	C4–C6, C10, D2–D9
1843–1844	Journal	wl (4)	E11
1844	A Week	bw (6)	D6
1844	A Week	ww 40.7 x 19.2	D5
1845–1846	A Week	bw (9)	D5, D7
1845–1846	Essays, A Week, Walden	ww (1a)	C7–C8, D1–D2, D4–D5, D7, D10
1846	Walden	ww (22)	D10, E12
1846–1847	Essays, A Week	ww (14)	C10, D3–D9
1846–1847	Maine Woods	gnw (2)	D24, E12
1847	Walden	gnw (2)	D10
1847	Walden	ww (22)	D10
1847	A Week	gyw (6)	D5, D7
1847	A Week, Walden	bw (1)	D5–D9, D12
1847–1848	Walden	gnw (2)	D10
1848–1849	Poems, Essays	bw (3)	C9
1848–1849	A Week, Walden Maine Woods, Cape Cod	ww (5)	C9–C10, D4–D9, D13–D14, D23–D24

Date	Contents	Paper	Items*
1848–1849	Poems, Surveys	ww (18)	F11
1848–1850	Journal, Essays, A Week, Yankee	bw (5)	C9, C15, D5–D7, D9, D20, E13
1849	Survey Notebook	bw 19.8 x 16.5	F12
1849	Indian Notebook	ww (23)	F10a
1850	Cape Cod	bw 25.1 x 20	D23
1850	Indian Notebook	ww 20.1 x 16.6	F10b
1850	Journal	bw (5)	E14
1850	Journal	ww (7)	E15
1850–1851	Journal	bw (11)	E16, E18
1850–1852	Canada Notebook	ww (21)	F9
1851	Indian Notebook	wl (6)	F10c
1851	Journal	bw (5)	E17
1851–1852	Essays, Walden, Yankee, Cape Cod	ww (18)	C11, C14, D15–D16, D20–D23
1852	Walden, Maine Woods	ww (5)	D18, D25
1852	Walden	gyw (5)	D15
1852	Indian Notebook	bw 20 x 16.2	F10d
1852	Journal	bw (10)	E19–E20
1852	Journal	bw 25.5 x 19.5	E21
1852	Journal	bw 24 x 19.3	E23
1852	Essays, Walden	bw (8)	C12–C14, D16–D17
1852–1853	Walden, Cape Cod	ww (16)	D15, D23, F9
1852–1853	Journal, Indian Notebook	bw (7)	E22, E24, F10f
1853	Journal	ww (24)	E25
1853	Notebooks	bw (12)	F15–F16
1853–1854	Journal, Indian Notebook	ww (20)	E26, F10g
1853–1854	Journal	ww 23.9 x 19	E27
1853–1854	Essays, Walden, Maine Woods	ww (12)	C11, C15, D25, G3–G15
1853–1854	Essays, Walden	ww (19)	C15, D15–D17, G16
1854	Walden, Cape Cod	ww (17)	D18, D23
1854–1856	Journal, Indian Notebook	ww (19)	E28–E29, F10h
1855	Cape Cod, Canada and Nature Notes	bl (1)	D23, F9, F28, F31
1855–1856	Journal	wl 25 x 19	E30
1855–1856	Journal, Indian Notebook, Nature Notes	bl (3)	E31, F10i, F25, F31–F32
1856	Journal	wl (3)	E32–E36

Date	Contents	Paper	Items*
1857	Indian Notebook	bw (4)	F10j
1858	Journal	bw 25.9 x 19.5	E37
1858	Journal	bl (3)	E38
1858	Journal, Indian Notebook	bl (4)	E39, E42–E43, F10k
1858–1859	Essays, Nature Notes	ww (13)	C15–C16, C20–C21, F18, F28–F29, F31
1858–1859	Essays, *Maine Woods*, Journal	wl (2)	C20, D24–D26, E38, E40
1858–1859	Nature Notes	wl (1)	F21, F29
1859	Essays, Nature Notes	wl (5)	C11, C16–C21
1859	Essays	ww (4)	C15, C20
1859	Essays	bl 25.2 x 19.3	C20
1859–1861	Journal	ww (6)	E41, E44
1860	Essays, *Maine Woods*, Nature Notes	bl (2)	C15, C18, D25, D26, F32
1860	Nature Notes	gnl (1)	F20, F27
1861	Nature Notes	ww 33.5 x 21.5	F28–F30, C20, D24–D26
1861	Essays, *Maine Woods*, Minn. Journey	wl (2)	E44

* General entry numbers only, with most from section B excluded. See the items for cross references to other contents or missing leaves.

INDEXES

These indexes permit readers to find manuscripts by title or location; they also list all proper names (excluding place names) that appear in the Calendar. Included are all "Citation" titles plus any variant manuscript "Titles". (Typographical peculiarities or line endings in titles are not noted in the index entry.) For several large public collections the index of repositories lists call numbers in their numerical order. Readers thus have several means of coordinating Calendar descriptions with the actual manuscripts. For aid in compiling these indexes, I again thank my research assistant, Elizabeth Friskey, and the Bureau of Student Aid, Princeton University.

Public Collections

(HM 13195), B16e, B19c–d, B95c, B97b, B121a, D4a, D5c, D6b, D7b, D8a, D9e
(HM 13196), B148b, B149b, B186, C12a, C13a
(HM 13197), B21a
(HM 13198), F19a
(HM 13199), D26a
(HM 13201), B10a–d, B11a, B13b, B13f, B14a, B16a–b, B28a, B29a, B30a, B31, B40d, E1b–c, F2b–c, F4c
(HM 13202), C16b, F18b
(HM 13203), C16a, F19b
(HM 13204), B103
(HM 13206), D23a, E13d
(PB 110229), D9i

CSdS   San Diego State College, San Diego
C20j¹
CU-S   University of California at San Diego, La Jolla
C21a

CONNECTICUT
CtLkH   Edsel Ford Memorial Library, The Hotchkiss School, Lakeville
C15s
CtY   Beinecke Rare Book Library, Yale University, New Haven
B24b
(Za 1), F23a
(Za 3,4), G10c
(Za 5), D15i
(Za 7), B118a, D8f
(Za 8), D16h
(Za 9), F19d
(Za 11), F31a
(Za 13), F24c
(Za 14), F22c
(Za T391 B906 1), C11i

DISTRICT OF COLUMBIA
DLC   Manuscript Division, Library of Congress
(Literary Miscellany) A18; (Poetry Archive) F7; (Batchelder Autograph Collection) G16f

IOWA
IaU   Iowa University, Iowa City
C20z

ILLINOIS
ICarbS   Morris Library, Southern Illinois University, Carbondale
B4, B13h, B23b, B28b, B29b, B30b, B46b, B93b, C11b, C11e, C15c, C20p, C21d, E10b, F31d, G3, G150, G15r

NRRI　　Rochester Institute of Technology, Rochester
C21e[1]
NSchU　　Schaffer Library, Union College, Schenectady
D23d
NYPL　　New York Public Library, New York
(Berg Collection) B7, B10e–f, B12, B13a, B14b, B16c, B40b, B41b,
B44b, B77c, B90, B116a–b, B139b, B196, C4a, C11d, C20b, C20v–w,
D2a, D3a, D8g, D10f, D17b, D21c, D21f, D24a–b, E12d, F16–F17,
F18c, F18e, F21a, F22a, F23c–d, F26, F27d, F28a, F28c, F28e, F29b,
F29e, F29h, F29j, F30, F31e, F32e
(Manuscript Division) B170, D23g, E13f, F6c, F8, G10b, G16a

PENNSYLVANIA
PPiU　　Darlington Library, University of Pittsburgh, Pittsburgh
H12

RHODE ISLAND
RPB　　John Hay Library, Brown University, Providence
A6, A28, B2, B165, B166a, B195, C15e, C15j, D5l, D9j, D24d, D25c,
F1f, F4d, F6d, F18a, G4, G9b, G15f, G15i, G15k, G15m–n, G15q

TEXAS
TxU　　Miriam Lutcher Stark Library, University of Texas, Austin
A11, B32, B144, B155b, B156b, B166b, C12b, C13b, C20e, D50, D7f,
D12b, D16f, E11a, E13c, E13i, G15c, G15l, G15p

VIRGINIA
ViU　　Alderman Library, University of Virginia, Charlottesville
(6329a), B112c
(6345), B9, D16b, D21e, F1b–e, F6b
(6345:2.25), F29g
(6345:13), F29a
(6345-e), A3, B25a, D6g, G8c, G15e, G15h, G16b
　(7), C16f
　(8), D25g
　(9–10), D23k
　(11), D23b
　(12), C21b
　(14), C15g
　(15), E29b
　(16), C20t
　(18), C20u, D13d
　(19), C20i
　(20), C20n
　(21), D23f
　(22), C11c
　(23), F2d
　(24), E11e

(6345-f), D23e
(6345-g), D21h–i

Addendum: The Robert H. Taylor Collection of Thoreau Manuscripts, Firestone Library, Princeton University

Just after the present Calendar went to press, I belatedly learned of a sizeable collection of Thoreau manuscripts owned by Robert H. Taylor and now on permanent deposit in the Taylor Room at Firestone Library, Princeton University. The Taylor Room was dedicated in April 1972, and only recently were its Thoreau items catalogued. With Mr. Taylor's kind permission, I am able to give the following descriptions, numbered according to their respective locations in the Calendar. Cross references and index entries do not appear for these items, but this listing at least acknowledges the existence of a major collection, representing every phase of Henry Thoreau's literary career.

A10¹.   Citation: [College Theme] A.ms., 2 sides. Ink (c). NjP (Taylor).

First line: find another perhaps no better satisfied than ourselves.

Collation: 1 leaf of white wove (type 3), 25.4 x 20.3 cm., pp. [1–2], formerly bound in *The First and Last Journeys of Thoreau* (Boston: Bibliophile Society, 1905).

Date: [Theme No. 22, 2–16 October 1835].

Contents: Portion of class exercise; text unpublished. For contents of verso see D4d¹.

B10c¹.   Citation: "The Fall of the Leaf" A.ms., 2 sides. Ink (c) Pencil (r). NjP (Taylor).

Title: The Soul's Season.

First line: Thank God who seasons thus the year,

Collation: 1 leaf of gray wove (type 3), 24.8 x 20.2 cm., pp. [1–2], paged* "334"; edge torn.

Date: [1841–1842].

Contents: Intermediate draft of 9 stanzas, 36 lines; text varies from *CP*, pp. 236–38.

Note: This draft precedes Item B10e, the first to bear Thoreau's final title, "The Fall of the Leaf".

D4d¹. Citation: *A Week*, "Sunday" A.ms., 1 side. Ink (c,r) Pencil (r). NjP (Taylor).

First line: There is no infidelity nowadays so great as that which prays—

Collation: 1 leaf of white wove (type 3), 25.4 x 20.3 cm., pp. [1–2], paged "6"; formerly bound in *The First and Last Journeys of Thoreau* (Boston: Bibliophile Society, 1905).

Date: [1842–1843].

Contents: Draft portion; text varies from *W* 1:77–78. For contents of recto see A10¹.

D12a¹. Citation: *Walden* [from draft A] A.ms., 1 side. Ink (c,r) Pencil (r). NjP (Taylor).

First line: I have seen some frozen-faced Connecticut | Or Down east man—

Collation: 1 fragment of blue wove (type 1), 20.1 x 19.7 cm., pp. [1–2]; formerly bound in *Echoes of Harper's Ferry*, ed. James Redpath (Boston: Thayer and Eldridge, 1860).

Date: [Before 10 February 1847].

Contents: Late draft of 13 lines; text unpublished. For an early and briefer version, partly used in *Walden*, see D10g.

D23k¹. Citation: *Cape Cod* A.ms., 1 side. Ink (c,r) Pencil (r,d). NjP (Taylor)

First line: early barren and desolate waste, and seemed good for nothing but to hold the Cape together.

Collation: 1 leaf of white wove (type 16), 24.4 x 19.3 cm., pp. [1–2]; mounted, formerly bound in the Manuscript Edition.

Date: [1853].

Contents: Portion of early draft; text varies from W 4:254–55.

G8a¹. Citation: [Moonlight: June] A.ms., 8 sides. Ink (c,r) Pencil (r,d). NjP (Taylor).

Title: June 21st '52

First line: To Cliffs. It is dusky now—a cool evening, past 8 o'clock.

Collation: 4 leaves of white wove (type 12), 24.5 x 19.3 cm., pp. [1–8].

Date: [Before 8 October 1854].

Contents: Transcripts of *Journal* entries for 21–30 June 1852.